Start a Business in North Carolina or South Carolina

Second Edition

Jacqueline D. Stanley
Jeffrey D. DeGood
Attorneys at Law

SPHINX® PUBLISHING
AN IMPRINT OF SOURCEBOOKS, INC.®
NAPERVILLE, ILLINOIS
www.SphinxLegal.com

Second Edition: 2007

Published by: **Sphinx® Publishing, An Imprint of Sourcebooks, Inc.®**

Naperville Office
P.O. Box 4410
Naperville, Illinois 60567-4410
630-961-3900
Fax: 630-961-2168
www.sourcebooks.com
www.SphinxLegal.com

This publication is designed to provide accurate and authoritative information in regard to the subject matter covered. It is sold with the understanding that the publisher is not engaged in rendering legal, accounting, or other professional service. If legal advice or other expert assistance is required, the services of a competent professional person should be sought.

From a Declaration of Principles Jointly Adopted by a Committee of the American Bar Association and a Committee of Publishers and Associations

This product is not a substitute for legal advice.

Disclaimer required by Texas statutes.

Library of Congress Cataloging-in-Publication Data
Stanley, Jacqueline D.
   Start a business in North Carolina or South Carolina / by Jacqueline D.
Stanley and Jeffrey D. DeGood. — 2nd ed.
       p. cm.
   Rev. ed. of: How to start a business in North Carolina or South Carolina.
1st ed.
   Includes index.
   1. Business enterprises—Law and legislation—North Carolina—Popular
works. 2. Business enterprises—Law and legislation—South
Carolina—Popular works. I. DeGood, Jeffrey D. II. Stanley, Jacqueline D.
How to start a business in North Carolina or South Carolina. III. Title.
KFN7605.Z9S73 2006
346.756'065—dc22
                                                                                    2006031232

Printed and bound in the United States of America.
RRD — 10 9 8 7 6

Contents

Website Design
Web Designers
Web Hosting
E-commerce
Website Promotion

Acknowledgments

I want to thank several people for making this book possible. My deepest appreciation goes to my husband, Tim Stanley, for his unflagging encouragement and support throughout this project. I owe my three daughters, Whitney, Sydney, and Symone, a special debt of gratitude for their patience and support. Jeff DeGood, thanks for being so easy to collaborate with. And a special thanks to entrepreneurs—past, present, and future—for having the courage to hang out your shingle!

Jacqueline D. Stanley

I would like to acknowledge my wife, Christine, without whose encouragement and understanding I would never have been able to bring myself to spend so many sunny Saturday afternoons in the library.

Jeffrey D. DeGood

Using Self-Help Law Books

Before using a self-help law book, you should realize the advantages and disadvantages of doing your own legal work and understand the challenges and diligence that this requires.

The Growing Trend

Rest assured that you will not be the first or only person handling your own legal matter. For example, in some states, more than 75% of the people in divorces and other cases represent themselves. Because of the high cost of legal services, this is a major trend, and many courts are struggling to make it easier for people to represent themselves. However, some courts are not happy with people who do not use attorneys and refuse to help them in any way. For some, the attitude is, "Go to the law library and figure it out for yourself."

We write and publish self-help law books to give people an alternative to the often complicated and confusing legal books found in most law libraries. We have made the explanations of the law as simple and easy to understand as possible. Of course, unlike an attorney advising an individual client, we cannot cover every conceivable possibility.

Cost/Value Analysis

Whenever you shop for a product or service, you are faced with various levels of quality and price. In deciding what product or service to buy, you make a cost/value analysis on the basis of your willingness to pay and the quality you desire.

When buying a car, you decide whether you want transportation, comfort, status, or sex appeal. Accordingly, you decide among choices such as a Neon, a Lincoln, a Rolls Royce, or a Porsche. Before making a decision, you usually weigh the merits of each option against the cost.

When you get a headache, you can take a pain reliever (such as aspirin) or visit a medical specialist for a neurological examination. Given this choice, most people, of course, take a pain reliever, since it costs only pennies; whereas a medical examination costs hundreds of dollars and takes a lot of time. This is usually a logical choice because it is rare to need anything more than a pain reliever for a headache. But in some cases, a headache may indicate a brain tumor, and failing to see a specialist right away can result in complications. Should everyone with a headache go to a specialist? Of course not, but people treating their own illnesses must realize that they are betting, on the basis of their cost/value analysis of the situation, that they are taking the most logical option.

The same cost/value analysis must be made when deciding to do one's own legal work. Many legal situations are very straightforward, requiring a simple form and no complicated analysis. Anyone with a little intelligence and a book of instructions can handle the matter without outside help.

But there is always the chance that complications are involved that only an attorney would notice. To simplify the law into a book like this, several legal cases often must be condensed into a single sentence or paragraph. Otherwise, the book would be several hundred pages long and too complicated for most people. However, this simplification necessarily leaves out many details and nuances that would apply to special or unusual situations. Also, there are many ways to interpret most legal questions. Your case may come before a judge who disagrees with the analysis of our authors.

Therefore, in deciding to use a self-help law book and to do your own legal work, you must realize that you are making a cost/value analysis. You have decided that the money you will save in doing it yourself outweighs the chance that your case will not turn out to your satisfaction. Most people handling their own simple legal matters never have a problem, but occasionally people find that it ended up costing them more to have an attorney straighten out the situation than it would have if they had hired an attorney in the beginning. Keep this in mind while handling your case, and be sure to consult an attorney if you feel you might need further guidance.

Local Rules   The next thing to remember is that a book which covers the law for the entire nation, or even for an entire state, cannot possibly include every procedural difference of every jurisdiction. Whenever possible, we provide the exact form needed; however, in some areas, each county, or even each judge, may require unique forms and procedures. In our state books, our forms usually cover the majority of counties in the state or provide examples of the type of form that will be required. In our national books, our forms are sometimes even more general in nature but are designed to give a good idea of the type of form that will be needed in most locations. Nonetheless, keep in mind that your state, county, or judge may have a requirement, or use a form, that is not included in this book.

You should not necessarily expect to be able to get all of the information and resources you need solely from within the pages of this book. This book will serve as your guide, giving you specific information whenever possible and helping you to find out what else you will need to know. This is just like if you decided to build your own backyard deck. You might purchase a book on how to build decks. However, such a book would not include the building codes and permit requirements of every city, town, county, and township in the nation; nor would it include the lumber, nails, saws, hammers, and other materials and tools you would need to actually build the deck. You would use the book as your guide, and then do some work and research involving such matters as whether you need a permit of some kind, what type and grade of wood is available in your area, whether to use hand tools or power tools, and how to use those tools.

Before using the forms in a book like this, you should check with your court clerk to see if there are any local rules of which you should be aware or local forms you will need to use. Often, such forms will require the same information as the forms in the book but are merely laid out differently or use slightly different language. They will sometimes require additional information.

Changes in the Law Besides being subject to local rules and practices, the law is subject to change at any time. The courts and the legislatures of all fifty states are constantly revising the laws. It is possible that while you are reading this book, some aspect of the law is being changed.

In most cases, the change will be of minimal significance. A form will be redesigned, additional information will be required, or a waiting period will be extended. As a result, you might need to revise a form, file an extra form, or wait out a longer time period. These types of changes will not usually affect the outcome of your case. On the other hand, sometimes a major part of the law is changed, the entire law in a particular area is rewritten, or a case that was the basis of a central legal point is overruled. In such instances, your entire ability to pursue your case may be impaired.

Foreword

In many ways, starting a business is as American as apple pie. This country, which is viewed by many as the land of opportunity, was built and continues to thrive on the vision and perspiration of small business owners.

The desire to start your own business or to be your own boss is linked to the intrinsic human desire to sail your own course and chart your own destiny. However, no matter how burning the desire, without a well thought-out plan, a new business venture lacks the tools necessary for success. To start on your path of being your own boss, begin by asking yourself some vital questions.

CAN I LIVE WITH THE UNCERTAINTY OF NOT HAVING A REGULAR PAYCHECK?

The biggest advantage of working for someone else is that you do not have to worry about how you are going to get paid. Meeting payroll is your employer's problem.

Example:

One small business owner said during her first six months in business, she did not generate enough revenue to pay herself one dime. Fortunately, she was able to live off her husband's income until her business grew to the point where she could pay herself a salary, but not everyone has those resources.

You need to be prepared for times when you will not have the funds to pay yourself. You need to plan on how you would survive if you had to go six months without a paycheck. Some ways to keep yourself going are to:

- ✪ have savings that can sustain you through the lean times (six months' worth is the general rule);

- ✪ have a spouse or other family member whose income can support you and your family without any financial contributions from your new business; or,

- ✪ budget a cushion in any start-up loans or new business loans you take out to get the business going.

DO I WORK WELL UNDER PRESSURE?

There is a universal assumption that is safe for all business owners to make—*what can go wrong will go wrong at a time when you desperately need everything to go right.* There will be times when large accounts will be lost, valued customers will complain, and reliable suppliers will fail to deliver. How you respond to these situations will dictate whether your business will fail or succeed.

Example:

Consider what happened to John. He owns a catering business. On the day before he was scheduled to cater an affair for a new client he desperately wanted to impress, a city water main burst, and his water was shut off, seemingly destroying his ability to prepare the food.

Instead of panicking, John got on the phone and called a company that sells bottled water. They agreed to supply him with the water he needed until the water to his building was turned backed on. John, by thinking on his feet, was able to avert disaster and keep his commitment to an important client.

As the person in charge, if you are confronted with a crisis, you must have the ability to immediately shift priorities and solve problems. Your ability to think on you feet and turn disaster into triumph is a sign of your future success.

DO I RESPOND POSITIVELY TO CHANGE?

A business is not a static enterprise; it may begin one way and then evolve into something else altogether. Business owners must be able to go with the flow in order to meet consumer demands and compete in a fluctuating economy.

Example:

Jan, an owner of a textbook company that caters to parents who teach their children at home, said her bottom line suffered because she was slow to add an Internet component to her business.Jan said that although she liked doing business through the old-fashioned way of storefront retail, many of her customers wanted the convenience of doing business online.

Examine yourself in different settings and determine how you respond to change. If you generally react negatively, then running your own business may not be the best path for you. Every day you will be confronted with situations that, even a day earlier, would require a different decision.

AM I WILLING TO WORK AT DRIVING REVENUE?

No matter what kind of business you start, you are going to have to go out and sell your product or service to consumers.

Example:

Sarah started a business selling hand-painted furniture to interior design companies. Because everyone who saw her work raved about the quality, she thought the chairs would sell themselves. This proved to be an almost fatal mistake that threatened the life of her business.

Sarah struggled through the first months of her business, barely making ends meet. It was not until she acknowledged her aversion to going out and getting business and began working to overcome it that was she able to turn her business around. Her new motto is, *Without sales, I fail*.

You must be willing to adopt a similar motto. Few products are so desirable or in such great demand that it will take no effort on your part to make sales. Even if you have such a product, others will be unaware that you are selling it because you are a new business. Making cold calls and soliciting business is not for everyone. You must decide if it is something you can do or at least afford to hire someone to do. No matter how good your product is, if it does not sell, you do not make a dime.

AM I WILLING TO WORK REALLY HARD?

You must be willing to break a sweat or work ten to twelve hours a day to turn your dreams into a reality. You are the one in charge, and it is ultimately up to you to make all major decisions, manage employees, work with vendors, and get the product or service to customers.

Example:

Brad, who owns and operates a chain of cleaners, said he works ten times harder as a business owner than he ever did when he was working for someone else as an employee.

AM I WILLING TO LEARN WHAT I DO NOT KNOW?

During the course of your business life, you will encounter situations that you will not know how to handle. Examples include how to motivate lackluster employees, or how to increase your referral business. When confronted with these issues, you have two choices. You can waste time and energy fighting your way through a problem, or you can go out and learn the things you do not know. A few suggestions on how you can get the information you need include the following:

- read books and listen to audiotapes;

- attend seminars;

- hire consultants;

- seek mentors; and,

- enroll in classes.

AM I WILLING TO ASK FOR HELP WHEN I NEED IT?

One of the biggest mistakes business owners make is that they try to fill all of the roles needed to operate their business. Sometimes they have control issues that cause resistance to letting go of the reins and sometimes it is because they have financial issues that make it difficult to hire help. Either way, the result is the same—instead of running the business, the business is running them. Before they know it, they are burned out, and they are too busy to focus on the things that will create revenue.

No matter how competent you are, it will not be possible (and even if it is possible, it is not smart) to try to do it all yourself. Smart and successful entrepreneurs find ways to delegate these tasks. Some of the tasks that should be delegated include:

- ✪ any task that keeps you from doing what you need to do to make money;

- ✪ any job that you absolutely detest; and,

- ✪ any job that you are not competent to perform.

DO I WANT TO MAKE MONEY?

The reason this question is important is because many people have notions that they describe as business ideas but are in fact something else, such as hobbies or causes. Businesses are created to make money.

Business owners can use the money they generate to do other things, nobler things, but generating revenue is the bottom line of every business. If you are not focused on the bottom line, you will not have the money you need to keep your doors open.

CONCLUSION

Ideally, someone starting a business should have answered yes to each of the questions asked here. However, your response to the questions is not as important as the fact that you took the time to ask them. The point of asking yourself the vital questions is that you enter into the process with your eyes wide open. What really matters is that you are aware of some of the challenges that lie ahead and that your passion is tempered with reasonable expectations.

Ultimately, the only sure way of knowing if you have what it takes to make your business a success is to go out and try it!

Introduction

Starting a business is one of the greatest challenges a person can undertake. One of the reasons for writing this book is to compile the information needed to make the undertaking a little less challenging. This book is designed to be a practical, how-to guide for people who want to start a business in North Carolina or South Carolina. We have dispensed with as much legal jargon and legal theory as possible. There will be no discussion of what the law *should* be. This book is a practical guide to what the law is and how it applies to business owners.

HOW TO USE THIS BOOK

Begin by reading the book from cover to cover. This will help you determine what is relevant to your venture and what is not relevant. A cover-to-cover reading will also help you distinguish what you think you already know from what the law really is. It will also make clear what you do not know and help you determine when you may need to go to a lawyer, accountant, or other professional.

Chapter 1 discusses matters business owners must consider when selecting a name for their business. Chapter 2 explains the pros and cons associated with the four most common forms of business organization. Chapter 3 helps you determine if there are any federal, state, or local licenses or permits you must obtain in order to operate. Chapter 4 examines the employment and labor laws that may apply to new business owners once they hire employees. Chapter 5 takes a look at insurance and explores the kind of coverage a business owner should obtain in order to protect his or her venture.

Chapter 6 assists you in making certain your marketing and advertising claims are in compliance with applicable state laws. Chapter 7 addresses questions relating to how businesses are taxed. Chapter 8 explores the concept of business franchises. Chapter 9 offers insight on e-business or doing business on the Web. Chapter 10 discusses collections and how you can get the money owed to you without breaking the law. Chapter 11 includes an overview of the Uniform Commercial Code and a discussion of intellectual property.

At the end of each chapter is a summary that you can use as a reference or checklist to make sure you have completed everything you need to get your business going.

An extensive glossary helps you understand the meanings of the legal terms used in the book that may be unfamiliar. Appendix A contains a six-step plan that allows you to put your business idea to the test. Appendix B contains an actual business plan. Appendix C contains sample forms that were cited throughout the text. These forms can be taken from the book, completed, and filed at the appropriate location.

Names, Trademarks, and Service Marks

Choosing a name for your business can be one of the most important decisions you make. If you are selling products or delivering services that you would like people to purchase or use repeatedly, then you will want a unique name that can be recognized and remembered by your customers. If your business becomes successful and people associate the name with quality products or services, then the name itself may become valuable. At that point, you will want to make sure that other businesses cannot use the name in association with their products or services.

Taking certain precautions when choosing a name for your business will give you the ability to protect your business if other businesses try to use the same or a similar name. If you can prove that you were operating your business under the name first and that consumers have been confused by the unauthorized use of the name, you will be entitled to damages from the unauthorized user. This could include the other business having to pay you for any damages or lost profits caused by the unauthorized use of your business name.

State and federal governments have developed ways to make sure that more than one business will not use the same name, to prevent consumers from becoming confused. The secretary of state offices of

North Carolina and South Carolina each keep official records of trade names and business entity names registered in their respective states. The United States Patent and Trademark Office (PTO) keeps official records of all trademarks and service marks registered with the federal government. Likewise, the North Carolina and South Carolina secretary of state offices keep official records of all trademarks and service marks registered with their respective states.

DISTINGUISHABLE BUSINESS NAMES

To register a business name in either North Carolina or South Carolina, you must choose a name that is distinguishable from every other business entity organized or authorized to do business within that state. The laws only require that a business name be somehow different from any other business names already registered. For example, if one business in North Carolina is organized under the name *Carolina Lawn, Inc.*, then the secretary of state of North Carolina may let a second business organize under the name *Carolina Lawn Service, Inc.*

You can make sure that no other business entity in your state operates under the same name by searching the online database for the North Carolina office of the secretary of state at **www.sosnc.com** or the South Carolina office of the secretary of state at **www.scsos.com**.

You can also contact the offices of the secretary of state and ask them to conduct the search for you.

North Carolina
Secretary of State
Corporations Division
P.O. Box 29622
Raleigh, NC 27626
919-807-2225

South Carolina
Secretary of State
Business Filings
Edgar Brown Building
1205 Pendleton Street
Suite 525
Columbia, SC 29201
803-734-2158

CONFUSINGLY SIMILAR BUSINESS NAMES

Registration of your business name with the secretary of state will allow you to create a business entity and begin conducting business within the state. However, if your business name is similar to another business name that was operating in your area before you, then the other business could sue you for lost profits or other damages resulting from confusion among consumers created by your business name. In order to protect yourself from liability in the future, you should make sure that no other businesses in the area you intend to operate in currently use a name so similar to the name you choose that consumers would likely become confused. Consumers may become confused by similar business names if:

- ✪ the two business names look or sound alike;

- ✪ the two businesses operate within related industries; or,

- ✪ the two businesses operate within nearby geographic areas.

Each of these factors will be considered individually and under the context of the specific businesses in question. For example, a hotel operating under the name *Carolina Sands, Inc.*, and a nearby excavating company operating under the name *Carolina Sand, Inc.*, have business names that look and sound similar, and they operate in close geographic areas, but it is unlikely that consumers would be confused because their industries are so unrelated. In such a case, both names would be allowed, as neither is *confusingly* similar in this context.

When considering a name for your business, you need to determine whether you expect to operate your business in a small, local area or in a statewide, regional, or national area. You will need to take precautions to make sure that no other business operates under the same or a similar name within a related industry in any area you expect to operate. This can be accomplished by thoroughly searching all area phone books and the Internet with the full name as well as any likely abbreviations, derivations, or segments of the name that could cause confusion.

Keep in mind that some business names are well known and would cause confusion regardless of whether the business currently operates in your area. Even if a *McDonald's* fast food restaurant does not operate in your town, it would still be confusing to consumers if you attempt to open a hamburger business under the name *McDonald's*.

RESTRICTIONS

The laws of North Carolina and South Carolina include certain rules limiting the name you may choose for a business entity. If you form your business as a corporation, the laws require that the name of a corporation must be followed by some word or abbreviation that indicates the business is incorporated. Words or abbreviations that convey this information include:

Corporation	Corp.
Incorporated	Inc.
Limited	Ltd.
Company	Co.

Similarly, the name of a limited liability company or a limited partnership must be followed by the words *Limited Liability Company* or LLC and *Limited Partnership* or LP, respectively.

Additionally, the name of a business entity may not suggest that it conducts some business that would be inappropriate or for which it is not authorized. For example, a business could not be organized under the name *Carolina Bank, Inc.,* if it is not truly an authorized banking institution.

Making sure that the business name you choose has not previously been registered with the office of the secretary of state by someone else and that you have complied with any restrictions on your name is only the first step in the naming process. Registration of a business name will stop other people from registering for the same business name in that state.

STATE REGISTRATION OF BUSINESS NAMES

After determining your name, there may be state registration requirements that you must follow. If your business is not a separate legal entity, such as a corporation or an LLC, and your business operates under a name other than your own legal name, then North Carolina law requires you to register the *trade name*. (South Carolina does not have this requirement.) Usually this is done at the local government level, in the office of the *register of deeds*, in the county where your business is located.

A trade name must be registered only if the name is different from the legal name of the person operating the business. For example, John Smith could operate a lawn care business under the name *John Smith Lawn Care* without registering it as a trade name. If he operates the business under the name *Smith Lawn Care* or *The Lawn Care Company*, then the name must be registered as a trade name.

To register a trade name, you should contact the register of deeds office in the county where your business is located. Local registration is not necessary if you create a separate business entity, unless you operate the business under a name other than the registered name of the business entity.

REGISTRATION FORMS

Once you have determined that the business name you have chosen is distinguishable from all other businesses currently registered with the office of the secretary of state in each state you wish to operate, and that the business name you have chosen is not so similar to that of another business that it would cause confusion among consumers, you should register your business name with the secretary of state. In North Carolina, file an **APPLICATION TO RESERVE A BUSINESS ENTITY NAME** (form 1, p.155). In South Carolina, if your business is a corporation or limited liability company (LLC), file an **APPLICATION TO RESERVE CORPORATE NAME** (form 2, p.157) or an **APPLICATION TO RESERVE A LIMITED LIABILITY COMPANY NAME** (form 3, p.159). You could also simply file your company's articles of incorporation if incorporating or Articles of

Organization if forming an LLC, as explained in Chapter 2. (Unlike North Carolina, South Carolina does not provide a way for an unregistered business to reserve an assumed name.)

If you file an application to reserve a name before filing your Articles, then you will have 120 days until the reservation expires. Before the expiration date, you will need to have your Articles filed and file a **Notice of Transfer of Reserved Entity Name** (form 4, p.161) in North Carolina. If you are in South Carolina, you will need to file a **Notice of Transfer of Reserved Corporate Name** (form 5, p.163) or **Notice of Transfer of a Reserved Limited Liability Company Name** (form 6, p.165).

If you organize your business in one state, and then operate your business in another state, you will need to file for *authorization to conduct business* in the other state. You can obtain authorization by filing an *Application for a Certificate of Authority to Transact Business* with the secretary of state of the state in which you wish to conduct business.

In North Carolina, file an **Application for Certificate of Authority** (form 7, p.167) if your business is a corporation or an **Application for Certificate of Authority for Limited Liability Company** (form 8, p.171) if your business is an LLC.

In South Carolina, file an **Application by a Foreign Corporation for Certificate of Authority to Transact Business** (form 9, p.173) or an **Application for a Certificate of Authority by a Foreign Limited Liability Company to Transact Business** (form 10, p.177).

The same rules apply to the name of a business organized in another state seeking authorization to do business. If you know that you will operate in another state, search the database of business names at that state's office of the secretary of state.

TRADEMARKS AND SERVICE MARKS

After you have been operating your business you may want to consider registering a trademark or service mark to further protect the value of your business's name. A trademark or service mark can also be registered to protect the name of your products or services, or any logo that your customers may associate with your products or services.

A *trademark* is any word, name, symbol, or device, or any combination of them used by you to identify and distinguish the *goods* you sell from the similar goods manufactured or sold by others. A *service mark* is any word, name, symbol, or device, or any combination of them used by you to identify and distinguish the *services* that you perform from the similar services performed by others.

Along with your business and product name, you can file a trademark for unique labels, logos, containers, displays, or some other identifying external characteristic of your goods or the package containing your goods. You can also file a service mark for the name of a unique process or procedure that you provide, or a logo that identifies the process or procedure.

While an attorney is not required to register a trademark or service mark, it is recommended that you consult an attorney that specializes in intellectual property law if you are considering registering a trademark or service mark.

The following discussion is meant only to provide you with a basic understanding of the requirements and procedures for both state and federal registration of a trademark or service mark.

STATE REGISTRATION

Both North Carolina and South Carolina have adopted a *Trademark Registration Act*. Registration of a trademark or service mark under state law gives you the exclusive rights to use that mark *within the state* you register in and to prevent others from using the mark *within that state*.

Registration of a mark is effective for five years from the date of registration in South Carolina and for ten years from the date of registration in North Carolina. Thereafter, registration can be renewed for another five-year period in South Carolina or another ten-year period in North

Carolina. Once you have registered a mark, the right to use the mark within that state becomes your property, and you may assign or sell it to anyone you wish.

Registration Requirements

Before you may register a trademark or service mark in North Carolina or South Carolina, you must *use* the mark within that state. There is no minimum time period that you must use the mark, but when you file the application for registration, you must be currently using the mark in the ordinary course of your business.

A trademark will be considered in use if your products are sold or transported within the given state and you put the mark:

- ✪ on your products or their containers or displays associated with your products or their containers;

- ✪ on tags or labels affixed to your products or their containers; or,

- ✪ on documents associated with your products if the nature of your products makes placement impracticable.

A service mark will be considered in use if your services are offered or available to be rendered in the given state and the mark is used or displayed in the sale or advertising of the services. Before the mark may be registered, your products must actually be for sale in the marketplace and you must be actually rendering your services.

Distinctness. Your trademark or service mark must be *distinguishable* from all other trademarks or service marks that have been registered in the state. Before you file an application for registration, the trademark office will not be able to tell you for certain if your mark or a similar mark has been registered by someone else. However, if you believe that your mark may cause confusion among consumers with another mark already used by some other business, the trademark office may be able to give you guidance as to what features they examine when determining if a mark is distinguishable.

Whenever two or more applications for confusingly similar marks are filed, the law requires that priority be granted to the first application *filed*, not the date the mark was first put into use. Therefore, if prior to registration, you discover that your mark may be similar to another unregistered mark used by another business, then you should file an application for registration as soon as possible.

Application for Registration

If you are currently using a mark that you believe is distinguishable and you wish to register the mark, then you must file a **TRADEMARK/SERVICE MARK REGISTRATION & RENEWAL** form (form 11, p.179) for North Carolina or an **APPLICATION FOR REGISTRATION OF A TRADEMARK OR SERVICE MARK** (form 12, p.189) for South Carolina. The application requires that you describe your mark, describe the specific goods or services the mark will cover, and provide the date the mark was first used in the state.

In addition, you must provide three *original specimens* of the mark to be registered. An original specimen of a trademark is either a *sample* of your product with the mark on it or a photograph of the mark on one of your products. An original specimen of a service mark is either a sample of marketing material used to promote the service or your business's letterhead, invoices, or envelopes containing the mark.

FEDERAL REGISTRATION

Registration of your trademark or service mark with the secretary of state gives you exclusive rights over the use of the mark within that state. However, if you would like to have exclusive rights over the use of the mark in any state, you should register the mark with the *United States Patent and Trademark Office* (PTO). The filing fee for a trademark application is $335 (at the time of this publication). You may file an application for registration with the PTO online at their website, **www.uspto.gov**, or you can call the PTO at 800-786-9199 to obtain a printed form to file by mail at the following address:

Commissioner for Trademarks
P.O. Box 1451
Alexandria, VA 22313

It is recommended that you conduct a search of the PTO prior to filing your application. The search may help you determine if a mark similar to yours has already been registered. You may conduct the search for free at the PTO website or at the Patent and Trademark Office Public Search Library for trademarks, located at the PTO office in Arlington, Virginia.

Application for Registration

Unlike registration for use within a state, you may file an application for registration with the PTO before you actually use the mark. If you file a *use-based* application, which is for a mark that is already used in commerce, the requirements are similar to the requirements for a state application. If you file an *intent-based* application, which is for a mark that is not already used in commerce, then in addition to the other requirements, you must have an actual intention to use the mark in commerce.

If the application is accepted by the PTO, then the mark will be published in the *Weekly Gazette*, a publication of the PTO. Any other business that believes that the mark will cause damage to the business will have thirty days from publication to file an *opposition* to the registration of the mark. A hearing will then be held before the Trademark Trial and Appeal Board, a PTO administrative tribunal, where each side can argue its position. If no opposition is filed or if the opposition is unsuccessful, the application will be granted. If you filed an application based on intent to use a mark, then you will have six months after the application is granted to actually start to use the mark in commerce.

Summary

✪ The secretary of state offices of North Carolina and South Carolina keep official records of trade names and business entity names registered in their respective states.

✪ The United States Patent and Trademark Office keeps official records of all trademarks and service marks registered with the federal government.

✪ To register a business name in either North Carolina or South Carolina, you must choose a name that is distinguishable from every other business entity organized or authorized to do business within that state.

✪ If you form your business as a corporation, the name of the corporation must be followed by some word or abbreviation that indicates the business is incorporated.

✪ A trade name must be registered only if the name is different than the legal name of the person operating the business.

✪ A trademark or service mark can also be registered to protect the name of your products or services, or any logo that your customers may associate with your products or services.

✪ Registration of a trademark or service mark under the state law will give you the exclusive rights to use that mark within the state you register in and prevent others from using the mark within that state.

✪ Registration of your trademark or service mark with the secretary of state will give you exclusive rights over the use of the mark within that state. However, if you would like to have exclusive rights over the use of the mark in any state, you should register the mark with the United States Patent and Trademark Office (PTO).

chapter 2

Selecting a Form of Business Organization

Selecting a form of business organization is an important consideration when starting a business. There are several forms you can choose from. The four most common forms of business organization include the following:

1. sole proprietorship;

2. partnership;

3. corporation; and,

4. limited liability company.

This chapter examines these forms and explains the pros and cons of each.

SOLE PROPRIETORSHIP

When most people want to start a business, they simply open shop and do what they can to get people to come through the door to buy their goods or services. A *sole proprietorship* is relatively simple to start. Due to its simplicity, most new businesses choose to take this form. When the business grows and develops, it changes forms to reflect the needs and vision of the company.

The most distinguishing characteristic of a sole proprietorship is that there is no legal difference between you and the business or between the business and you. This can be a benefit or a liability, depending on the circumstance.

Advantages   As a sole proprietor, *you* are the business. Because you already exist, there are no formalities creating the business. There are no agreements to sign or forms to file with the secretary of state. The minute you open the door, you are in business. Conversely, there are also no formalities associated with ending the business. You can close shop and be out of business as quickly as it began.

Disadvantages   The biggest drawback to a sole proprietorship is that there is nothing standing between you and the business should something go wrong. While this is extremely unlikely if you are properly insured, it is conceivable that you could lose everything you own in a single lawsuit. Before deciding to just open a business, you need to consider the risks associated with your enterprise.

If you are someone starting a business selling the crafts you create out of your home, the risk of someone suing you is extremely small. However, if you are opening a restaurant, the risk increases. It is easy to imagine someone slipping and falling, or claiming an allergic reaction to your special sauce. In cases like this it might be worth going through the formalities and selecting a form of organization that will protect your personal assets.

PARTNERSHIP

Partnerships are formed when two or more people start a business. The benefits of this type of business are that you have someone with whom to share the load. One partner might be responsible for making the product, while the other focuses on getting people in the door and making sure the bills are paid on time.

Creating a partnership does not require any formalities, although it is wise to have a written agreement. Areas that you must make certain are covered in any agreement include the following.

- ✪   How will liabilities be divided?

- ✪   How will assets/profits be divided?

- ✪   What are the responsibilities of each partner?

- ✪   How can partners be added?

- ✪   What happens if a partner dies?

- ✪   How will conflicts be resolved?

- ✪   What happens if a partner wants out?

- ✪   What if one partner wants to buy out the other partner?

- ✪   What happens if a partner wants to begin a competing venture?

- ✪   How will growth and expansion will be handled?

Partnerships are great when they work well, but they can be the most difficult of all forms of business to resolve when they do not. Two types of problems that can undermine business partnerships and should be avoided are:

- ✪   poor communication—partners must be on the same page and know when to speak up and when to listen, and

- ✪   interest—if one partner has an outside interest that is greater than the interest in the partnership, it can tear the partnership apart.

Partnerships require no legal formality to dissolve if there is no partnership agreement that dictates what will be done in the event of a breakup. However, because you are involved with at least one other person, it will be more complicated to dissolve a partnership than to end a sole proprietorship.

Selecting a Partner

Deciding on a business partner is something that should be given careful consideration. Your best friend may be the best friend in the world, but he or she could be the worst business partner imaginable. The only way you are going to find out is by asking each other tough questions, taking off the rose-colored glasses, and looking at what each person has to bring to a business relationship. Keep in mind that you may be too close to a friend or family member to make a good decision about your compatibility as business partners. Starting a business with someone who is neither a family member or friend allows you the objectivity to do what is best for the business without worrying too much about the relationship going sour.

Things you might consider when taking on a partner include the following.

- Do you share the same vision for the company?

- Do you share the same core values?

- Do you have compatible temperaments?

- Do you share the same work ethic?

Before you go into business with someone, you should do a thorough investigation into the person's background.

Liabilities

Individual members of a partnership are vulnerable to the same liability issues as a sole proprietorship. In a partnership agreement, the partners can decide how liability will be apportioned between the partners, but this would not apply to a third party.

CORPORATION

A *corporation* is a legal business entity that has a life of its own. Its existence is separate and apart from the owners or the individuals who incorporated the business. It is created by filing a document called *articles of incorporation* with the secretary of state in the state you are incorporating in.

Articles of Incorporation

The *articles of incorporation* must include some basic information about the business. You can file *articles of incorporation* with the forms provided in Appendix C. For North Carolina, file **ARTICLES OF INCORPORATION** (form 13, p.195) and for South Carolina, file **ARTICLES OF INCORPORATION** (form 14, p.199). Some of the requirements for the articles are discussed in the following section.

The name of your corporation. Generally, one of the following words or abbreviations must be included in whatever name you select—Company, Corporation, Incorporated, Limited, Co., Corp., Inc., or Ltd. (see page 4 for more information.)

Example:
John and Joe decided to incorporate and use their names in the business name. These are some possible names for their company.

John and Joe's Company	John and Joe's Co.
John and Joe's Corporation	John and Joe's Corp.
John and Joe's Incorporated	John and Joe's Inc.
John and Joe's Limited	John and Joe's Ltd.

The classes of stock issued by your corporation. Generally, corporations issue one class of *stock*. This is typically the *common stock* of the corporation. A discussion of classes of stock is beyond the scope of this book. Consult an attorney for advice regarding which class would best serve the needs of your business.

The registered office and the name of your registered agent. The *registered office* is the designated place where your business can be reached for official (government) notices or by those needing to sue the corporation. Often, it is the place where you receive your mail. Your registered office does not have to be the same location as the place where you conduct your day-to-day business. It can be, but there is no requirement that it has to be.

The *registered agent* is the person authorized to accept or sign for official documents like legal papers. In small companies, the owner or person who incorporates the business generally serves in the role of registered agent.

In North Carolina, there is a requirement that the registered agent and the registered office be *continuously situated* in North Carolina. There is a procedure requiring a small fee that allows you to change the agent or office if that becomes necessary. There are also companies that perform this function for you. A small business generally would not need to go to this expense.

The name and addresses of the incorporators. The *incorporators* are the people who actually go through the task of completing the *articles of incorporation* and filing them with the state. There must be at least one incorporator, but there is no upper limit on the number possible (one to three is the norm). The incorporators must actually sign the articles of incorporation.

Once the articles of incorporation have been completed, they must be filed with the secretary of state. There is a filing fee that must accompany the Articles. The secretary of state will then send you a certified copy of the Articles.

Organizational Meeting

Once you receive the certified copy of the articles of incorporation, the incorporators must hold an organizational meeting before you can officially open for business. At the *organizational meeting*, the following matters should be addressed:

- ✪ elect a board of directors;

- ✪ elect officers;

- ✪ adopt a set of corporate *bylaws* (a document that spells out the inner workings of the business);

- ✪ issue shares of stock;

✪   establish the corporate fiscal year; and,

✪   formally adopt any agreements or contracts needed by your corporation.

Additionally, before opening for business, you will need to apply for a federal and state tax identification number (see Chapter 3); apply for any relevant business licenses (see Chapter 3); buy a company seal from an office supply company; and, create a bookkeeping system.

Annual Reports

A copy of the annual report form will be sent to you at the address listed on the *articles of incorporation*.

North Carolina. Corporations are required to file annual reports along with a filing fee. In North Carolina, they are filed with the North Carolina Department of Revenue. The reports must be filed by the 15th day of the third month following the close of their fiscal year. That means if the Home Co. fiscal year ended March 31st, its annual report would be due June 15th. Failure to complete an annual report in a timely manner could result in your corporation being dissolved. The filing fee is $20.

South Carolina. You must consult an attorney regarding the filing of annual reports in South Carolina. The South Carolina legislature has decided that the assistance of an attorney is *necessary* to complete this process.

Advantages

There are considerable advantages to incorporating your business. Consider these benefits of incorporation, in order of importance.

Liability protection. Because the incorporators are a separate entity from the corporation, the business could go bad without it impacting your personal affairs.

Tax breaks. While a discussion of taxes falls outside the scope of this book, there are tax breaks available to corporations that are not otherwise available to unincorporated businesses. Contact an accountant to discuss this issue.

Credibility. Because it is a separate entity from the owners, an incorporated business can be appraised and sold. This makes it more attractive to investors.

Disadvantages The major disadvantages of incorporating your business are the formalities and fees associated with creating and running a corporation. The same formalities that go into creating a corporation must be followed when it is dissolved.

LIMITED LIABILITY COMPANY

You can have limited liability without the formalities of a corporation by forming a *limited liability company* (LLC). An LLC is an unincorporated association that offers a combination of liability protection and tax benefits. There is some formality associated with creating an LLC, but not as much as those formalities associated with a regular corporation.

Formation To form an LLC, you must file an **ARTICLES OF ORGANIZATION** form with the secretary of state. (Form 15, p.___, for North Carolina information or form 16, p.___ for South Carolina information.) It must include the following information.

Name. The name you select for your company must contain the following words or abbreviations—L.L.C., LLC, ltd. liability co., limited liability co., or ltd. liability company.

Example:
If John and Joe form an LLC using their names in the business name, they would have these options.

John and Joe's L.L.C.   John and Joe's ltd. liability co.
John and Joe's LLC   John and Joe's limited liability co.
        John and Joe's ltd. liability company

Dissolution date. The dissolution date is the date—month, day, and year—the company will be dissolved. This applies in situations where a company is formed for a specific purpose, and when the purpose is complete, the company will be dissolved. If you leave the space blank, the LLC will be deemed to continue indefinitely.

Organizers/Members. The name and address of each person signing the *Articles of Organization* must be listed. You must also indicate whether you are completing the Articles in the capacity of a member or an organizer.

Registered office and agent. The owner of the LLC generally serves as the registered agent. Generally, the registered agent must reside in the state where the LLC is filed.

Finalizing Formation

Once you complete the *Articles of Organization,* they must be filed with the secretary of state along with a filing fee. A certified copy will be returned to you. At that point, you must take the following steps.

Execute an operating agreement. This is similar to bylaws adopted by corporations. It details how the LLC will be managed.

Select a manager. Generally, the organizational structure of LLCs consists of managers who are responsible for the internal management of the company and members who have certain rights in the operation of the company. Unless you indicate otherwise, the members of a limited liability company are also managers.

Additionally, before opening for business, you will need to apply for a federal and state tax identification number (see Chapter 3); apply for any relevant business licenses (see Chapter 3); and, create a bookkeeping system.

Annual Reports

A copy of the annual report form will be sent to you at the address listed on the *Articles of Organization*.

North Carolina. Each year, the company must file an annual report with the North Carolina secretary of state. The report is due on the fifteenth day of the fourth month following the close of the company's fiscal year. For example, if your company's fiscal year ends on April 30th, the annual report would be due on August 15th. The annual report filing fee is $200.

South Carolina. The first annual report must be delivered to the secretary of state between January 1st and April 1st of the year following the calendar year in which a limited liability company was organized. Subsequent annual reports must be delivered to the secretary of state on or before the 15th of the fourth month following the close of the taxable year. The annual report filing fee is $10.

Advantages There are considerable advantages to forming your business as a limited liability company.

Minimal Paperwork. The forms associated with forming a limited liability company are significantly less than those associated with forming a regular corporation.

Fewer Formalities. Limited liability companies are not required to conduct regular meetings or to engage in many of the other ongoing formalities that regular corporations are required to perform.

Legal Protection. The owners, or members, of a limited liability company are not personally liable for the debts and liabilities of their company.

Disadvantages While there are tax benefits to operating a limited liability company, they sometimes are not as generous as those available to a regular corporation.

Using an Attorney In North Carolina, you do not need a lawyer to file either *articles of incorporation* or *Articles of Organization*. If you need assistance completing the forms, you can consult an attorney or you can go to **www.secretary.state.nc.us/Corporations** and download a pamphlet titled *Incorporating Your Business in North Carolina* or *Organizing Your Limited Liability Company In North Carolina*.

As mentioned earlier, South Carolina law specifically requires that a licensed attorney certify or sign off on the *articles of incorporation*. However, you do not need an attorney to establish your business as an LLC.

Summary

- ✪ The four most common forms of business organization include the following: sole proprietorship, partnership, corporation, and limited liability company.

- ✪ The most distinguishing characteristic of a sole proprietorship is that there is no legal difference between you and the business or between the business and you.

- ✪ Partnerships are formed when two or more people start a business.

- ✪ Creating a partnership does not require any formalities, although it is wise to have a written agreement.

- ✪ A corporation is a legal business entity that has a life of its own. Its existence is separate and apart from the owners or the individuals who incorporated the business.

- ✪ A limited liability company (LLC) is an unincorporated association that offers a combination of liability protection and tax benefits.

chapter 3

Business Licenses and Permits

Before opening a business, a business owner must determine if there are any federal, state, or local licenses or permits he or she must obtain in order to operate.

FEDERAL LICENSES OR PERMITS

In an effort to encourage entrepreneurship, the federal government takes a *hands-off* approach when it comes to the regulation of small businesses. If you only have a few employees, it is not likely you will need to obtain any federal licenses or permits. However, the operative word is *small*. Once your business grows beyond a few employees, the likelihood of your needing federal licenses or permits will increase.

Regardless of the number of people you employ, if your business falls into certain categories, then you can be fairly certain that there is a federal regulation you should know about. Those categories include:

- ✪ sale or use of hazardous materials;

- ✪ sale of goods or services across state lines;

- ○ sale of food or drugs; and,

- ○ sale of alcohol, firearms, or tobacco.

To help determine what federal licenses or permits are needed for your business, it may be beneficial to contact one of the following.

- ○ The Small Business Administration at **www.sba.gov**.

- ○ A trade association for your industry. They will have information that will ensure you are in compliance with all applicable federal laws. They may require you to join the association before providing information. However, they are usually an invaluable resource for new business owners.

- ○ The federal government via the Internet. A website that should be able to answer your questions or point you in the right direction can be found at **www.dol.gov/esa**.

EMPLOYER IDENTIFICATION NUMBER

If you answer yes to any of the following questions, you will need to apply for a federal *employer identification number* (EIN).

- ○ Do you have employees?

- ○ Do you operate your business as a corporation or a partnership?

- ○ Do you file any of these tax returns—Employment, Excise, or Alcohol, Tobacco, and Firearms?

- ○ Do you withhold taxes on income, other than wages, paid to nonresident aliens?

- ○ Do you have a Keogh plan?

- ○ Are you involved with any of the following types of organizations?

- Trusts

- Estates

- Real Estate Mortgage Investment Conduits

- Nonprofit Organizations

- Farmers' Cooperatives

- Plan Administrators

You have four options for filing for an EIN number. You can do it online at the IRS website **www.irs.gov**. You can also use **IRS FORM SS-4** (form 17, p.211) and file in one of the following ways:

✪ By mail:
   Internal Revenue Service Center
   Attn: EIN Operation
   Holtsville, NY 00501

✪ Over the phone:
   800-829-4933

✪ By fax:
   631-447-8960

STATE LICENSES AND PERMITS

Not every new business venture needs a business license. Whether your business will need a license or permit depends on the type of business it is. For example, ABC Company might be a business that provides typing services to law firms. There are no state licensing requirements for that type of business. However, DEF Company might own a restaurant, in which case there are several licensing requirements that must be satisfied.

North Carolina   In North Carolina you can contact the *North Carolina Business License Information Office* (BLIO) to assist you in determining the licenses or permits your business needs. The office can be reached at 919-715-2864 or 800-228-8443. They have consultants who can guide you through the process and help you determine compliance with all state licensing and permit requirements.

There are added benefits of using the BLIO service. Ordinarily, if you fail to meet compliance, you might be subject to a fine. However, if you follow the advice of the BLIO consultant and do not get a permit you are supposed to get, you will not be subject to a fine if the consultant failed to properly advise you.

Example:

Donna was opening a child care center. She contacted a BLIO consultant about relevant licenses. Through an oversight, the BLIO consultant neglected to inform her about a license she needed to operate the center. Six months into the business, Donna received notification that she was not in compliance and her business was fined. Donna notified the state of the advice she received from the BLIO. The state waived the fine and gave Donna additional time to obtain the license she needed.

South Carolina   The most effective way to determine compliance with the South Carolina license and permit requirements is to log on to the Internet. Through a program called *Business One Stop,* it is possible in many instances to start a business in South Carolina online.

Business One Stop was created to make it easier to start a business in South Carolina. If you plan to apply online, you will need the following information:

- Social Security number;

- federal employer identification number;

- type of ownership;

- address of business; and,

- payroll information.

You should also be prepared to pay with a credit card. In order to access this site, log on to **www.myscgov.com.** Click the "Business" link and then click "Starting a Business."

LOCAL LICENSES AND PERMITS

When establishing a business, you must also consider the licenses the city or county may require. You may need either, or you may need both. The only way to find out is to ask.

In North Carolina, the *Business License Information Office* will also provide direction in getting this information. South Carolina residents should consult **www.myscgov.com**. Businesses that fail to obtain the proper licenses may be subject to fines and other penalties.

Lastly, there are certain businesses, like child care centers, restaurants, and hair salons, that need to obtain special permits from one or more of the following entities:

- ✪ health department;

- ✪ fire department;

- ✪ police department; or,

- ✪ sanitation department.

ZONING AND ORDINANCES

Most cities, counties, and townships have local ordinances that govern residential and business zones. That is what keeps an airport from being built in the middle of a suburban neighborhood or a neighborhood from being built in the center of an office park. It is important to check on how a location is zoned before agreeing to rent or buy any retail or manufacturing space.

This is also true for people who open home-based businesses. Usually there is no problem, but if parking is a problem or you are going to have lots of deliveries, you should ensure that you are not violating any local zoning ordinances. Problems are easier to prevent than to solve.

North Carolina Occupational Licensing Boards

Certain occupations and types of business have their own licensing requirements. The following list provides contact information for the most common in North Carolina.

Board of Examiners of Electrical Contractors
P.O. Box 18727
Raleigh, NC 27619
www.ncbeec.org

Board of Electrolysis Examiners
Pinehurst Building
Box 34
2 Centerview Drive
Greensboro, NC 27407

Board of Examiners
for Engineers and Surveyors
4601 Six Forks Road
Suite 310
Raleigh, NC 27609
www.ncbels.org

Board of Registration for Foresters
P.O. Box 27393
Raleigh, NC 27611

Board of General Contractors
3739 National Drive
Suite 225
Raleigh, NC 27612
www.nclbgc.net

Board of Licensed Geologists
P.O. Box 41225
Raleigh, NC 27629
www.ncblg.org

Board of Hearing Aid Dealers and Fitters
P.O. Box 966
Raleigh, NC 27602
www.nchalb.org

Home Inspectors Licensing Board
410 North Boylan Avenue
Raleigh, NC 27603

Board of Landscape Architects
P.O. Box 41225
Raleigh, NC 27629
www.ncbola.org

Landscape Contractors Registration Board
P.O. Box 1578
Knightdale, NC 27545
www.nclcrb.state.nc.us

Board of Law Examiners
P.O. Box 2946
Raleigh, NC 27602
www.ncble.org

Public Librarian Certification Commission
109 East Jones Street
Raleigh, NC 27601

NC Locksmith Licensing Board
P.O. Box 10972
Raleigh, NC 27605
www.nclocksmithboard.org

Marriage and Family Therapy Licensure Board
P.O. Box 37669
Raleigh, NC 27627
www.nclmft.org

Board of Massage and Bodywork Therapy
P.O. Box 2539
Raleigh, NC 27602
www.bmbt.org

Midwifery Joint Committee
P.O. Box 2129
Raleigh, NC 27602
www.ncbon.com

Board of Mortuary Science
1033 Wade Avenue
Suite 108
Raleigh, NC 27605
www.ncbms.org

Board of Nursing
3724 National Drive
Suite 201
Raleigh, NC 27612
        or
P.O. Box 2129
Raleigh, NC 27602

Board of Examiners of Nursing Home Administrators
3733 National Drive
Suite 228
Raleigh, NC 27612
www.ncbenha.org

Board of Occupational Therapy
P.O. Box 2280
Raleigh, NC 27602
www.ncbot.org

Board of Opticians
P.O. Box 25336
Raleigh, NC 27611

Board of Examiners in Optometry
109 North Graham Street
Wallace, NC 28466
www.ncoptometry.org

Board of Practicing Pastoral Counselors
3000 Bethesda Place
Suite 503
Winston Salem, NC 27103

Board of Pharmacy
P.O. Box 4560
Chapel Hill, NC 27515
www.ncbop.org

Board of Physical Therapy Examiners
18 West Colony Place
Suite 140
Durham, NC 27705
www.ncptboard.org

**North Carolina
Medical Board**
P.O. Box 20007
Raleigh, NC 27619
www.ncmedboard.org

**Board of Plumbing, Heating
and Fire Sprinkler
Contractors**
1109 Dresser Court
Raleigh, NC 27609
www.nclicensing.org

Board of Podiatry Examiners
1500 Sunday Drive
Suite 102
Raleigh, NC 27607
www.ncbpe.org

Private Protective Services
9001 Mail Service Center
Raleigh, NC 27699

Real Estate Commission
P.O. Box 17100
Raleigh, NC 27619

**Board of Refrigeration
Examiners**
893 Highway 70 West
Suite 208
Garner, NC 27529
www.refrigerationboard.org

**North Carolina Respiratory
Care Board**
1100 Navaho Drive
Suite 242
Raleigh, NC 27609
www.ncrcb.org

**Board of Sanitarian
Examiners**
P.O. Box 610
Lumberton, NC 28359
www.rsboard.com

**Certification Board
for Social Work**
P.O. Box 1043
Asheboro, NC 27204
www.ncswboard.org

**Board of Licensing Soil
Scientists**
659 Cary Towne Boulevard
PMB 281
Cary, NC 27511
www.ncblss.org

**Board of Speech and
Language Pathologists and
Audiologists**
P.O. Box 16885
Greensboro, NC 27416
www.ncboeslpa.org

**Substance Abuse
Professionals
Certification Board**
P.O. Box 10126
Raleigh, NC 27605
www.ncsapcb.org

**Board of Recreational
Therapy Licensure**
P.O. Box 67
Saxapahaw, NC 27340

Veterinary Medical Board
P.O. Box 37549
Raleigh, NC 27627

South Carolina Occupational Licensing Boards

Certain occupations and types of business have their own licensing requirements. The following list provides contact information for the most common in South Carolina.

Foresters
P.O. Box 11329
Columbia, SC 29211
803-896-4498

Board of Funeral Service
P.O. Box 11329
Columbia, SC 29211
803-896-4497

Registration for Geologists
P.O. Box 11329
Columbia, SC 29211
803-896-4498

Long Term Health Care
P.O. Box 11329
Columbia, SC 29211
803-896-4544

Manufactured Housing Board
P.O. Box 11329
Columbia, SC 29211
803-896-4682

Massage/Bodywork Therapy
P.O. Box 11329
Columbia, SC 29210
803-896-4490

Board of Medical Examiners
P.O. Box 11289
Columbia, SC 29211
803-896-4500

Board of Nursing
P.O. Box 12367
Columbia, SC 29211
803-896-4550

Board of Occupational Therapy
P.O. Box 11329
Columbia, SC 29211
803-896-4683

Board of Examiners in Opticianry
P.O. Box 11329
Columbia, SC 29211
803-896-4681

Board of Examiners in Optometry
P.O. Box 11329
Columbia, SC 29211
803-896-4679

Board of Pharmacy
P.O. Box 11927
Columbia, SC 29211
803-896-4700

Board of Physical Therapy
P.O. Box 11329
Columbia, SC 29211
803-896-4655

The Pilotage Commission
P.O. Box 11329
Columbia, SC 29211
803-896-4415

Board of Podiatry Examiners
P.O. Box 11289
Columbia, SC 29211
803-896-4685

**Board of Examiners in
Psychology**
P.O. Box 11329
Columbia, SC 29211
803-896-4664

Board of Pyrotechnic Safety
P.O. Box 11847
Columbia, SC 29211
803-896-4420

Real Estate Commission
P.O. Box 11847
Columbia, SC 29211
803-896-4400

Real Estate Appraisers Board
P.O. Box 11847
Columbia, SC 29211
803-896-4400

**Residential Builders
Commission**
P.O. Box 11329
Columbia, SC 29211
803-896-4696

**Board of Social Work
Examiners**
P.O. Box 11329
Columbia, SC 29211
803-896-4665

**Speech, Language
Pathology/Audiology**
P.O. Box 11847
Columbia, SC 29211
803-896-4650

**Veterinary Medical
Examiners**
P.O. Box 11329
Columbia, SC 29211
803-896-4598

Summary

- If your business falls into one of these categories, then you can be fairly certain there is a federal regulation you should know about:

    - sale or use of hazardous materials;

    - sale of goods or services across state lines;

    - sale of food or drugs; or,

    - sale of alcohol, firearms, or tobacco.

- You can obtain a federal employer ID number (EIN) online or by telephone, mail, or fax.

- In North Carolina, you can contact the North Carolina Business License Information Office (BLIO) to assist you in determining the licenses or permits your business needs.

- In South Carolina, it is possible in many instances to start a business online through a program called Business One Stop.

- When establishing a business, you must also consider the licenses the city or county may require.

- Most cities, counties, and townships have local ordinances that govern residential and business zones. This also applies to home-based businesses.

Employment and Labor Laws

Most states have enacted laws to protect the interests and well-being of employees in the workplace. This chapter examines the employment and labor laws that may apply to new business owners once they hire employees.

HIRING EMPLOYEES

Generally, employers are permitted to hire whomever they choose. The exceptions to this general rule include situations in which a business is the recipient of certain state and federal contracts. In an effort to promote diversity, these contracts are awarded to businesses committed to hiring practices that promote *equal opportunity employment*.

Effective Hiring Policies

Always hire the most qualified applicant. This is important because your business will only be as successful as the people who work for you. Another benefit of this policy is that it will protect you against claims of *discrimination*. These actions can be costly to defend and can create a public relations nightmare.

Do not hire anyone you cannot fire. It is not unusual for new business owners to hire friends and relatives. In most cases, this works well for everyone involved. However, if an employee is not working out and it is in the best interests of the business to let him or her go, he or she must be let go, no matter how difficult. If you know you do not have the heart to fire your mother, do not hire her.

MINORS

If you decide to hire minors, make certain you are in compliance with all relevant *Child Labor Laws*.

North Carolina   In North Carolina, no person under age 18 can be hired without a *youth employment certificate*. Children under age 18 who are employed by their parents are exempt from most of these provisions. However, they still need a permit. They are prohibited from working in hazardous or detrimental occupations and someone 21 years or older must be present on the premises.

The following outlines the general child labor work scheduling rules, giving the maximum daily and weekly hours children under age 16 can work.

- ✪ Non-school day—8

- ✪ Non-school week—40

- ✪ School day—3

- ✪ School week—18

Children under age 16 are prohibited from working between the hours of 7 p.m. (9 p.m. during summer vacation) and 7 a.m.

Children between ages 16 and 17 are prohibited from working between 11 p.m. and 5 a.m. before a school day while school is in session. (The law is waived with written permission from both parent and school.)

South Carolina   In South Carolina, a minor needs to be 14 years old before he or she can begin work. However, the child labor laws have restrictions on what type of work can be performed.

The following outlines the general child labor work scheduling rules, giving the maximum daily and weekly hours children under age 16 can work.

- ✪ Non-school day—8

- ✪ Non-school week—40

- ✪ School day—3

- ✪ School week—18

Children under age 16 are prohibited from working between the hours of 7 p.m. (9 p.m. June 1 through Labor Day) and 7 a.m.

CITIZENSHIP VERIFICATION

Employers are responsible for making certain that the people they hire are either U.S. citizens or authorized to work in the United States. Before you actually hire an employee, he or she must provide you with one or more of the following forms of documentation:

- ✪ birth certificate;

- ✪ driver's license;

- ✪ state-issued ID card;

- ✪ Social Security card;

- ✪ passport;

- ✪ certification of U.S. citizenship;

✪   certificate of naturalization; or,

✪   alien registration card.

Once you determine a potential employee is eligible for employment, you must then complete an **EMPLOYMENT ELIGIBILITY VERIFICATION** form, commonly referred to as **FORM I-9** (form 18, p.219) and keep it with your employee records.

The responsibility is the employer's to check an employee's eligibility status within three days of the person being hired. Stiff penalties can be imposed for failing to do so. If you later discover that the employee is not eligible to work, you cannot knowingly continue to employ this individual. However, if you properly completed the paperwork, you will not be penalized for hiring an unauthorized alien unless the government can prove you had actual knowledge of the unauthorized status of the employee at the time of hire.

While it may be tempting to avoid hiring noncitizens in order to avoid the paperwork, keep in mind that it is illegal to discriminate against employees because of their national origin or citizenship status. To learn more, contact the United States Citizenship and Immigration Services (USCIS) at:

United States Citizenship and Immigration Services
425 I Street, NW
Washington, DC 20536
800-870-3676
www.uscis.gov

WAGES

Employers are generally required to inform employees of certain financial matters relating to their employment at the time of hire. This notification can be verbal or in writing. A written notice will eliminate any confusion and prevent problems from occurring down the road. Failure to provide this information can result in a penalty. The following describes what information employers are required to give employees at the time of hire:

✪   rate of pay;

✪   vacation time and pay policy;

✪   sick leave; and,

✪   day and place for payment of wages.

A written notice must be posted in a prominent place in the workplace that states the company's policy regarding wages and notice of any changes. Employers may be also be required to maintain records of each employee's wages, hours, and vacation. Again, good recordkeeping will minimize any disputes that might arise in the future.

North Carolina   Certain North Carolina laws impose additional requirements over the federal regulation of wages.

Minimum wage. States possess the right to set a minimum wage. It cannot be lower than what is set by the federal government, but it can be higher. In North Carolina, the minimum wage is $5.15 per hour (at the time of the printing of this title).

Payday. Employees must be paid on the regular pay day. Pay periods can be daily, weekly, biweekly, semimonthly, or monthly. Bonuses and commissions can be paid at other intervals, assuming the employee is given proper notice.

Tips. Any tips earned by an employee can be counted as wages only up to 50% of the applicable minimum wage for each hour worked, and:

✪   the employee must be notified in advance;

✪   the employee must be allowed to retain all tips;

✪   the employer must maintain and record the amount of tips received by each employee; and,

✪   the employee must comply with other standards.

Training wage. Employers may impose a training wage on new employees. The rate cannot be lower than 85% of the minimum wage and is restricted to a ninety-day, on-the-job training limit. It is illegal for employers to cycle people in every ninety days to save money on labor. If found guilty of this practice, the Department of Labor can ban an employer's use of the training wage permanently.

Overtime. If an employee works more than forty hours per week in any given work week, he or she must be paid no less than 1.5 times his or her regular pay rate for those hours in excess of forty.

South Carolina   Certain South Carolina laws impose additional requirements over the federal regulation of wages.

Minimum wage. South Carolina has not established a set minimum wage; therefore, it is set by federal law and the minimum wage is $5.15 per hour (at the time of the printing of this title).

Payday. Employees must be paid on the regular pay day. Pay periods can be daily, weekly, biweekly, semimonthly, or monthly. Bonuses and commissions can be paid at other intervals, assuming the employee is given proper notice.

Tips. Employers of *tipped employees* (those who customarily and regularly receive more than $30 a month in tips) may consider such tips as part of their wages. However, employers must pay a direct wage of at least $2.13 per hour if they claim a tip credit. They must also meet other certain conditions. (Visit **www.irs.gov** for more information.)

Overtime. If an employee works more than forty hours per week in any given work week, he or she must be paid no less than 1.5 times his or her regular pay rate for those hours in excess of forty.

BENEFITS

Although these benefits will be needed to attract quality employees, there is no requirement that employers provide sick leave, vacation, or health insurance.

However, if you do not notify employees at the time of hiring that they have these benefits, you must offer time off or compensation. Notifying employees in writing is best with regard to what conditions exist to earn vacation and what conditions result in losing vacation time or pay. Any change in policies must be given to employees in reasonable time—before it is time to take the vacation.

SAFETY IN THE WORKPLACE

The purpose of the *Occupational Safety and Health Act* (OSHA) is to encourage employers and employees to reduce the occupation and safety health hazards at the work place. Both South Carolina and North Carolina have adopted a state version of this federal law. It mandates that a workplace must be free from hazards that cause or are likely to cause death, serious injury, or physical harm. A *reasonable man standard* will be applied to determine whether a recognized hazard exists in the workplace.

To learn more about compliance, contact:

North Carolina—OSHA
1101 Mail Service Center
Raleigh, NC 27699
800-NC-Labor
www.nclabor.com

South Carolina—OSHA
Division of Labor
P.O. Box 11329
Columbia, SC 29211
www.llr.state.sc.us/labor/osha

TERMINATING EMPLOYMENT

North Carolina and South Carolina are both *employment at will* states. This means employees may be terminated for any reason—a good reason, a bad reason, or no reason at all. Likewise, employees have the same option to terminate their employment without offering notice or an explanation.

Employers are prohibited from terminating an employee based on his or her race, color, age, sex, handicap or disability, national origin, or religion. It may also be illegal to fire an employee for the following reasons:

✪ retaliation for filing a discrimination complaint with a state or federal agency;

✪ retaliation for workers' compensation claim;

✪ retaliation for filing an OSHA complaint; or,

✪ refusal to do something illegal.

Final Pay Requirements

When an employment relationship ends, the employer is under certain obligations as to when any remaining wages or bonuses are paid to the parting employee.

North Carolina. In North Carolina, all wages must be paid on or before the next payday. If there is a dispute over wages, the employer should pay the wages or part of wages that he or she concedes is not in dispute. The employee can take steps to obtain the balance that is in dispute.

Failure to follow this requirement can result in a penalty that includes unpaid wages and interest. Additionally, other damages equal to the amount of unpaid wages can be charged to employers who did not act in good faith and are not reasonable. Employers may also be ordered to pay the employee's attorney's fees.

South Carolina. In South Carolina, employers must pay employees all wages due within forty-eight hours of the day of separation or on the next regularly schedule payday as long as it does not exceed thirty days from the date employment ended.

EMPLOYMENT NOTICES

The Department of Labor in both North Carolina and South Carolina requires employers to post certain information throughout the workplace to ensure employees are aware of their rights.

North Carolina

In North Carolina, employers with five or more employees must keep posted (in a conspicuous place) in every room, a printed notice stating the provisions of law relative to the employment of adult persons and children and the regulation of hours and working conditions. You can obtain a printed copy of the notice from the State Department of Labor at **www.dol.state.nc.us** or 800-NC-Labor.

South Carolina   In South Carolina, employers can obtain an All-in-One poster that contains required employment notices from these four agencies:

○ South Carolina's Department of Labor, which includes *Licensing and Regulation's OSHA Requirements*, *Payment of Wages, Child Labor*, and *Right-to-Work Laws*;

○ Employment Security Commission, which contains *Workers Pay No Part of the Cost for Job Insurance* and *If You Become Unemployed*;

○ Workers Compensation Commission, which contains *Workers Comp Works for You*; and,

○ Human Affairs Commission, which contains *Equal Opportunity is the Law*.

You can receive an *All-in-One* poster by calling 803-896-4380.

Summary

✪ Generally, employers are permitted to hire whomever they choose. The exception to this general rule includes situations where a business is the recipient of certain state and federal contracts.

✪ In North Carolina, no person under age 18 can be hired without a youth employment certificate.

✪ In South Carolina, a minor needs to be 14 years old before he or she can begin work.

✪ Employers are responsible for making certain that the people they hire are either U.S. citizens or authorized to work in the United States.

✪ The minimum wage in North Carolina and South Carolina is $5.15 per hour.

✪ Both North Carolina and South Carolina have adopted the state version of the federal Occupational Safety and Health Act (OSHA).

✪ North Carolina and South Carolina are both employment at will states. This means employees may be terminated for any nondiscriminatory reason.

✪ In North Carolina, a terminated employee's wages must be paid on or before the next payday. In South Carolina, employers must pay employees all wages due within forty-eight hours of the day of separation or on the next regularly scheduled payday as long as it does not exceed thirty days from the date employment ended.

✪ The North Carolina and South Carolina Departments of Labor require employers to post certain information throughout the workplace to ensure employees are aware of their rights.

Insurance

Obtaining proper insurance coverage should be at the top of every new business owner's to-do list. This chapter explores three important types needed by most businesses—*business liability insurance, workers' compensation insurance,* and *unemployment insurance.*

BUSINESS LIABILITY INSURANCE

As part of the research for this book, an experienced insurance agent was asked, "Who needs to buy business liability insurance?" He quickly responded by saying, "Any business owner who is interested in staying in business." Business owners must take precautions to protect their ventures against losses that might be incurred as a result of lawsuits and unexpected calamities. The two primary areas of concern are *property damage* and *personal injury.*

Property Damage

It is important that business owners protect against damage to their property as well as damage committed by the business or its employees to another person's property. It is not hard to imagine how devastating it would be to a printing company if it had to pay the out-of-pocket cost to replace a $100,000 piece of printing equipment that was damaged as a consequence of a break-in or vandalism.

Personal Injury

The claims that might arise in the area of *personal injury* can cover the span of everything from a customer slipping and falling while shopping in your store to a client's hair turning green after having his or her locks dyed in your salon. The types of exposure a business may encounter are only limited by the imagination of the people filing the lawsuits and the attorneys who represent them. Whoever thought fast-food restaurants would be defending claims that they are responsible for obesity? That is why it is important for business owners to obtain insurance coverage against property damage and personal injury, as well as for:

- product liability;

- loss of business income;

- advertising irregularities;

- employee dishonesty;

- contractual liability;

- business continuation insurance (benefits to cover salaries and rents in the event of temporary disability);

- commercial auto insurance; and,

- business life insurance (often referred to as *keyman insurance*— the business can be the beneficiary in the event of the death of one of the partners or vital employees).

Amount of Insurance Needed

An experienced commercial insurance agent can assist a business owner in determining how much coverage is appropriate. There are several factors insurance agents use to make this determination. They include the following:

- the nature of the business;

- the number of employees;

✪   the value of the business assets;

✪   estimate of next year's sales and payroll;

✪   sales and payroll costs for the past year;

✪   the structure of the business; and,

✪   the geographic reach of the business—local, national, or international.

Finding an Agent

The best place to begin your search for an agent to provide insurance for your business is with the agent who handles your home and automobile coverage. If he or she does not handle commercial business insurance, the agent should be able to refer you to a commercial agent.

Experience matters most when selecting your agent. Your business is important to you. Make sure you get the coverage you need to make certain your business is protected. You will be able to recognize an experienced agent by the following three qualities.

1. The agent asks questions. Insurance is designed to give people peace of mind. How will an agent know your concerns if he or she does not ask questions?

2. The agent listens to you. Listening means he or she behaves as if what you have to say is as important as what he or she has to say.

3. The agent customizes coverage to suit your needs. Businesses are as unique as the individuals who launch them. There is no such thing as one-size-fits-all coverage.

Using Your Homeowner's Policy

Most homeowner policies specifically exclude business claims related to businesses beyond $2,500 unless the homeowner specifically pays for increased coverage. When one considers that a $3,500 computer system would not be covered under a standard homeowner's policy, it is probably a good idea for home-based business owners to take the following steps to protect their home-based ventures:

- review your homeowner's policy to determine your level of coverage;

- calculate the value of your business assets; and,

- if assets exceed coverage limits, contact your insurance agent about either increasing your homeowner's coverage or obtaining business coverage. Your agent can best advise which would better serve your interests.

WORKERS' COMPENSATION INSURANCE

Workers' compensation is insurance that reimburses an employer for damages that must be paid to an employee for injuries occurring in the course of employment. Deciding what is a work-related injury and what is not accounts for much of the litigation that occurs in this country each year.

Generally, a work-related injury is an injury that occurs to an employee during the normal course of employment. For example, a painter who is injured by falling off a ladder while painting a house would be entitled to be compensated by his or her employer. However, if a painter is injured changing a light bulb, lawyers will have to litigate to decide whether that employee would be entitled to coverage.

Independent Contractors

It is important to note that employers are only required to provide coverage for employees—not independent contractors. *Independent contractors* are generally regarded as consultants who perform specific tasks for a business. They control the manner and method of the work performed.

The fact that the *Internal Revenue Service* (IRS) has accepted that the person who works for you is an independent contractor does not necessarily mean that person will be deemed an independent contractor for purposes of workers' compensation coverage. Most states' *Workers' Compensation Act* tends to have a narrower definition of independent contractor. It is a good business policy, when in doubt, to assume the independent contractor is an employee.

Businesses Requiring Coverage

Only business owners who regularly employ a certain number of employees must be insured. The law in North Carolina provides that business owners who employ fewer than three employees are not required to carry workers' compensation coverage. However, the Workers' Compensation Act in South Carolina exempts employers with fewer than four employees. (Sole proprietors are not included as employees for purposes of the Workers' Compensation Act.)

Obtaining Coverage

Business owners have three options when seeking workers' compensation insurance.

Obtain commercial insurance. Business owners can contact their homeowners or car insurance agents about obtaining coverage for their businesses.

Self-insure. A business, in order to *self-insure*, must apply and meet certain financial or other requirements and be approved by the commission that oversees workers' compensation.

Seek placement in a self-insured fund. Self-insured employers are regulated by the *Workers' Compensation Commission*. They are required to maintain excess insurance, obtain a surety bond or letter of credit in an amount specified by the commission, provide audited financial statements annually, pay annual self-insurance tax, and undergo a second injury fund assessment.

Cost

The specific cost of workers' compensation insurance varies and depends on many factors. There are rates for each specific type of classification. These rates are applied on a percentage basis. The percentage is then applied according to the amount of dollars of the total payroll. An insurance agent will be able to provide the rates and help you calculate the actual costs of coverage for your business.

Penalties

The Workers' Compensation Act in both North Carolina and South Carolina is *compulsory*. This means a business that fails to obtain the proper coverage will be subject to penalties. Fines may be imposed for each day of noncompliance until such time as the business receives proper coverage.

All employers operating under the Workers' Compensation Act are required to post a *Compliance Poster*. For information on obtaining the poster, as well as other workers' compensation questions, contact:

North Carolina
Industrial Commission
4340 Mail Service Center
Raleigh, NC 27699
919-807-2500
www.comp.state.nc.us

South Carolina
Workers' Compensation
Commission
1612 Marion Street
Columbia, SC 29202
803-737-5700
www.wcc.state.sc.us

UNEMPLOYMENT INSURANCE

Most states are part of a federal program that was designed to provide temporary financial benefits to eligible employees. Each state administers a separate unemployment insurance program within the guidelines established by federal law.

There are two forms of unemployment. *Separated unemployment* is what happens when an employee is out of work for an indefinite period and no longer has any connection with employer. *Attached unemployment*, sometimes known as *layoffs*, relates to a situation in which an employee's normal work hours have been cut because the employer can no longer provide work.

Someone who loses a job through no fault of his or her own is eligible for unemployment benefits. To maintain that eligibility, the person must:

- ✪ have worked during a specified period time;

- ✪ have received a minimum amount of wages during that period;

- ✪ be able and available for work; and,

- ✪ be actively seeking new employment.

(The spouse, parent, or child (under the age of 21) of an individual business owner is not considered an employee for unemployment insurance coverage purposes.)

The unemployment benefits paid to eligible employees are paid by employers into a *fund*. No money is withheld from workers' checks to pay for unemployment benefits. Unemployment insurance tax is a tax on employer payrolls paid by employers and used to provide funds from which unemployment benefits are paid to qualified unemployed workers. (See Chapter 7 for a more detailed explanation of the Unemployment Insurance Tax.)

For more information on unemployment insurance coverage and requirements, contact:

North Carolina
Employment Security Commission
P.O. Box 25903
Raleigh, NC 27611
www.ncesc.com

South Carolina
Employment Security Commission
P.O. Box 995
Columbia, SC 29202
www.sces.org

Summary

✪ The two primary areas of business liability are property damage and personal injury.

✪ Most homeowner policies specifically exclude business claims related to businesses beyond $2,500 unless the homeowner specifically pays for increased coverage.

✪ Worker's compensation is insurance that reimburses an employer for damages that must be paid to an employee for injuries occurring in the course of employment.

✪ In North Carolina, business owners who employ fewer than three employees are not required to carry workers' compensation coverage. South Carolina law exempts employers with fewer than four employees.

✪ Business owners have three options when seeking workers' compensation insurance: obtain commercial insurance, self insure, or seek placement in a self-insured fund.

✪ A business that fails to obtain the proper coverage will be subject to penalties.

✪ North Carolina and South Carolina are a part of a federal program that was designed to provide temporary financial benefits to eligible employees.

✪ There are two forms of unemployment: separated unemployment and attached unemployment.

Marketing and Advertising

Advertising is defined as any oral, written, or graphic statement made by a seller to solicit business. Advertising is considered *speech* and therefore protected by the First Amendment because it furthers the societal interest in free flow of commercial information. However, advertising is less protected than other types of speech because of its nature and the danger that false or misleading advertising can pose to consumers.

You will undoubtedly want to conduct some sort of advertising of your products or services. You should use any advertisement with caution. If you make untrue or even exaggerated claims in your advertisements, you could be subject to penalties.

Both the state and federal governments are allowed to and actively do regulate advertising. As a general rule, governmental controls on advertising focus on misleading or deceptive statements that could affect a consumer's choice to purchase or not purchase the advertised product or service. The federal and state governments have an interest in ensuring that consumers do not receive information that would unfairly or inaccurately affect the decision to purchase a product or service.

STATE LAWS

Both North Carolina and South Carolina have developed laws and regulations to control advertising related to specific businesses and industries. If you intend to conduct business within any of the following categories, you should consult the accompanying regulations to learn more about advertising limitations.

Type of Business or Industry	North Carolina Law or Regulation	South Carolina Law or Regulation
Accountants		S.C. Bd. Of Accountancy, Acct. R. 1-33
Alcoholic Beverages	N.C. Gen. Stat. Sec. 18B-105	S.C. Al. and Bev. Cont. Comm'n., Al. Bev. C.R.7-34
Architects	N.C. Gen. Stat. Sec. 83A-6	S.C. Code Ann. Sec. 40-3-130
Art Dealers	N.C. Gen. Stat. Sec. 25C-11	
Athletic Agents	N.C. Gen. Stat. Sec. 78C-76	
Auctions and Auctioneers	N.C. Gen. Stat. Sec. 85B-8	
Automobile Dealers	N.C. Gen. Stat. Sec. 20-305	S. C. Code Ann. Sec. 56-15-40
Barbers		S.C. Code Ann. Secs. 40-7-220 to 40-7-240
Cemeteries	N.C. Gen. Stat. Sec. 65-63	
Chiropractors	N.C. Gen. Stat. Sec. 90-154	S.C. Code Ann. Sec. 40-9-90
Cosmetologists	N.C. Gen. Stat. Sec. 88-26	S.C. Code Ann. Sec. 40-13-250
Counselors and Therapists	N.C. Gen. Stat. Sec. 90-332.1	State Bd. Of Examiners for Lic. of Prof. Counselors, Assoc Counselor, and Mar. and Fam. Therap., Cours & Ther. R. 36-51
Diamonds	N.C. Gen. Stat. Sec. 66-74	
Funeral Homes	N.C. Gen. Stat. Sec. 90-210.20	S.C. Code Ann. Sec. 32-7-90 State Bd of Funeral Svcs., Funeral R. 57-26

Insurance	NC Stat Secs. 58-29-1(m) to 58-29-25	S.C. Dept. of Insurance, Ins. R. 69-17
Landscape Architects		S.C. Land. Arch. Bd. Of Reg., Land. Arch. R. 74-9
Opticians	N.C. Gen. Stat. Sec. 90-249	State Bd. Of Opticianry, Opticianry R. 96-20
Personnel Placement Services	N.C. Gen. Stat. Sec. 95-47.26	S.C. Code Ann. Sec. 41-25-50
Real Estate Sales	N.C. Gen. Stat. Sec. 93A-1	S.C. Code Ann. Secs. 27-29-70 to 27-29-120 S.C. Real Est. Comm'n, Real Est R. 105-2
Rental Vehicles	N.C. Gen. Stat. Secs. 66-200 to 66-206	

Both the North Carolina and South Carolina legislatures have created criminal penalties for disseminating an advertisement that is intentionally untrue or obtaining money or other property through the use of false pretenses. If you make false advertisements, you could be punished with fines and jail time.

Unfair Trade Practices

The laws against untrue advertisement and false pretenses do not create a civil cause of action that would allow one citizen to sue another citizen for violation of the law. However, both North Carolina and South Carolina laws prohibit unfair trade practices. *Unfair trade practices* are unfair methods of competition and unfair or deceptive acts or practices in the conduct of trade or commerce.

In South Carolina, advertising is specifically included within the definition of trade or commerce. The laws against unfair trade practices provide for a civil right of recovery for any person who is injured as a result of a violation of the law. If the violation is willful, the violator could be held liable to the injured person for three times the actual damage as well as attorney's fees. (If you make false advertisements, your competitors could sue you and recover up to three times their damages or lost profits.)

FEDERAL LAWS

The federal government regulates the advertising of any products or services that could be considered *interstate commerce* through the *Federal Trade Commission* (FTC). If you sell goods or services to residents of a state other than the one in which your business is located, or your advertisements could reach states other than the one in which your business is located, then the advertising you do should conform to the rules set forth by the FTC.

The FTC requires that advertisements be truthful and nondeceptive. An advertisement is *truthful* if there is a reasonable basis to support the claims made in the advertisement. A *reasonable basis* could be any form of objective evidence such as tests, studies, or surveys, as long as the evidence is accurate and reliable. An advertisement is *deceptive* if a statement in the advertisement or information omitted from the advertisement is material and would likely mislead a reasonable consumer. A statement or information is *material* if it would be important to a consumer's decision to buy or use the advertised product or service. If you advertise your products or services, you must have evidence to back up any claims you make. You must present those claims in a way that is not misleading to consumers.

The FTC will not prescreen an advertisement to determine if it is truthful and nondeceptive. The FTC acts as an enforcement agency and its job is enormous. Generally, the FTC pays more attention to advertisements for products that could cause health risks to consumers, such as dietary supplements, over-the-counter drugs, and weight loss products. However, the FTC provides many publications that explain how the agency regulates specific products and services such as clothing and textiles, 900 numbers, food, jewelry, tobacco, and consumer leases. The FTC's website, **www.ftc.gov**, can offer more information about advertising specific products and services, as well as guidance for making advertising truthful and nondeceptive.

Specific Claims Made in Promotions

The FTC has issued publications and advisory opinions on the use of many specific claims or statements often found in advertisements, as well as common practices used to promote a product or service. The following are some of the most common claims and promotions that could be considered untruthful or misleading if not used properly.

New. When a product is first exposed to the market, advertisements may freely state that the product is *new*. However, after a period of time, a statement in an advertisement that the product is new will be considered misleading. The FTC has not determined a set time limit for when a product may be advertised as new without being misleading. Generally, the determination will be made on a case-by-case basis in light of the specific product and the context of the advertisement. However, an FTC advisory opinion suggests that products should not be advertised as new for more than six months.

In addition, a claim of new in an advertisement may not be made in reference to goods that have been *previously sold*, *used*, or *reconditioned*. For instance, a car that has previously been used by a dealer or by another consumer could not be advertised as a new car. Likewise, tires that have been used and then retreaded or respun for resale could not be advertised as new tires. The FTC has issued rules for the use of the claim *new* in reference to specific products such as tires and textiles.

Free. The FTC has stated that when a product or service is offered as *free,* consumers have a right to assume that they are paying nothing for that product or service. If that is not the case, any conditions to the free offer must be clearly and conspicuously disclosed in any advertisement of the offer. For instance, an advertisement that makes the claim or offer that some product or service is free with some other purchase must also state the specific products or services that must be purchased to trigger the free offer. Additionally, if one product is offered as free with the purchase of another product, the price of the purchased product cannot be increased or adjusted to recover the cost of the free product. These rules apply to any term that conveys similar meaning to free, such as *bonus*, *gift*, or *without charge*.

On sale. The FTC has stated that when an advertisement claims that a product is *on sale*, the sale price must be lower than the regular price by an amount not so insignificant as to be meaningless. In addition, the regular price must not be one that was used for the purpose of establishing a fictitiously high price to which a sale price could later be compared.

A product should not be advertised as on sale unless the sale price is significantly lower than the price at which the product was recently offered for sale, for a reasonably substantial period of time, in the regular course of business. Before you advertise your products or services as on sale, you must establish the regular price and then the sale price must be a meaningful discount.

Made in the USA. The FTC also regulates claims that products are *Made in the USA* or *American Made*, and similar statements that suggest a product is made in the United States. Such a statement should only be made upon a reasonable basis that the product is all or *virtually* all made within the United States.

There is no definitive test established to determine when a product is all or virtually all made within the United States. At a minimum, the final assembly or processing of the product must take place within the United States. Beyond that, other factors are considered on a case-by-case basis, including the proportion of total manufacturing costs attributable to parts and processing within the United States.

Generally, a product should not be advertised as *Made in the USA* unless that product and the components of that product have had only negligible contact with foreign manufacturing processes. If you are considering advertising your product as *Made in the USA,* you should consult the FTC publication, *Enforcement Policy Statement on the use of U.S. Origin Claims*. For more information on obtaining this and other FTC publications, go to the FTC website at **www.ftc.gov**.

Environmental claims. Claims in advertisements such as *recycled, biodegradable, ozone friendly*, or *environmentally safe* should be used with caution. Any time an environmental claim is expressed or implied, like any other claim, it must be substantiated by a reasonable basis. A reasonable basis for environmental claims will often require scientific evidence such as tests, analyses, or studies conducted by environmental experts. Any time an environmental claim is made it should be specific and not lead consumers to believe that the attributes are greater than they truly are. If you are considering using an environmental claim in an advertisement, you should consult the FTC publication, *Guides for the Use of Environmental Marketing Claims*.

Endorsements and testimonials. Endorsements can be an effective way to convince consumers that the performance of your product complies with the claims made or that your product is preferred over other similar products. Like any other form of advertising, endorsements should not mislead consumers. Therefore, an endorser may not make a statement or representation that would be deceptive if it were coming from you directly.

To ensure that consumers are not misled by glowing testimonials, the FTC requires that an endorsement must reflect the honest opinion of the endorser. It also requires that any material connection between the endorser and the business benefited by the endorsement must be disclosed to consumers. For instance, if the endorsement comes from an employee of the store who sells the product or a relative of the person providing the service, then consumers should be informed, since the endorser may have other motives influencing his or her testimony.

You may try to obtain endorsements for your products or services from a celebrity or public figure, a typical consumer, or an expert in a field pertaining to your products or services. If your advertisement includes an endorsement from a celebrity or public figure, the testimonial must be that person's honest experience or opinion. If your advertisement includes an endorsement from a typical consumer, the testimonial must reflect the typical experience or opinion of consumers. If the results are not typical, the advertisement must clearly state that the testifying consumer had uncommon results. If your advertisement includes an expert's endorsement, the expert must be qualified, and the expert's conclusions must be supported by actual evidence that would typically be used by other experts in the field to support such a conclusion.

Rebates. Offering *rebates* on the purchase price can be an effective way to draw consumer attention to your product. The FTC requires that any offer for a rebate must prominently state the price before rebate as well as the amount of the rebate being offered. In addition, the offer must state any additional conditions, requirements, or fees required to obtain the rebate and a time frame for when consumers can expect to receive the rebate. If you are considering offering a rebate in an advertisement, you should consult the FTC publication, *Big Print, Little Print, What's the Deal?*

Guarantees and warranties. Offering a *guarantee of satisfaction* or *warranty of fitness* with a product may be another effective marketing tool. If you advertise a satisfaction or money-back guarantee with your product or service, the FTC requires that you must be willing to return the full purchase price for any reason if the consumer is unsatisfied. In addition, any conditions or limitations, such as a requirement to return the goods or a limitation on how long after the purchase the warranty is valid, must be clearly disclosed to the consumer.

If you advertise a warranty for a product or service that costs more than fifteen dollars, the FTC requires that you provide consumers with access to a copy of the warranty before the sale. An advertisement promoting a warranty must clearly disclose how consumers may obtain details about the warranty, as well as any conditions or limitations to the warranty. If you are considering offering a guarantee or warranty in an advertisement, you should consult the FTC publication, *Guides for the Advertising of Warranties and Guarantees*.

Shipping claims. Recent increases of Internet and mail order sales have given rise to FTC regulation of shipping claims. These rules are detailed, and if your business includes Internet, telephone, or mail order sales, you should consult the FTC's publication, *A Business Guide to the FTC's Mail or Telephone Merchandise Rule*.

Generally, consumers should be able to rely on any claims you make regarding shipping time. Therefore, you must have a reasonable basis supporting any claim you make as to how soon the consumer may expect to receive the product. If no claim is made, the FTC has determined that consumers should be able to expect that you will ship the product within thirty days.

If a delay occurs, the consumer must be informed and given a right to cancel the transaction. Any subsequent delays also require the consumer's consent. If you fail to gain the required consent, you must promptly refund any purchase price paid *without* request from the consumer. Offering discounts or gift certificates for future purchases will not be an adequate substitute for refund.

Internet advertising. All of the same rules apply to any promotion or advertising of products or services on the Internet. Any claims you make must not be misleading or deceptive. Disclosures must be clear and conspicuous. You may use hypertext and links to provide access to such information as disclosure of conditions or warranty information. However, the link should be in close proximity to the product that it supports, and it should be very obvious. Keep in mind that you are the advertiser for any products found on your Web page. If you plan to include retail of another manufacturer's products on your Web page, you should ask for and review the information used by the manufacturer to substantiate its claims, rather than simply repeat the information. If you are considering using a Web page or some other form of Internet advertising, you should consult the FTC publication, *Dot Com Disclosures*.

•   •   •   •   •

Any advertising you choose to conduct to promote your business, products, or services should be done with caution. You may think that the FTC or your state government will not be aware of your advertisements or will not bother with enforcement of advertising regulations against your small business, but there are many private consumer watchdog agencies that may bring your advertisements to the attention of the authorities. Remember, once an advertisement is published, it cannot be taken back. If you choose to advertise any products or services, the advertisements should be well thought-out and thoroughly reviewed for any statements or omissions that could mislead consumers.

Summary

✪ As a general rule, governmental controls on advertising focus on misleading or deceptive statements that could affect a consumer's choice to purchase or not purchase the advertised product or service.

✪ If you make false advertisements, you could be punished with fines and jail time.

✪ Both North Carolina and South Carolina laws prohibit unfair trade practices, which are unfair methods of competition and unfair or deceptive acts or practices in the conduct of trade or commerce.

✪ The federal government regulates the advertising of any products or services that could be considered interstate commerce through the Federal Trade Commission (FTC).

✪ The following are some of the most common claims and promotions that could be considered untruthful or misleading if not properly used:

- New
- Free
- On sale
- Made in the USA
- Environmental claims
- Endorsements and testimonials
- Rebates
- Guarantees and warranties
- Shipping claims

Taxes

As a business owner, you will be required to file tax returns and pay taxes on the net profits from your business. The following discussion is meant to give you a general understanding of how businesses are taxed. It is not intended to be legal advice.

The Internal Revenue Service (IRS) conducts tax workshops designed to help small business owners understand tax laws. The seminars are conducted on many different dates throughout the year and in many different cities throughout North Carolina and South Carolina. Consult the IRS website, **www.irs.gov**, for dates and locations. Attending one of these workshops can give you a greater understanding of the tax laws and how they will affect your business.

Understanding the tax implications of your business decisions could greatly increase your success. Before filing a tax return for your business, you should either attend one of the IRS seminars or consult a certified public accountant or an attorney specializing in taxation.

RECORDKEEPING

As a business owner, you must become a diligent recordkeeper. You should keep records of every receipt, sales slip, invoice, bank deposit, cancelled check, or any other record that evidences a transaction of your business. You will need these records at the end of the year to substantiate your business income as well as any deductions or credits that you take to reduce your business income tax. You will also need to save these records in case the IRS ever decides to audit you or your business. The IRS says that you should save all records pertaining to a tax year for three years after the date the tax return is due or filed, or two years after the taxes are paid, whichever comes later. Any records for *employment taxes* should be saved for four years after the date the tax return is due or filed or after the taxes are paid.

NET PROFITS

A business must pay taxes on its *net profits*. It may be able to carry forward any *net losses*, as well as certain costs, to reduce tax liabilities in future years. The following are simplified accounting equations to compute net profits.

Net profit is calculated by subtracting all of the expenses that are ordinary and necessary for the operation of your business from the gross profit of your business.

$$Net\ Profit = Gross\ Profit - Expenses$$

Gross profit is calculated by subtracting the cost of the goods that you sell or the services that you provide from the net sales of your business.

$$Gross\ Profit = Net\ Sales - Cost\ of\ Goods\ Sold$$

Net sales is calculated by subtracting any money that you refunded to customers from the gross receipts that your business took in from sales.

$$Net\ Sales = Gross\ Receipts - Returns$$

The *cost of goods sold* is calculated by starting with the inventory your business has at the start of the period, adding any purchases you made to increase that inventory, and then subtracting out the inventory your business has at the end of the period.

Cost of Goods Sold = Beginning Inventory +
Purchases – Ending Inventory

INCOME TAXATION OF BUSINESS ENTITIES

Some business entities allow for *pass through* taxation, meaning that the net profits from your business will pass through the business itself and be taxed directly to you, the business owner, as part of your income. Other business forms require the business itself to pay income tax on the net profits. The following is a summary of the ways different business entities are taxed and the ways that income tax returns should be filed with the IRS. All of the forms referenced in this section may be obtained from the IRS at **www.irs.gov**.

Sole Proprietor or Single Member LLC

The net profits from a business operated through a sole proprietorship or through a limited liability company with only one member are taxed as income directly to the owner. You should file a *Schedule C* or *Schedule C-EZ, Net Profit From Business* with your individual Form 1040 to report profits and losses from the business. In addition, you will need to file *Schedule SE, Self-Employment Tax*.

Partnership or Multiple Member LLC

The net profits from a business operated through a partnership or a limited liability company with more than one member are also taxed as income directly to the owners. The total income or loss should be divided between the owners in proportion to each individual's ownership interest, if no other arrangement for dividing profits and losses has been made between the parties.

The business should file a *Form 1065, Partnership Tax Return Income* with the IRS to provide a summary of the business activities of the partnership or LLC. The business should also give each owner a *Schedule K-1, Partner's Share of Income, Credits, Deductions, Etc.*, which each partner should attach to Part II of Schedule E, *Supplemental Income and Loss*, on his or her individual Form 1040 return.

Subchapter S Corporation

In order to make the Subchapter S election, the corporation should file a **Form 2553, Election by a Small Business Corporation** (form 19, p.223) within the first seventy-five days of the tax year. If Form 2553 is filed after the first seventy-five days of the tax year, then the election will not be effective until the following tax year. The net profits from a business operated through a corporation that has been qualified as a Subchapter S corporation does not pay tax on income from operations if the gains are passed on to the shareholders as dividends.

> **NOTE:** *Dividends paid to shareholders of a corporation are subject to income tax, but are not subject to self-employment tax. A Subchapter S corporation, although somewhat more complicated to form than an LLC, could save a single-owner business some tax liability for self-employment taxes.*

If net profits are not distributed to shareholders, then some tax liability may be due. A Subchapter S corporation will also incur tax liability for any capital gains realized when corporate assets are sold. To report earnings and losses, the corporation should file a *Form 1120S, US Income Tax Return for an S Corporation*. The corporation should also give each shareholder a Schedule K-1, which each shareholder should attach to Part II of *Schedule E, Supplemental Income and Loss*, on his or her individual Form 1040 return.

C Corporation

The net profits from a business operated through a corporation (sometimes called a C corporation) are subject to income tax at the corporate level. If dividends or distributions are made to shareholders, then those dividends are also subject to income tax as regular income to the shareholders. The corporation should file *Form 1120 or Form 1120(A), US Corporation (Short Form) Income Tax Return*. If dividends or distributions are made to shareholders, then the corporation should give each shareholder a *Form 1099, Dividend Statement for Receipt of Dividends and Distributions*, to complete their individual Form 1040 return.

Self-Employment Tax

In addition to income tax, if the net profit you receive from your business totals more than $400, then you could be subject to self-employment tax. Regular wages and salary are subject to payroll taxes. Profits you receive from your business are not wages or salary, and therefore are not subject to payroll taxes. The IRS imposes the self-employment tax on profits that you receive from your business to mirror the payroll taxes.

The self-employment tax rate is 15.3%, but could change in future years. The rate consists of 12.4% for Social Security and 2.9% for Medicare. For tax year 2006, only the first $94,200 of your combined income, either from net profits you receive from your business or from any other income, including regular wages or salary, will be subject to the 12.4% tax for Social Security. All of your self-employment income and any other regular income will be subject to the 2.9% tax for Medicare. The amount of income is subject to the tax changes with inflation.

NOTE: *Dividends and distributions on shares of corporate stock are not considered regular income, and therefore are not subject to either payroll taxes or self-employment taxes. As a result, you may avoid both taxes by operating your business through a Subchapter S corporation and distributing the net profits as dividends.*

Withholding Taxes for Employees

If you choose to employ others as part of your business, then you take on the responsibility of withholding federal and state income and payroll taxes on behalf of your employees. The IRS will hold you, as an employer, personally liable for all amounts that you should withhold from your employee's paychecks, regardless of whether the amounts were actually withheld.

If you do have any employees, then you need to file **FORM SS-4, APPLICATION FOR EMPLOYER IDENTIFICATION NUMBER** (form 17, p.211). Your *employer identification number* (EIN) is the number that the IRS uses to identify your business. You will need an EIN to open a bank account in the name of the business, as well as to deposit the funds you will withhold from your employees' paychecks for income and payroll taxes.

Federal income tax withholding. Any employee you hire should complete a *Form W-4, Employee Withholding Allowance Certificate*, when he or she begins work. The W-4 allows your employee to claim his or her expected income tax exemptions, deductions, and credits, also known as *withholding allowances*. Consult IRS Publication 15,

Circular E, Employer's Tax Guide, which includes tables that help you to determine the amount that you should withhold for federal income tax from the wages and salary that you pay to each employee.

Generally, the income tax withholding amount will be based on the amount of the paycheck and the number of withholding allowances that the employee claims on Form W-4. If a new employee does not give you a Form W-4, you should withhold tax as if he or she is single with no withholding allowances.

Federal payroll tax withholding. In addition to income tax, you must withhold federal payroll taxes in the form of Social Security and Medicare taxes from your employees' wages. You are also required to pay a matching amount. The payroll tax rate is 15.3%. Social Security tax accounts for 12.4% of the payroll tax, 6.2% of which is paid by the employee, and 6.2% of which is paid by the employer. Social Security tax is paid on the first $94,200 of income earned by an employee. Medicare tax accounts for 2.9% of the payroll tax, 1.45% of which is paid by the employee, and 1.45% of which is paid by the employer. Medicare tax is paid on all income earned by an employee.

For the first $94,200 in wages and salary paid to any employees, you should withhold 7.65% of each paycheck, and for all wages and salary paid over $94,200 you should withhold 1.45% of each paycheck. Ultimately, you as the employer will match the amount of the withholding to satisfy the employee's payroll tax liability.

Depositing Withheld Income and Payroll Taxes

Generally, you must deposit all withheld income taxes, all withheld payroll taxes, and your employer match amount of all withheld payroll taxes in a bank that is authorized to accept federal tax deposits. Within five to six weeks after you receive your EIN, the IRS will send you a book of *Federal Deposit Coupons*. On or before each deposit date that you are required to deposit withheld taxes and match amounts, you should mail or deliver one Federal Deposit Coupon and a single check or money order to an authorized bank.

Within one month after the end of each calendar quarter (January 1–March 31, April 1–June 30, July 1–September 30, and October 1–December 31), the IRS requires every employer to file *Form 941, Employer's Quarterly Tax Return*.

Federal unemployment taxes. In addition to income taxes and payroll taxes, your business may be required to pay unemployment taxes. Federal unemployment taxes, along with state unemployment taxes, provide for payments of unemployment compensation to workers who have lost their jobs. If you pay wages totaling $1,500 or more in any given calendar quarter, or if you have one or more employees working for at least some part of the day in twenty or more different weeks, then you must pay federal unemployment taxes. The rate for federal unemployment tax is generally .08% of the first $7,000 in wages and salary paid to each employee during the year. You should stop paying unemployment taxes on an employee's wages when he or she has been paid $7,000 for the year.

Generally, you should deposit the unemployment tax liability accumulated during each quarter within one month after the end of that quarter. If less than $100 has accumulated, then you may make the deposit or carry the accumulated liability forward to the next quarter. For each deposit, you should mail or deliver one Federal Deposit Coupon and a single check or money order to an authorized bank. You should file *Form 940 (EZ), Employer's Annual Federal Unemployment Tax Return* in order to report this tax.

STATE TAXES

In addition to federal taxes, your business will be subject to state and local taxes wherever you operate. You should register your business with the Department of Revenue in any state that you do business. In North Carolina, this is accomplished by filing a **REGISTRATION APPLICATION FOR SALES AND USE TAX AND INCOME WITHHOLDING FORM** (form 20, p.229) with the North Carolina Department of Revenue. In South Carolina, you can register your business for state tax purposes by filing a **FORM STC-111, BUSINESS TAX APPLICATION** (form 21, p.231) with the South Carolina Department of Revenue.

Once you have registered your business, the Department of Revenue will identify your business by a license number based on the type of business that you operate. The registration number you receive is permanent and will not be issued to any other business or person. If you buy a business from someone else, you should file another registration form and obtain another number. After registration, you may also be allowed to file various tax returns and pay tax liabilities electronically. This could save you time and money. Contact the Department of Revenue in your state for more information:

North Carolina
Department of Revenue
P.O. Box 25000
Raleigh, NC 27640
877-252-3052
www.dor.state.nc.us

South Carolina
Department of Revenue
P.O. Box 125
Columbia, SC 29214
803-898-5822
www.sctax.org

Sales Tax

If your business includes the retail sale of any goods or provides certain services, then you will be required to collect *sales and use taxes* in both North Carolina and South Carolina. You should charge sales tax any time you sell your products to a consumer who is not a wholesaler. If the person you are selling your products to intends to resell the products to consumers, then sales tax will not apply. You should keep any amount that you collect for sales taxes and deposit them periodically with the state.

After you have registered your business with the Department of Revenue in the state that you operate, you will receive detailed information about state sales taxes and preprinted forms for reporting and paying sales tax. Generally, sales taxes for North Carolina and South Carolina are due on or before the 15th or 20th day of each month, respectively, for all taxes due for the preceding calendar month. The South Carolina Department of Revenue offers a discount of 3% of liabilities less than $100 and 2% of liabilities greater than $100 for all sales taxes that are paid in a timely manner by a retailer, with a maximum discount of $3,000 ($3,100 if filed electronically) per year.

Generally, in North Carolina, the sales tax rate consists of $4\frac{1}{2}\%$ state tax and either 2%, $2\frac{1}{2}\%$ or 3% local tax. In South Carolina, the sales tax rate consists of 5% state tax and either 1% or 2% local tax. Contact the Chamber of Commerce in any county that you operate to determine the exact local tax rate.

In both North Carolina and South Carolina, many specific products are exempt from sales taxes. You can find these exemptions and much more information on sales taxes on the website for your state's Department of Revenue.

Property Taxes   The assets of your business will be subject to *property taxes*, assessed by the local government wherever you operate. Property taxes will be due on both personal property (furniture, fixtures, equipment, etc.) as well as real property (land and buildings). In North Carolina, you are required to file a business personal property return at the county assessor's office for the county in which you do business. In South Carolina, you are required to file a business personal property return with the South Carolina Department of Revenue. All furniture, fixtures, and equipment are to be reported on the return at *acquisition cost* with a deduction allowed for depreciation. The tax liability is assessed based on the acquisition value of the property, reduced by a statutory depreciation method, and multiplied by the local tax rate for property of that kind. In North Carolina, the tax liability is assessed based on the *current fair market value* of the property, multiplied by the local tax rate for property of that kind.

Franchise Tax and License Fee   Both North Carolina and South Carolina have a corporate *franchise tax* or *license fee* that is assessed against any corporation organized within the state or that has been authorized to do business in the state. The tax or fee is solely for the privilege of being organized or authorized to do business in the state. In North Carolina, the franchise tax is based on the greater of the values of:

❂   the corporation's capital stock, surplus, and undivided profits;

❂   the corporation's investment in tangible property located in North Carolina; or,

❂   the appraised value of the corporation's investment in tangible property located in North Carolina.

In South Carolina, the license fee is based on the value of the corporation's capital stock and paid in capital accounts.

In North Carolina the tax rate is $1.50 per $1,000, with a minimum tax of $35. In South Carolina, the license fee is .001% plus $15, with a minimum fee of $25. In both states, the tax or fee is calculated and paid when filing a corporate tax return.

State Income Taxes

Both North Carolina and South Carolina state income tax structures follow the federal income tax laws. The following is a summary of the ways different business entities are taxed and the ways that income tax returns should be filed with North Carolina and South Carolina. The forms mentioned are supplied to the business by the respective state. If you fail to receive a form or need additional information, contact your state's Department of Revenue.

Sole proprietorship and single-member LLC. The net profits from a business operated through sole proprietorship or through a limited liability company with only one member are taxed as income directly to the owner. In North Carolina, you should file a *Form NC-40* to report profits and losses from the business. In South Carolina, you should file a *Form SC 1040* to report profits and losses from the business.

Partnership or multiple-member LLC. Similar to federal income taxes, North Carolina and South Carolina tax the net profits from a business operated through a partnership or a limited liability company with more than one member as income directly to the owners. The total income or loss should be divided between the owners in proportion to each individual's ownership interest if no other arrangement for dividing profits and losses has been made between the parties.

The business should file (as applicable) a North Carolina *Form D-403, Partnership Income Tax Return* or a South Carolina *Form SC 1065, Partnership Return of Income* with the appropriate state's Department of Revenue. These forms provide a summary of the business activities of the partnership or LLC to the state. The business should also give each owner (as applicable) a North Carolina *Schedule NC K-1, Partner's Share of Income, Credits, Deductions, Etc.,* or a South Carolina *Form SC-K*, which each partner should file along with his or her individual *Form NC-40* or *SC-1040*.

Subchapter S corporation. Both North Carolina and South Carolina will recognize a corporation that has been qualified as a Subchapter S corporation. The net profits from a business operated through a Subchapter S corporation will not pay taxes on income from operations if the gains are passed on to the shareholders as dividends.

To report earnings and losses, the corporation should file a North Carolina *Form CD 401S, S Corporation Tax Return* or a South Carolina *SC 1120S, S Corporation Income Tax Return*. The corporation should also give each shareholder a North Carolina *Schedule NC K-1, Shareholder's Share of North Carolina Income, Adjustments and Credits* or a South Carolina *Schedule SC-K*, which each shareholder should file along with his or her individual *Form NC-40 or SC-1040*.

C corporation. Both North Carolina and South Carolina tax the net profits from a business operated through a corporation other than a qualified Subchapter S corporation at the corporate level. If dividends or distributions are made to shareholders, those dividends are also subject to income tax as regular income to the shareholders. The corporation should file North Carolina *Form CD-405, Corporate Tax Return* or South Carolina *Form SC 1120, C Corporation Income Tax Return*.

Withholding Income Taxes for Employees

If you choose to employ others as part of your business, then you take on the responsibility of withholding state income taxes on behalf of your employees. If you have employees, you must register for a withholding number with Department of Revenue in the state you operate. In North Carolina, this is accomplished by filing a **REGISTRATION APPLICATION FOR SALES AND USE TAX AND INCOME WITHHOLDING FORM** (form 20, p.229) with the North Carolina Department of Revenue. In South Carolina, you can register your business for withholding state tax purposes by filing a **FORM STC-111, BUSINESS TAX APPLICATION** (form 21, p.231) with the South Carolina Department of Revenue.

After you register, you will become a withholding agent and begin to receive withholding packages annually from the Department of Revenue with forms for filing and remitting the taxes. The amount you withhold from each employee's paycheck will be based on the federal Form W-4. The withholding packages will contain charts to determine the applicable withholding amount based on the amount of the paycheck and the number of withholding allowances that the employee claims on Form W-4. If a new employee does not give you a Form W-4, then you should withhold tax from his or her paycheck as if he or she is single with no withholding allowances.

Depositing and Reporting Withheld State Income Taxes

All withheld state income taxes should be deposited in your local bank at the same time that you are required to deposit federal withholdings. You should make the deposit along with the withholding tax payment coupons sent to you by the Department of Revenue. In North Carolina you must file a *Form NC-5, Withholding Return* quarterly, if you withhold less than $250 each month; monthly, if you withhold more that $250, but less than $2,000 each month; and, semiweekly if you withhold more than $2,000 each month. In South Carolina you must file a *Form WH 1605, Quarterly Withholding Tax Return* at the end of each quarter, regardless of the amount of taxes that you withhold.

State Unemployment Taxes

Generally, if you are liable for federal unemployment taxes, then you are also liable for state unemployment taxes. Unemployment taxes are paid by employers, not deducted from employee wages. If you pay wages totaling $1,500 or more in any given calendar quarter or if you have one or more employees working for at least some part of the day in twenty or more different weeks, then you must pay federal unemployment taxes.

The North Carolina rate for unemployment taxes is 1.2% of the first $15,900 paid to each employee. The South Carolina rate for unemployment taxes is 2.64% of the first $7,000 paid to each employee. After an employee's wages and salary have totaled over $15,900 or $7,000 (as applicable), you should no longer pay unemployment taxes on that employee.

Unemployment taxes are paid to the North Carolina Employment Security Commission or South Carolina Employment Security Commission. You must also file quarterly reports with the commission on North Carolina—*Form NCUI 101, Employer's Quarterly Tax and Wage Report* or South Carolina—*Form UCE-120, Employer Quarterly Contribution and Wage Reports*.

Summary

✪ Save all records pertaining to a tax year for three years after the date the tax return is due or filed, or two years after the taxes are paid, whichever comes later.

✪ The net profits from a business operated through a sole proprietorship, partnership, or limited liability company are taxed as income directly to the owner.

✪ The net profits from a Subchapter S corporation are not taxed on income from operations if the gains are passed on to the shareholders as dividends.

✪ The net profits from a C corporation are subject to income tax at the corporate level. If dividends or distributions are made to shareholders, then those dividends are also subject to income tax as regular income to shareholders.

✪ Your business will be subject to state and local taxes wherever you operate. You should register your business with the Department of Revenue in any state that you do business.

✪ If your business includes the retail sale of any goods or provides certain services, then you will be required to collect sales and use taxes in your state.

✪ The assets of your business will be subject to property taxes, assessed by the local government wherever you operate.

✪ Both North Carolina and South Carolina have a corporate franchise tax or license fee that is assessed against any corporation organized within the state or that has been authorized to do business in the state.

Business Franchises

Rather than beginning a new business from the ground up, many entrepreneurs choose to buy a franchise or business opportunity. Generally, the purchaser of a *franchise* will be allowed to distribute goods or services under a well-known company name and receive significant assistance with management and operations from a parent company. The purchaser of a *business opportunity* will gain access to wholesale products or services and to previously established distribution networks or practices, but will not operate under the name of a parent company and will not receive assistance with management and operations. There are currently more than 1,500 companies in the United States that offer to sell franchise rights.

In many ways, buying a franchise will limit the risk associated with starting your own business. Instead of creating your own products or services and business model that may or may not be successful, you will be allowed to sell products and services that have already proven popular in other markets. You may also be given instruction and guidance on how to organize and run your business in a form that has already been established. However, remember that even buying the franchise rights to a business that was successful in another market does not guarantee that the same business will be successful in your market.

The specific benefits of a franchise or business opportunity may include some or all of the following:

○ use of patented products or processes;

○ use of protected trademarks, service marks, and trade names;

○ use of predesigned forms and methods for formation, management, accounting, and bookkeeping;

○ access to special contract prices from wholesalers and distributors; and,

○ cost sharing with other franchise purchasers for marketing and advertising.

Franchise or business opportunity rights for successful businesses are usually expensive. Therefore, buying the right to sell a proven product in a demonstrated form is often cost prohibitive.

If you are considering buying a franchise, it is important to shop around. Because the prospect of starting a business that seems risk-free is enticing, swindlers and con artists will often hide their scam within what seems to be a legitimate franchise or business opportunity. You should be especially cautious of sellers that make high earnings claims, sellers that make the job sound easy, and sellers that use high-pressure sales tactics. Remember, if it sounds too good to be true, it most likely *is* too good to be true.

FEDERAL LAWS

The Federal Trade Commission (FTC) has published the *Franchise and Business Opportunity Rule*. This requires anyone selling franchise rights to give a potential purchaser a written franchise or business opportunity agreement and a detailed *disclosure document*. The agreement must be given before any payment is received. The disclosure document must be given at either the first face-to-face meeting between the seller and potential purchaser or ten days before a purchaser pays any money or commits to any purchase—whichever occurs first. The disclosure document must contain all of the following:

- ✪ details of the franchise agreement, including the term of the agreement; the renewal, repurchase, and termination provisions; and, any rights for the purchaser to assign or resell the franchise rights;

- ✪ an accurate description of the costs required to start and maintain a franchise operation, including fees, rent, inventory and equipment purchases, royalties, training and operating expenses, and contributions for marketing or advertising;

- ✪ any and all responsibilities of the seller and the purchaser after the franchise rights have been purchased;

- ✪ any restrictions on territory, customer base, or operating site selection;

- ✪ fully audited financial statements of the selling company for the past three years;

- ✪ the background and expertise of each of the key executives and officers in the selling company;

- ✪ whether, during the past seven years, any of the key executives or officers in the selling company have been convicted or pleaded *nolo contendere* (no contest) to any felony charge, been party to a civil lawsuit, or subject to any government enforcement action involving fraud, embezzlement, or other deceptive acts;

- ✪ whether the selling company, any of its subsidiaries, key executives, or officers have filed for bankruptcy protection or been reorganized;

- ✪ the name, address, and phone number of at least ten other purchasers in your geographic area; and,

✪ written bases for any earnings representations made by the seller, including the number and percentage of other franchisees who have achieved the stated claims.

The Franchise and Business Opportunity Rule applies to all business format franchises, all product franchises, and all vending machine or display rack business opportunity ventures. Some exemptions do exist; however, they are very limited. For example, the rule will not apply to a franchise sale if:

✪ all of the payments to the franchisor for the first six months of operations do not exceed $500;

✪ the arrangement is limited to a single trademark license offered to a single licensee; or,

✪ the arrangement is deemed to be an employment contract or partnership arrangement.

If a franchise seller tells you that his or her offer is exempt from the disclosure requirements of the Franchise and Business Opportunity Rule, be wary of any claims made—especially as to earnings.

STATE LAWS

Franchise and business opportunity sellers are required to comply with the Franchise and Business Opportunity Rule (as well as any more stringent state law requirements in the states in which they offer to sell their franchise or business opportunity). If a seller offers to sell you a franchise or business opportunity in either North Carolina or South Carolina, then additional restrictions and disclosures are required by each state to protect you and make sure you receive adequate information.

Business Opportunity Sales Act

Both North Carolina and South Carolina have adopted the *Business Opportunity Sales Act*. This act applies to the sale or lease of any products, equipment, supplies, or services for the purpose of enabling you to start a business if you are required to pay the seller a fee greater than a minimum amount, and the seller represents at least one of the following promises:

- that the seller will provide or assist you in finding locations for the use or operation of vending machines, racks, display cases, or similar devices;

- that the seller will purchase products made by you using the supplies he or she sold to you;

- that the seller guarantees that you will derive income exceeding the purchase price or that he or she will refund the purchase price or repurchase any products sold to you if you are unsatisfied; or,

- that the seller will provide a sales or marketing program that will enable you to derive income exceeding the purchase price.

Exceptions. The Business Opportunity Sales Act specifically excludes:

- the sale of an ongoing business when the owner of that business intends to sell only that one business;

- the sale of all or substantially all of the assets of an ongoing business;

- a not-for-profit sale of sales demonstration equipment or a sale of product inventory sold to the purchaser at a bona fide wholesale price; or,

- the sale of products, equipment, or supplies where the seller has a net worth of at least ten million dollars.

If a seller tells you that his or her offer is exempt from the Business Opportunity Sales Act, be wary of any claims made—especially as to earnings.

State Law Disclosure Document

If the Business Opportunity Sales Act applies to the sale in question, then in addition to the disclosure document required by the Franchise and Business Opportunity Rule, the seller must also provide a disclosure document in compliance with the Business Opportunity Sales Act. The disclosure must come at the earlier of forty-eight hours before signing a contract or receiving any payment for the business opportunity. The document must disclose the following:

- any names under which the seller and any of its parents or subsidiaries have done business or intend to do business in the future;

- the names and addresses of all persons charged with responsibility for the seller's business activities;

- the length of time the seller has been involved in such transactions;

- current financial statements of the seller;

- a description of the business opportunity, including details about any services, training, or placement of products that the seller undertakes to perform; and,

- a notice that you may cancel the transaction within forty-five days if the seller fails to deliver the product, equipment, or supplies necessary to begin operations.

State Law Contract Requirements

The Business Opportunity Sales Act requires that, in addition to receiving the written disclosures discussed above, all purchasers of business opportunities must receive a written contract that includes the following:

- the terms and conditions of payment;

- a detailed description of all services that the seller will perform for the purchaser;

- the seller's business address; and,

- the approximate delivery date of any products, equipment, or supplies that the seller is to deliver to the purchaser.

Additional Obligations and Restrictions of the Seller

In order to further protect purchasers, the Business Opportunity Sales Act puts additional obligations and restrictions on sellers of franchises or business opportunities. If a seller guarantees that you will derive income exceeding the purchase price, or he or she will refund the purchase price or repurchase any products sold to you if you are unsatisfied, then the seller must establish a trust account or surety bond to satisfy this obligation.

To ensure that a seller will not mislead the potential purchaser, the Business Opportunity Sales Act prohibits a seller from:

- using any trademark, service mark, or other commercial symbol not in control of the seller;

- suggesting that any person profited from the business opportunity without offering a current address for that person as well as a description of the circumstances under which the profit was earned; or,

- making any reference to compliance with the Business Opportunity Sales Act.

Finally, the seller of every business opportunity subject to the Business Opportunity Sales Act must file a copy of the disclosure, as well as the details of any trust account or surety bond required by the Act, with the secretary of state. The seller must also update the filing when any material change occurs as to the information contained therein, as well as annually.

CONSIDERATIONS FOR PURCHASERS

The disclosures required by both federal and state laws will ultimately be helpful to a prospective purchaser of a franchise or business opportunity in determining whether or not to enter into the arrangement. Franchise or business opportunity agreements are generally uniform among all buyers of a given franchise or business opportunity. Therefore, the agreement is generally written to favor the seller. These agreements and the accompanying disclosure documents should be read carefully and thoroughly. Many factors should be considered when examining the agreement and disclosure documents. The following is a list of factors that may be helpful in analyzing a franchise or business opportunity.

Overhead Costs

You should determine the total amount of fees or costs involved in the arrangement. In addition to the initial fee to purchase the franchise or business opportunity, the contract could require renewal fees, periodic royalty fees, or fees to be paid into common funds for advertising or marketing. All of these fees will increase your overhead and cost of doing business.

Training and Support

You should consider the amount of training and support services offered by the seller and the price at which it is offered. If you have experience operating a similar business, then the training and support offered may be of little value to you. A franchise agreement that includes a premium for such services would not be beneficial. However, if you have limited experience, then you would want to make sure that more training and support services are available at a cost that will not be prohibitive.

Operational Controls

You should consider the amount of operational controls that the seller may use if he or she intends to direct certain aspects of your business operations. Common restrictions will include limitations as to the location of your business, the selling area that you may operate within, and the processes that you must use to ensure quality control. Some things, such as a predetermined storefront design, may appear to require less planning on your part, but in reality would limit the manner in which you may conduct business. Consider all contractual terms that limit the freedom with which you may operate your business and how those restrictions may affect your profits.

Other Operators

The single most beneficial disclosure to a prospective purchaser may be the telephone number and address of other franchise or business opportunity operators in your geographic area. You should at least call these other operators and confirm your understanding of the arrangement, the cost, and the expected profits. If possible, you should visit some of the operating sites to further confirm your understanding. Also, ask the listed franchise purchasers if they know of any unlisted or terminated franchise purchasers. Contact some unlisted or terminated franchise purchasers, as the seller may only list franchise purchasers that have been successful.

•   •   •   •   •

A franchise or business opportunity can be an excellent way to start a business for someone who does not have much business experience but does have the money to purchase the franchise or business opportunity. If you spend time researching for an operation that fits your skills, your needs, and your market, a franchise or business opportunity can supply you with a demonstrated business model and proven products or services that may reduce the risk that goes along with starting your own business.

Summary

✪ Generally, the purchaser of a franchise will be allowed to distribute goods and services under a well-known company name and receive significant assistance with management and operations from a parent company.

✪ The purchaser of a business opportunity will gain access to wholesale products or services and to previously established distribution networks or practices, but will not operate under the name of a parent company and will not receive assistance with management and operations.

✪ The Federal Trade Commission (FTC) requires anyone selling franchise rights to give a potential purchaser a written franchise or business opportunity agreement and a detailed disclosure document.

✪ If a seller offers to sell you a franchise or business opportunity in either North Carolina or South Carolina, then additional restrictions and disclosures are required by each state to protect you and make sure you receive adequate information.

✪ Both North and South Carolina have adopted the Business Opportunity Sales Act. This Act applies to the sale or lease of any products, equipment, supplies, or services for the purpose of enabling you to start a business if you are required to pay the seller a fee greater than a minimum amount, and the seller makes a certain representation.

✪ The following is a list of factors that may be helpful in analyzing a franchise or business opportunity:

   • Overhead cost
   • Training and support
   • Operational controls
   • Other operators

Internet Business

The rise in the popularity of the Internet gives small business owners opportunities that were never before available. If you choose to create a Web page as a part of your business, you may be able to reach customers around the world, increase your customer service and efficiency, and allow your customers to shop and purchase your products twenty-four hours a day, seven days a week.

A website will be an added expense, both with initial start-up costs and periodic fees. These expenses can be high and may not be an option if your business is just starting, but a website could benefit your business so much that the added profits would exceed the costs. A website will not be a good idea for all businesses. That is why you should carefully plan a strategy to optimize your use of the Internet.

PURPOSE

The first and most important consideration is what *purpose* a website would serve to your business. A website could simply give a list of your products or services and contact information for your business. A website could provide related information or a service to your existing customers or people you would like to entice into becoming customers. A website could include online shopping and e-commerce so that customers can make purchases directly from your inventory, regardless of their location, and have your products shipped to them.

COST AND BENEFIT

A simple website including information about your business can be very inexpensive and easy to design. There are many places on the Web that will host your site for free or for a very low cost. However, this type of website will probably only be useful if people are looking for information about your business and they already know the Web address. It would do little to attract new customers or to increase your sales market.

More expensive websites could provide the people who visit your site with the option to make purchases without coming to your store, increasing your sales without increasing the size of your store or the number of employees you have for customer service. Designing a website that includes *e-commerce*, or online shopping, will be a cost in excess of $500 and as much as several thousand dollars. Web hosting and servicing your website will be an additional periodic cost ranging upwards from $25 to several hundred dollars per month. In addition to that, the most successful websites devote a good amount of money to online marketing and promotion of the website to draw more attention from Internet users. Like most other things, the more you spend, the more attention your website is likely to receive.

TIME RESTRAINTS

The effectiveness of your website and the costs of maintaining your website will both be affected by the amount of time that you put into creating and servicing it. If you are not computer savvy and do not wish to learn, you can pay a webmaster to create, maintain, and enhance your website. However, if a website will not add profits to compensate for that cost, you may want to do some of the work yourself. This will undoubtedly increase the amount of time you spend working on your business.

Learning to create and design Web pages takes time. Once your website is up and running, you can not simply ignore it, even if there are no operational problems. To make your website effective, you should constantly be changing it by adding new products, advertising special offers, or simply changing the design or graphics so that customers are enticed to return. This will all take time.

BUSINESS CAPABILITIES

If a website is effective, it will increase the demand for your products or services. Consider how much increased demand your business can handle when deciding how much money and effort you want to put into your website. If your products are labor intensive or take a long time to complete, a website with high volume could create a demand that you cannot handle and force you to compromise quality to meet that demand. A successful website could also drain your business of inventory, leaving your store with empty shelves and disappointing your existing customer base.

DOMAIN NAME

If you decide to create a website, you will want a *domain name* that is easily recognized by your customers. A domain name is the address on the Internet where your Web page is located. If you have a domain name in mind, you can go to one of several website registration services and search to see if your domain name is available. The *Internet Corporation for Assigned Names and Numbers* (ICANN) is a nonprofit corporation formed to assume responsibility for regulating the registration of domain names. You can go to the ICANN website to learn more about domain name registration at **www.icann.com**. The ICANN website has a list of companies that can register a domain name for you. The price of registering a name varies depending on the company, and many times this price is reduced if you agree to use other services provided by that company.

In a perfect world you would be able to register for the domain name that matches your business name. However, that domain name may already be occupied. Regardless of whether your business name is a registered trademark or service mark, you may have a difficult time getting the occupant to give up control of the domain name without paying for it or taking costly legal action. Generally, the domain name is less important than most people think, and you can have just as much success by choosing to operate your website at a domain name that closely matches your business name.

WEBSITE DESIGN

A website can be as simple or as complicated as you want it to be. If you want the site to be simple, you may be able to design and build it yourself with the help of some inexpensive software tools. If you want a more complicated site, you may need to enlist the help of a friend with more computer knowledge or even a *site designer*.

The best way to figure out what you want on your website is to visit other websites. Start by searching the Web for products or services that are similar or related to yours. By looking at what your competition is doing, you may get a better idea of how the Internet could benefit your business. However, do not limit your searches to similar businesses. You may see an idea on a website for another type of product that you think could work well with your products. Do not worry about not knowing intimidating Internet jargon. Take specific notes in common language of the designs that you like, and eventually you will be able to translate that into technical terms once you learn more.

Design Tools   If you know what type of website you want to build and you are somewhat computer savvy, inexpensive off-the-shelf software tools are available to help you build it yourself. There are many website design tools out there that you can research by reading online or going to a computer store and asking questions. A good website design software package should cost between $500 and $1,000, which can be much less expensive than paying a designer to build your website. You should check out several different software packages. Many demos are available on each software company's website. How-to books have been written about many of them to supplement the materials provided by the software company.

A good design tool will have two elements—a Web page development tool and an image editor. The *Web page development tool* actually creates the foundation and frame of each of the Web pages that will be on your website. A good Web page development tool will allow you to create Web pages by manipulating the image of the pages themselves, rather than requiring you to write in a computer code language. A good Web page development tool will also have the ability to manipulate templates or forms so you can create several similar pages for your site at a time if you will have a separate page for each product.

The *image editor* will allow you to create and manipulate pictures and graphics. A good image editor should let you edit an image by taking it apart and adding or changing the elements of the graphic. This will allow you to optimize your use of graphics by changing the color and image quality to strike a balance between clarity and the time that it takes to download the Web page.

WEB DESIGNERS

Web designers can be found almost everywhere today. By simply searching online or in the phone book you will easily be able to find hundreds of people offering to design and create a website for you. There are huge companies that do website design work with hundreds of programmers, as well as individuals who do freelance website design work out of their homes. Because there are so many designers and so many options for website designs, pricing is irregular. It is extremely important to shop around. Many times a designer will listen to what you want and then quote a price based on how much he or she thinks you are willing to pay rather than how much effort will go into the site. Many times the design for a new website will take less effort if the structure and format will be a close copy of the design of a website that the designer previously created. A good website designer will be able to point you to several sites that he or she has already created and give you price quotes a la carte based on what you see on the sites.

You may choose to have your website designed by someone located in the area that you operate, but that is not necessary. Your website can be designed anywhere in the world and accessed by you and your customers from where you are located. Several existing websites, such as **www.programmingbids.com** and **www.elance.com**, offer the services of many different designers in a bidding format. You can go to the site and input the details of the website you would like to have built, and then many different designers will present their respective prices to build the website you specified. If you choose to use one of these services, make sure you get a written contract from the designer that includes a price term as well as the specifications of the site to be designed, and a deadline for completion.

WEB HOSTING

A Web host is the actual computer that powers your website. Like a Web designer, you may choose to use the services of a Web host located in the area you operate, but that is not necessary. Web hosting services are offered by huge companies that power hundreds or thousands of websites, as well as individuals who have powerful computers in their homes that power a few websites.

As with website designers, it is very important for you to shop around. A good Web host will generally cost between $25 and $50 per month for a standard website (up to 50 MB of space).

There are several hosting companies that you may find on the Internet that offer free hosting services. These companies are not recommended for Internet commerce websites. The sites go down often, and they offer little or no support services. If you are going to spend your money and time on a website for your business, you will want to make sure that your customers can access it and that you will be able to get help when you have a problem.

Several websites exist where you can compare the price, reliability, customer support, and specific services that many different hosts offer. These websites include:

- ✪ **www.tophosts.com**;

- ✪ **www.hostsearch.com**; and,

- ✪ **www.webhostdir.com**.

Customer Support

The customer support services offered to you by a Web host may be the single most important factor in your decision of which host to use. Many hosts will set up step-by-step methods for you to use for many administrative and housekeeping tasks on your website, such as changing pictures, text, and email addresses. However, if something goes wrong or if you want to make more dramatic changes, you may want the help of customer support. You should ask any Web host that you are considering for references from other customers, and you should contact the references and talk to them about their experience with the Web host.

Other Factors for Web Hosting

At a minimum, if you are considering a website that will include Internet commerce, then you want a Web host to provide the following:

✪ reliable tech support twenty-four hours a day, seven days a week;

✪ rights to your domain name;

✪ 10 GB monthly transfer traffic;

✪ 20 MB to 50 MB server space for your website;

✪ ability to run CGI scripts on the server;

✪ unlimited email accounts;

✪ unlimited automatic responding to customers;

✪ ability to change your site design and content; and,

✪ statistics on visits to your site and access to the server logs.

In addition, you may want to consider the following list of other factors before deciding which Web host to use:

✪ the connection speed of the host computer;

✪ the extent of any backup systems;

✪   any advanced payment required;

✪   the length of the Web hosting contract;

✪   fees for setup and customer support;

✪   any software offered in connection with the hosting services; and,

✪   whether the host offers a secure server for processing commerce transactions and if there is any extra cost associated with use of the secure server.

Whoever you decide to use as a Web host should be someone that will be around for a long time and can grow with you and your business. Changing Web hosts can be a difficult and costly process. If you anticipate your website being only a small part of your business, you should be sure that the Web host will be providing hosting services for a long time. If you feel that your website may develop into a very active and busy site, then you will want to make sure that your Web host will be able to support this expansion.

E-COMMERCE

E-commerce, put simply, is conducting business over the Internet. This can be accomplished in several ways. You can list your products on your website and allow customers to order your products by sending you an email or simply calling your store directly. You can also provide an order form that customers can print and then mail or fax to your store. However, e-commerce is usually a little more complicated.

The main reason that the Internet has become so popular is convenience. Consumers have the ability to shop at many different retail stores from the comfort of their own home and make their purchases from their computer. This saves consumers time and usually saves them money because they can easily compare prices. If you wish to give your customers this convenience, you must have access to a *secure server* to allow *real time* credit card purchasing services on your website.

At first this may seem too complicated, but not to worry, many Web hosts will provide a secure server dedicated to e-commerce. Since e-commerce has become so popular, many companies have popped up specifically to serve Internet merchants and help them process their credit card purchases.

Shopping Cart Software

There are two basic functions that must occur for an e-commerce credit card purchase to be completed. Just like in a regular store, the customer must pick out the merchandise he or she wishes to purchase, and the customer must pay you for those items by transmitting a credit card number. If you have done much purchasing over the Internet, then you will know that the first step, much like in a regular store, is accomplished with the help of a *shopping cart* function.

An Internet shopping cart does exactly the same thing as a shopping cart at the market. Consumers pick out what they want as they are browsing the pages of your website and then make one transaction to purchase all of the items when they are done shopping. Your website can include a shopping cart function, or you can link to another website and pay that site a fee. If you wish to include the shopping cart on your website, purchase one of many shopping cart software tools (this will usually not be included in your website design software), which range in price between $400 and $600. If you are using a website designer, ask him or her about including a shopping cart on your site. If you accomplish the shopping cart function by linking to another site, the total cost will usually include a set monthly fee, around $50, plus a small percentage of your sales. Ask your website designer or your Web host about shopping cart services that he or she recommends.

Merchant Account Provider

The second function required to complete an e-commerce credit card purchase is for the customer to pay for the goods by transmitting a credit card number. This step can also be accomplished on your website or by linking your website to the website of a dedicated merchant account provider. A *merchant account provider* accepts and processes the credit card transaction and then sends you the funds along with an invoice for the goods that the customer has purchased. A merchant account provider will charge you a fee—usually a percentage of your sales. Linking to a merchant account provider is more cost effective for a small business website. However, as your website business grows, you may want to consider getting your own merchant account—adding this function, as well as the shopping cart function—directly to your site. Ask your website designer or Web host about merchant account providers that he or she recommends.

WEBSITE PROMOTION

Once your website is up and running, you want to attract attention to it so that customers will visit and purchase your products or services. This task is much easier said than done. One option is to pay someone to promote your website. There are many websites that claim to be website promotion services that will make sure your website is listed on search engines and trade registries. However, unless you know what to look for and how to check up on them, you will have no way of knowing if they are actually doing what they say. Also, you do not have a way of knowing if what they say they are doing will be effective.

You can also go to websites dedicated to providing advice for small business Internet merchants and read their recommended website promotion techniques. Each list will recommend different strategies and methods, and none will guarantee success.

Free Promotion

The most important thing to remember is to not get carried away spending money to promote your website. The following is a list of several ways that you can inform your customers about your website and attract new customers without spending any money.

- ✪ Include your website address on all of your traditional print promotions, including stationary, business cards, brochures, pamphlets, and print advertising.

- ✪ Submit your website to any industry websites or directories related to your products. If your goods or services are specialized, there may be a website dedicated to informing consumers about merchant websites that carry products of that kind.

- ✪ Begin collecting an email registry of your customers and send out an email newsletter with special offers and promotions. You can allow your customers to sign up for the email newsletter on your website and in your regular store.

✪ List your website with search engines that offer free registration. Although not as heavily trafficked and therefore less effective than the *pay-per-click* search engines, registering with free search engines will only cost you time. You can go to websites such as **www.addme.com** and register for several search engines at once. However, it may be more effective to visit these search engines individually and complete their sign-up forms.

✪ Contact webmasters of nonmerchant websites dedicated to topics related to your products and ask if they would place a link on their websites that will direct visitors to your website. Many times a webmaster will see this as another way to serve the people visiting his or her website.

Cost Effective Paid Promotion

As with the free promotion methods discussed, there are many different paid promotions methods that vary in cost and effectiveness. You should shop around and consider more than just the cost. Do not be fooled by online promotion sites that claim to reach hundreds or thousands of people. You can spend a lot of money on these services, and you may or may not reap any benefit. Most likely, you will have a difficult time checking up on these services to see if they are doing what they say.

Banner ads and pop-up ads on popular sites may reach lots of people, but they will be expensive. Many Internet users habitually ignore these promotions. Instead of trying to reach as many people as you can, you want any paid promotions to reach people who will be interested in buying your products or services. The following is a list of low-cost, popular, paid promotional techniques that may be an effective way to attract more people to your website.

Marketplace shops. Several incredibly popular websites have begun to offer small businesses an opportunity to take advantage of the traffic on their site by paying for a small marketplace within a highly trafficked website. These *storefront services* allow small business to pay a fee, usually a flat monthly fee or a percentage of sales, and then put a selection of products in a small section of the highly trafficked website. Popular storefront services include *Yahoo Shopping*, *Amazon Zshops*, and *eBay*.

Affiliate programs. Opinions on the effectiveness of affiliate programs are varied. An *affiliate program* is a revenue sharing program whereby a merchant is allowed to place a banner add or a link on other websites. If a sale is generated by someone who clicks on the banner or link, then the merchant pays a commission to the owner of the other website. The problem is that you will not always get to choose which other websites will have a link to your website. The affiliate sites may have little or no traffic by people who would be interested in your products. Again, this is a service for which you should shop around. There are several websites, such as **www.refer-it.com**, that are dedicated to searching for and reviewing revenue sharing programs.

Shopping bots. Several websites, commonly known as *shopping bots*, exist solely to aid consumers in comparing products and prices. Some shopping bots, like **www.froogle.com**, offer free registration for merchants, while others, such as **www.pricegrabber.com**, **www.dealtime.com**, and **www.bizrate.com** require you to pay them a fee if a consumer visits your site by way of their site. This *pay-per-click* technique can be very cost effective for you, as you will only pay for the service if a consumer actually visits your site.

Register with business directories. Several respected and highly trafficked business directories exists with websites that provide thousands of different products and services organized by topic. Most of these directories will require a fee to place your website on the list, but paying the fee may be worth the listing if you think that your products will stand out against similar products offered by other merchants. Some of these directories include **www.dmoz.com**, **www.about.com**, and **www.business.com**.

Pay-per-click search engines. Most people will tell you that the most effective method to direct traffic to your website is through pay-per-click search engines. Many of the most popular search engines will allow you to list your site for free, but then will require you to pay a fee if you would like to ensure that your website receives prominence when a consumer searches with certain terms that may be associated with your products. For instance, if your Web page sells sports memorabilia, you may want to be one of the sites that appears in the list whenever a consumer enters search terms such as "baseball cards." Some of the more popular pay-per-click search engines are:

- ✪ **www.ah-ha.com**;

- ✪ **www.kanoodle.com**;

- ✪ **www.google.com**; and,

- ✪ **www.mamma.com**.

Many of the search engines listed above are linked to other popular search engines that will conduct a search by combining results from other search engines.

As you can imagine, common search terms can return a list of hundreds or thousands of websites. That is why some search engines have developed ways for you to pay more to ensure your website will appear at the top of the returned list. Some search engines will let you pay a flat fee for your site to be associated with certain search terms. Some search engines allow you to bid with other merchants for association with certain search terms.

The fee structures vary, but usually the fee is based in paying per click. This will require you to pay the fee only if the search engine user actually visits your website. Be cautious, as not all of these search engines will allow you to set a budget. You could register for a popular search term at what seems like a great price, but when you get the bill and find out that thousands of people have clicked through to your site, it may not be cost effective.

Search engine positioning. Making sure that your website is at the top of the returned list when certain keywords are searched on popular search engines is called *search engine positioning*. Many complicated and intricate strategies have been developed to effectively accomplish the task. If Internet-based sales will be a big part of your business, you may want to consider outsourcing your search engine positioning to a company that specializes in that service. If you want to attempt to do your own search engine positioning, many articles and how-to books have been written on the topic.

Summary

✪ Your domain name should be easily recognized by your customers. A domain name is the address on the Internet where your Web page is located.

✪ A Web host is the actual computer that powers your website. Web hosting services are offered by huge companies that power hundreds or thousands of websites, as well as individuals who have powerful computers in their homes that power a few websites.

✪ You should ask any Web host that you are considering for references from other customers, and you should contact the references and talk to them about their experience with the Web host.

✪ E-commerce is conducting business over the Internet.

✪ There are both free and cost effective ways to promote your website.

Collections

Naturally, most small business owners would prefer to always be paid for their products and services with cash or by credit card at the time the goods are sold or the services are provided. Unfortunately, requiring your customers to pay only in cash or by credit card could limit the number of people interested in purchasing your products or services. Most businesses find it profitable to accept checks or provide credit accounts for their customers, notwithstanding the fact that accepting non-cash forms of payment will usually lead to collection hassles.

BOOKKEEPING

There are no laws that require any specific kinds of bookkeeping for your small business. If you have experience keeping financial books and records, you may want to choose a format with which you are familiar. If you do not have experience, there are numerous self-help books for small business owners to get their arms around the basic concepts of bookkeeping. The IRS also provides Publication 583, *Starting a Business and Keeping Records* on it website, **www.irs.gov**. This publication will serve as an excellent guide to setting up your business records.

You may choose to use one of several small business bookkeeping computer programs that will allow you to easily input invoices and receipts directly into your computer and will automatically return computations as well as provide detailed analyses and reports of your business's strengths and weaknesses. Some programs will also help you figure your business taxes and even create the forms to file with the IRS or connect to a website that will allow you to file your taxes online.

Regardless of what format you choose, bookkeeping is a part of your business that should not be taken lightly. You will be required to produce accurate records of gross receipts, purchases, expenses, and assets if your business is audited by the IRS. In addition, accurate bookkeeping can be an immeasurable benefit when you are reviewing and trying to learn from previous successes or failures, and to assist in collection activities. Too often, beginning small business owners focus all their efforts on building the business, and forget or neglect to keep good records. This can easily lead to headaches and even failure in the future. Do not wait until you have amassed a volume of receipts and invoices that need to be recorded; rather, develop and set up your bookkeeping system early and diligently maintain your business records.

CHECKS

Accepting checks as payment for your products or services may significantly increase the number of customers you have. Generally, the added expense of collections will be made up by increased sales. It is important to establish a standard check policy for your business. First and foremost, you should be sure to get a current address and driver's license number with each check that you accept. This information will aid in the collection process if the check is ultimately denied payment by your bank.

If you do receive payment by a check that is ultimately not honored, in both North Carolina and South Carolina you must send the customer a *demand letter* by certified mail requiring him or her to pay you the face amount of the check as well as a fee (not to exceed $20 in North Carolina or $30 in South Carolina). This letter may not include any threats other than the promise to pursue legal action if the debt is not paid.

If the check remains unpaid for thirty days, you may file a claim against the customer in court to collect the debt. As a small business owner, you will need to weigh the circumstances, most importantly the amount of the check, to determine if collecting the debt will be worth the time required to file and follow through with the lawsuit.

CONSUMER CREDIT LAWS

Both federal and state laws exist that may require disclosures and reporting requirements for businesses that extend credit to their customers, including the Truth in Lending Act, the Fair Credit Billing Act, the Equal Credit Opportunity Act, the North Carolina Consumer Finance Act, and the South Carolina Consumer Credit Act, among others. These laws are detailed and difficult to understand. If you are considering extending credit to your customers, then you should become familiar with these laws or consult a lawyer who is familiar with these laws.

Truth in Lending Act

The *Truth in Lending Act* requires that you disclose to the consumer the exact terms of the credit arrangement in a format that can be easily understood. The Act also regulates how you may advertise any consumer credit arrangement. Each consumer must be told the monthly finance charge, the annual interest rate, the due dates for all payments, the total price of any product or service, including all interest and finance charges, and the amount of any penalty charges and the terms under which they will be imposed.

The Fair Credit Billing Act

The *Fair Credit Billing Act* outlines requirements for how you must respond to a consumer who claims you made a mistake in billing. Generally, if a consumer notifies you in writing within sixty days after receiving a bill that the bill contains a mistake, you must:

- ✪ respond to the consumer within thirty days after receiving notification of the alleged mistake;

- ✪ conduct an investigation into the alleged mistake; and,

- ✪ within ninety days after receiving notification, explain to the customer why the bill is correct or correct the error.

Failure to follow these procedures will require you to give the consumer a $50 credit regardless of the accuracy of the bill.

The Equal Credit Opportunity Act

The *Equal Credit Opportunity Act* prohibits you from discriminating against a consumer credit applicant based on race, color, religion, national origin, age, sex, or marital status. You may consider factors that would legitimately indicate creditworthiness, such as the applicant's employment status and credit record.

If you do offer credit to consumers, you need to consult an attorney familiar with consumer credit protection laws. The attorney should help you draft a standard credit application for your business that includes all necessary information as to the terms of the credit arrangement. In addition, you and the attorney should establish an organized and accurate system of billing, dealing with billing inquiries and collection practices that will be used for all consumer credit arrangements.

CREDIT ACCOUNTS

Generally, if you are extending credit to another business, you are less likely to run afoul of the federal and state credit Acts. Most of the laws are directed at *consumer protection*, and therefore will not apply to credit transactions between two businesses. North Carolina does have a *usury law*, which will apply to credit transactions between businesses as well as consumer credit. The usury law limits the legal rate of interest that may be charged on several different types of credit transactions. The maximum rate limits are posted monthly on the website for the North Carolina Commissioner of Banks at **www.nccob.org**. If the maximum rate limit is exceeded, the borrower may be allowed to escape interest charges entirely. South Carolina does not have a usury law.

Summary

- ✪ There are no laws that require any specific kinds of book-keeping for your small business.

- ✪ Begin developing and setting up your bookkeeping system early and diligently maintaining your business records.

- ✪ Accepting checks as payment for your products or services may significantly increase the number of customers you have. Generally, the added expense of collections will be made up by the increased sales.

- ✪ If you do receive payment by a check that is ultimately not honored, in both North Carolina and South Carolina you must send the customer a demand letter by certified mail requiring him or her to pay you the face amount of the check as well as a fee (not to exceed $20 in North Carolina or $30 in South Carolina).

- ✪ The Truth in Lending Act requires you to disclose to the customer the exact terms of the credit arrangement in a format that can be easily understood. The Act also regulates how you may advertise any consumer credit arrangement.

- ✪ The Fair Credit Billing Act outlines requirements for how you must respond to a consumer who claims that you made a mistake in billing.

- ✪ The Equal Credit Opportunity Act prohibits you from discriminating against a consumer credit applicant based on race, color, religion, national origin, age, sex, or marital status.

- ✪ Generally, if you are extending credit to another business, you are less likely to run afoul of the federal and state credit acts. Most of the laws are directed at consumer protection, and therefore will not apply to credit transactions between two businesses.

Business Relations

This chapter examines the laws that govern business relations. Business relation laws are designed to regulate business in a way that will ensure every new entrepreneur has the opportunity to succeed.

CONTRACTS

Formation of a valid *contract* that is binding on parties agreeing to the contract requires three basic elements. One party must make an offer; another party must accept that offer; and, some form of payment must be exchanged.

What constitutes an offer is a difficult question to answer. Generally, a public advertisement of your products or services will not be considered an offer; however, something that resembles an estimate or a bid to provide your products or services would be considered an offer. If you make an offer to provide your products or services or to purchase another's products or services and someone accepts that offer, then you have likely obligated yourself to provide or purchase those products or services regardless of any change in circumstances that makes the offer less appealing to you.

If you believe that another person is not honoring a valid contract with you or if another person is claiming that you are bound by a contract that you do not believe exists, you can choose to either abandon or honor the obligation in question, or you can press your rights in a court of law. As a business owner, you will need to weigh the circumstances, including the possible negative effect that a reputation for not honoring contracts may have on your future business. You also need to determine the cost of legal representation and whether you could obtain or sell the products from or to another source.

The general rule is that a contract does not have to be written in order to bind the parties. Several exceptions exist to this rule that require parties to put a contract in writing before one party may enforce the agreement against another party. Contracts that are required to be in writing before they are enforceable include:

- contracts which, by their terms, will require longer than one year to fully perform all the obligations;

- contracts for the sale of an interest in real estate or for the lease of an interest in real estate that will last longer than one year;

- contracts for the sale of goods with a purchase price of more than $500; and,

- contracts for the lease of goods with a total lease price of more than $1,000.

If you require a written contract in your business, the safest way to ensure that your rights in the contract will be protected is to have an attorney draft the contract for you. You may also be able to find standard form contracts for your business in industry publications or through trade groups.

UNIFORM COMMERCIAL CODE

The *Uniform Commercial Code* (UCC) is an extensive set of laws governing commercial transactions. The UCC was created by a national commission to ensure that all of the individual state laws governing commercial transactions are based on the same model. Each state then has the choice of whether to adopt the code as part of their state law. Both the North Carolina and South Carolina legislatures have adopted the Uniform Commercial Code (UCC) as state law.

Transactions Governed by the UCC

An extensive discussion of the UCC is well beyond the scope of this book; however, what is important is that new business owners are aware of its existence and the types of businesses and transactions that it regulates.

The UCC is divided into different subject parts titled *Articles*. Each Article covers a different area of commercial concern. The following are generally the most important to new businesses.

- *Article 2: Sales.* This article applies to contracts or agreements for the sale of *goods*. For example, among other things, the UCC specifically provides that a contract for the sale of goods priced for $500 or more must be in writing in order to be enforceable in court. It also provides the rules governing contracts or agreements made between merchants as well as laws that dictate when a contract may be terminated or cancelled.

- *Article 2A: Leases.* This article applies to *any* transaction that creates a lease. A lease is created when there is a transfer of the right to possession and use of goods for a specified period of time in exchange for payment.

- *Article 3: Negotiable Instruments. Negotiable instruments* are documents that are signed by the maker and include an unconditional promise to pay a specific sum of money on demand or at a specified time. *Checks, certificates of deposit,* and *promissory notes* are examples of negotiable instruments.

- *Article 4: Bank Deposits and Collections.* This article applies to banking and collection transactions.

- *Article 4A: Funds Transfers.* This article applies to the series of transactions associated with the transfer of funds between banks.

○ *Article 5: Letters of Credit.* A *letter of credit* is a promise by a bank that it will honor demands for payment to a third party on behalf of one of its customers. Customers have to meet certain requirements before the bank will issue a letter of credit.

○ *Article 6: Bulk Sales.* This article covers transactions involving the bulk sales of a debtors' assets. For example, if a company owes your business money, then pursuant to this Article, it has to notify you before it can sell its assets in a bulk sale.

○ *Article 7: Warehouse Receipts, Bills of Lading, and Other Documents of Title.* This article governs any transaction involving documents that serve as evidence that the person in possession of it is entitled to the goods described in the document.

○ *Article 8: Investment Securities.* This article applies to transactions involving stocks and bonds.

○ *Article 9: Secured Transactions.* Transactions that involve the use of collateral would be covered by this provision of the UCC.

UCC Filings Both South Carolina and North Carolina have a system, pursuant to the UCC, whereby a person or business can give notice of security interest in the personal property owned by another person or business to interested third parties. Lien information on any person or business may be obtained, upon the payment of a small fee, from the state UCC section upon request. Contact your secretary of state concerning UCC filings at the following addresses:

North Carolina
Uniform Commercial Code Section
Department of the Secretary of State
P.O. Box 29626
Raleigh, NC 27626
www.secretary.state.nc.us/ucc

South Carolina
Uniform Commercial Code Section
Department of the Secretary of State
P.O. Box 11350
Columbia, SC 29211
www.scsos.com/uccsearch.htm

FEDERAL BUSINESS RELATIONS LAWS

There must be an even playing field if businesses are to thrive in a capitalistic society. That is why the federal government has stepped in to enact laws that promote fairness in the marketplace. The Robinson-Patman Act and the Sherman-Clayton Anti-Trust Act are two examples of these types of laws. The discussion that follows concerning these laws is designed to make new business owners aware of their existence so they can govern themselves accordingly and know when they need to seek professional help.

Commercial Discrimination

The *Robinson-Patman Act* includes prohibitions against *commercial discrimination*. The Act prohibits discrimination in the sale of goods among purchasers. For example, if you start a business that sells lumber to companies that build homes, it would be illegal for you to sell the lumber to Company A for one price and to Company B and Company C at another price.

There are two important points to consider with respect to the Robinson-Patman Act.

- ✪ The law requires that goods of the *same quality* must be the *same price*. However, different quality of goods can be sold for different prices. A lumber company could sell the highest grade of lumber to Company A for $1,000 and a lower grade to Company B for $100.

- ✪ The Act really only applies in situations where the discrimination is having a *negative impact* on competition. For example, if there is only one lumber company in a state and it was allowed to discriminate in its pricing, it could drive those not benefiting from its pricing out of business. The federal government recognized the negative impact this could have on competition and the economy and enacted this Act.

Monopolies and Price Fixing

The *Sherman Anti-Trust Act* (which was amended by the *Clayton Anti-Trust Act*) forbids two or more persons from engaging in activities that create monopolies or price fixing. A *monopoly* exists when one business controls all aspects of a market. Monopolies eliminate or erode the development of competition. *Price fixing* is an illegal agreement among two or more businesses to set prices at a certain level.

Not every monopoly is illegal. The Sherman Anti-Trust Act is designed to target situations where the monopoly is created or maintained by the deliberate act of a business owner to shut out or squelch the competition. In these situations, the Justice Department, on behalf of the federal government, can file charges and take steps to break the monopoly.

It is important to note that the Act was not designed to target a monopoly that is created through no fault of the business owner, but is a by-product of the business's growth and expansion.

INTELLECTUAL PROPERTY

Intellectual property is any product of the human intellect that is unique, novel, and unobvious, and has some value in the marketplace. This section will examine the types of intellectual property entrepreneurs commonly use as the basis for starting a business and its effects on business relations.

Patents

A *patent*, which is issued by the United States Patent and Trademark Office (PTO), gives an inventor the right to exclude others from making, using, offering for sale, or selling the invention in the United States or importing the invention into the United States. A patent granted by the U.S. Patent and Trademark Office is only good in the United States and its territories and possessions. Generally, a patent is good for twenty years from the date on which the application was filed with the Patent and Trademark Office.

If someone *infringes* on a patent, the owner of the patent must file a lawsuit in order to get the court to order him or her to stop the infringement. The court in these situations can also award the patent owner monetary damages. These types of lawsuits generally will require the assistance of an attorney and are very expensive.

For more information on patents, visit the U.S. Patent and Trademark Office at:

U.S. Patent and Trademark Office
Crystal Plaza 3
Room 2C02
P.O. Box 1450
Alexandria, VA 22313
800-786-9199
www.uspto.gov

Copyrights   *Copyright* is a form of legal protection provided to the authors of *original works of authorship* including literary, dramatic, musical, artistic, and certain other intellectual works—both published and unpublished. Copyrights are registered by the Library of Congress. The owner of a copyright has the exclusive right to do the following:

❂   reproduce the copyrighted work;

❂   prepare derivative works;

❂   distribute copies or phone records of the copyrighted work; and,

❂   perform the copyrighted work publicly or display the copyrighted work publicly.

A copyright is designed to protect the form or method of expression, not the subject matter or the content of the expression. For example, if you copyright a manual on how to build bridges, it would prohibit someone from copying your description of how to build bridges. However, it would not preclude someone from using your description to build a bridge or from creating his or her own description of how to build a bridge.

For more information on copyrights, visit the Copyright Office of the Library of Congress at:

U.S. Copyright Office
101 Independence Avenue, SE
Washington, DC 20559
www.loc.org

Trade Secrets

A *trade secret* is any information—process, formula, tool, or innovation—that gives a business an advantage over its competition. The courts consider trade secrets to be confidential business information. Examples of trade secrets might include the recipe for a gourmet cookie, a dry cleaning process for removing grape juice from white garments, or a tool that allows a manufacturer to make twice as many widgets in less than half the industry standard time.

It is illegal to obtain trade secrets through theft, deception, or other fraudulent means. If your competition were to obtain your trade secrets through any of these means, you would be able to get a court of law to prohibit them from taking advantage of your trade secret and to pay you damages for any losses you may experience as a consequence.

However, if your trade secret is discovered through legal means, the law does not prohibit your competition from using it to their advantage. For example, if a competitor concludes through the process of elimination, research, and analysis that the special ingredient in your chocolate chip cookies is oatmeal, they could lawfully begin adding oatmeal to their recipe.

Summary

- Formation of a valid contract that is binding on the parties agreeing to the contract requires three basic elements: an offer, acceptance of the offer, and an exchange of some form of payment.

- Generally, a contract does not have to be written in order to bind the parties.

- The Uniform Commercial Code (UCC) is an extensive set of laws governing commercial transactions.

- The Sherman Anti-Trust Act forbids two or more persons from engaging in activities that create monopolies or price fixing. A monopoly exists when one business controls all aspects of a market.

- Intellectual property is any product of the human intellect that is unique, novel, unobvious, and has some value in the marketplace.

- A patent, which is issued by the United States Patent and Trademark Office (PTO), gives an inventor the right to exclude others from making, using, offering for sale, or selling the invention in the United States or importing the invention into the United States.

- Copyright is a form of legal protection provided to the authors of original works of authorship including literary, dramatic, musical, artistic, and certain other intellectual works—both published and unpublished.

- A trade secret is any information—process, formula, tool or innovation—that gives a business an advantage over its competition. The courts consider trade secrets to be confidential business information.

Conclusion

In conclusion, we wish you great success in your business endeavor. In the days ahead, keep in mind that the only sure way to conquer is to continue. While the road that lies before you may not be easy, the rewards from staying the course are immeasurable in terms of both financial success and personal satisfaction. As this book was designed to make entrepreneurs aware of the legal issues that arise when starting or running a business in North Carolina or South Carolina, we are hopeful that it will be a resource you turn to again and again as your business grows and evolves.

Business Start-Up Checklist

❑ Select a name that is distinguishable from every other business entity in your state.
  ✪ Contact the secretary of state to conduct a name search:

North Carolina Secretary of State	**South Carolina Secretary of State**
Corporations Division	Business Filings
P.O. Box 29622	Edgar Brown Building
Raleigh, NC 27626	1205 Pendleton Street
919-807-2225	Suite 525
www.sosnc.com	Columbia, SC 29201
	803-734-2158
	www.scsos.com

❑ Select a Form of Business Organization
  ✪ Sole proprietorship
  ✪ Partnership
  ✪ Corporation
  ✪ Limited Liability Company

❑ Obtain Any Necessary Business Licenses and Permits
  ✪ Contact one of the following to determine what federal licenses or permits are needed for your business:
    www.sba.gov
    www.dol.gov/esa
  ✪ If applicable, apply for a federal employer identification number (EIN). (See Chapter 3 for requirements)
  ✪ Contact the following to determine what state licenses or permits are needed for your business:

North Carolina Business License Information Office (BILO)
800-228-8443 or 919-807-2166.

South Carolina Business One Stop
www.myscgov.com. (Click the "business" link.)

❏ Before you hire or fire an employee, familiarize yourself with the employment and labor laws relating to the following (see Chapter 4):
  ✪ Minors
  ✪ Citizenship verification
  ✪ Minimum wage
  ✪ OSHA
  ✪ Terminating employees
  ✪ Employment notices

❏ Obtain Insurance
  ✪ Contact an insurance agent about insurance protection against property damage and personal injury.
  ✪ Obtain workers' compensation insurance. (North Carolina business owners who employ fewer than three employees and South Carolina business owners who employ fewer than four employees are exempt.)

❏ Develop a Marketing and Advertising Plan
  ✪ Review Chapter 6 to see if your business is governed by specific regulations.
  ✪ Visit the FTC website **www.ftc.gov** for information about advertising specific products and services.

❏ Set up a recordkeeping system to ensure your taxes are paid in a timely manner.
  ✪ Visit **www.irs.gov** for dates and locations of tax workshops conducted in your area.
  ✪ Consult the website for the Department of Revenue in your state for more information:

North Carolina
www.dor.state.nc.us

South Carolina
www.sctax.org

Glossary

A

acceptance. A term used in contract law that describes what happens when a party agrees to an *offer* made by another party. Acceptance is a necessary element of a valid contract.

affirmative action. A plan employers implement in order to improve the employment opportunities for members of minority groups.

alien. A person who is not a citizen of the country where he or she resides.

articles of incorporation. The legal document that formally creates a corporation.

B

bait and switch advertising. An illegal sales practice that attracts customers into a business establishment by advertising low-priced goods and then encourages customers to purchase higher priced goods once they are in the establishment.

blue laws. Any state law or local ordinance that prohibits activities, such as the sale of goods on Sunday.

Bulk Sales Act. A provision of the *Uniform Commercial Code* that requires a debtor to notify his creditor prior to the bulk sale of his assets.

C

common law. The body of law, derived from England, that is based on judicial decisions as opposed to legislative enactments.

consideration. The inducement to a contract. In order for a contract to be valid, each party must promise to give up something in exchange for whatever it is he or she is to receive.

contract. A binding agreement. In order for a contract to be legally enforceable there must be an *offer, acceptance*, and *consideration*.

copyright. The exclusive legal right an author or artist has to the ownership and control of his or her original creative work product.

corporation. A legal entity created upon filing of the *articles of incorporation* with the Department of the secretary of state. It has a legal status that is separate both from the individual(s) who forms it and its owners.

D

deceptive pricing. An illegal tactic designed to mislead consumers about the actual cost of a good or service.

discrimination. To make a difference in the treatment of an individual on a basis other than merit.

domain name. An Internet address.

E

employee. An individual who provides a service in exchange for wages or a salary.

endorsement. A provision added to an insurance contract altering its coverage.

excise tax. A tax imposed upon the purchase of certain items.

express warranty. An overt assurance made by a merchant or manufacturer regarding their goods or products.

F

fictitious name. The name, other than a person's legal name, used by an entity to transact business.

G

general partners. Individuals who manage a limited partnership and are subject to unlimited liability.

goods. Refers to all things exchanged in commerce except real estate.

guarantee/guaranty. An assurance or promise with respect to the quality of goods or service.

I

implied warranty. An unexpressed assurance made by a merchant or manufacturer.

independent contractor. A person who performs work for another person while maintaining control over the manner and method by which the work is performed.

intangible property. Property that represents value but has no intrinsic value, such as promissory notes or stock certificates.

intellectual property. Any product of the human intellect that is unique, novel, and unobvious (and has some value in the marketplace).

L

liability. A person's responsibility for his or her goods or services.

limited liability company. An unincorporated association that offers a combination of limited liability and special tax treatment.

limited liability partnership. A business entity which is formed and operated as a partnership, and which is registered as a limited liability partnership within the state where it operates its principle place of business.

limited partnership. A business form comprised of one or more general partners who actively manage the business and are personally liable for debts of the business and one or more limited partners who contribute capital but do not manage and are not personally liable for the debts of the business.

limited partner. A partner in a limited partnership who contributes capital to the business but does not actively manage the business and is not personally liable for the debts of the business.

M

merchant. A person who produces goods or purchases goods at wholesale with the intent to sell the goods at retail.

merchant's firm offer. An offer to purchase or sell products or services that (1) is made by a merchant, (2) is in writing, (3) is signed by the merchant and (4) states that the offer will remain indefinitely or for a period of time.

N

nonprofit corporation. A corporation that is both organized for a purpose other than making a profit and does not distribute income to its shareholders.

O

offer. A promise to do or refrain from doing some thing in the future, which, if accepted by the person to whom the promise is made, will create a binding contract.

overtime. Hours worked beyond the regular fixed hours for employment.

P

partnership. An association of two or more persons to carry on, as co-owners, a business for profit.

patent. A government grant of the right to stop others from producing, using, or selling an invention without the permission of the person holding the grant.

personal property. Anything that is subject to ownership other than real estate.

pierce the corporate veil. Disregarding the normal liability limitations that protect the officers, directors, and shareholders of a corporation and imposing personal liability on all or some of them for damages caused by wrongful acts done in the name of the corporation.

professional association. A business form compromised of two or more professionals and organized to practice their profession together.

proprietorship. A business owned and operated by one person, which is not organized into a registered business form.

R

real property. Land and whatever is permanently built on the land.

resident alien. A person who is not yet a citizen of this country but is living in this country intending to become a citizen of this country.

S

S corporation. A corporation with limitations as to total assets and number of shareholders and which has elected to be taxed as a partnership for federal and state income tax purposes.

securities. Stocks, bonds, and other documents that represent an ownership interest in a company or a debt owed by a company.

service mark. Any word, name, symbol, or device, or any combination of them used by you to identify and distinguish the services that you perform from the similar services performed by others.

sexual harassment. Improper sexual advances or other verbal or physical conduct in the workplace.

shares. A unit of ownership or membership in a company.

statute of frauds. The law requiring some contracts to be made in writing before they will be binding on both parties.

stock. A unit of ownership or membership in a company.

sublease. A lease given by the current tenant, which conveys the tenant's remaining obligations under the lease to another party.

T

trade secret. A secret formula, process, pattern, or device not patented but known only to the person or business claiming it, which gives that person or business some advantage over competitors.

trademark. Any word, name, symbol, or device or any combination of them used by you to identify and distinguish the goods you sell from the similar goods manufactured or sold by others.

U

usury. The act of charging an illegally high rate of interest on a credit account or loan.

W

withholding tax. A tax collected by deduction from wages.

workers' compensation. Laws that require employers or their insurance companies to pay fixed awards to employees or their dependents in case of a work-related injury.

Putting Your Business Idea to the Test

To evaluate whether your idea for a new business is something that others would be interested in, follow the six steps outlined below. Taking the time to formulate a well thought-out idea in the beginning will save immeasurable amounts of time and headache later on.

Step One—Describe your business idea in fifty words or less. Write your description on a 3 x 5 note card. Place the note card in an envelope. Seal the envelope and place it in your desk drawer and do not look at what you have written for two weeks. During that time do all you can to not think about or discuss your business idea.

Step Two—Once the two weeks have passed, open the envelope and reread your idea. Revise as needed until your description is reduced to a single sentence.

Step Three—Share your idea with three of your strongest supporters, such as spouses, parents, children, and friends, who think everything you do is wonderful.

Step Four—Share your idea with three people you know who never have a positive thing to say about anything.

Step Five—Share your idea with five people who already own their own business. Invite them to lunch and tell them what you hope to accomplish. Ask them to share what they consider to be the pros and cons of being business owners.

Step Six—If you are still excited about your business idea, outline the specific goals you hope to achieve during the first five years of your business life. This is an important step. Research has shown that writing down goals makes them 95% more achievable.

Creating a Business Plan

A *business plan* is the blueprint for building the business of your dreams. Creating a business plan will allow you to outline the launch, development, management, and growth of your business on paper before you open the doors. This can save you both time and money once your business is off the ground.

A business plan is important for other reasons. It is what banks and investors use to evaluate your idea and determine whether to extend credit or invest in your enterprise. It can also serve as a compass to keep you focused on the vision that inspired you to start a business in the first place.

Business plans can be tailored many different ways, depending on the type of business you plan to open. However, there are a few key components common to every plan that you should be familiar with.

Executive Summary—This section includes a concise overview of the business you are planning to open.

Description of Product or Service—This section should provide a thorough response to what it is that you plan to sell.

Market Analysis—In this section, identify the consumers whom you plan to target and how you plan to get them interested in buying your product or service.

Financial Analysis—This section should include profit and loss projections as well as information on how you plan to finance your enterprise until it becomes self-funding.

Management—This section provides background information on the people who will be running the day-to-day operations of the business.

You can use the following sample business plan as a guide when creating your plan. If you need additional help, consider consulting one of the following sources.

❂ *The Complete Book of Business Plans* by Joseph A. Covello and Brian Hazelgren (an excellent source that includes eleven sample plans).

❂ *Business Plan Pro* by Palo Alto Software (one of the highest rated business plan software programs on the market).

❂ *Professional Consultants.* Search the Internet to locate writers, MBAs, and accountants who specialize in assisting entrepreneurs with business plans.

❂ *Small Business Administration.* This government agency is an invaluable resource for anyone interested in starting a business. They offer a wide range of support including financing, mentoring, and business plan development. You can visit their website at **www.sba.gov** or contact them at:

**North Carolina
SBA District Office**
6302 Fairview Road
Suite 300
Charlotte, NC 28210
704-344-6563

**South Carolina
SBA District Office**
1835 Assembly Street
Room 358
Columbia, SC 29211
803-765-5377

Business Plan for:

Residential Realty, Inc.

2222 West DiamondBack Road

SUITE B-1200

Raleigh, NC 00000

(555) 555-0204

January, 2007

Business Plan Copy Number _____

This Business Plan is confidential and the proprietary property of Residential Realty, Inc. No reproduction of any kind, or release of this document is permissible without prior written consent of Residential Realty, Inc.

Executive Summary

Residential Realty, Inc., was formed to provide a professional real estate service to buyers and sellers of residential real estate in the Greater Metropolitan Raleigh area. Tom and Randy Jones are the founders of the company.

Residential Realty, Inc., opened its doors for operation January 1, 2007. The office is located in the DiamondBack Corridor, to provide services to the higher income sections of Metropolitan Raleigh.

Residential Realty, Inc., is part of the Worldwide International System of independently-owned offices. The company is proud of its association with Worldwide International.

In two recent surveys of homeowners, buyers and sellers of residential real estate and potential sales associates preferred to do business with a Worldwide office. Worldwide continuously ranked higher than any other real estate organization.

The Joneses chose to become a part of this organization because of the high success ratio of the Worldwide System.

Statement of Purpose

For many years Tom and Randy Jones have been involved in the real estate market as investors. The primary reason for establishing Residential Realty, Inc., was to develop a profitable business enterprise from which other investments may be developed.

Each of the business investments is planned to have a future acquisition value at the end of three years. The Joneses plan to review the investments at the end of three years, and evaluate whether to continue to nurture the investment or to offer it for acquisition.

While so doing, the company will always continue to strengthen its position in the target market area by providing superior customer service to clients and to sales associates.

The objective of our extensive recruiting process is to hire at least 25 sales associates by January 2008. At present, we have hired 13 sales associates, and we expect to reach our intended goal ahead of schedule.

Management

Our management team consists of experienced managers whose backgrounds consist of more than 50 years of combined marketing, real estate, and sales experience.

Tom Jones has several years' experience as a successful entrepreneur in the real estate industry. Prior to operating his own business, he developed a solid background in the same field with other well-known agencies in North Carolina.

Randy Jones has extensive experience as a corporate vice-president in the cellular phone industry for Southern Bell Telephone Co.

Our sales manager and designated broker is Bill Thomas. He brings to our team 25 years of successful real estate experience in sales and as an investor.

Marketing

The fundamental thrust of our marketing strategy consists of recruiting the very best personnel available, many of whom live within our targeted market area. We intend. to reach six primary market segments in the affluent areas of Raleigh.

Our company can be characterized as an aggressive marketing company that is very serious about the quality of service we provide to our clientele. We intend to continue our advances in the marketplace by following this plan of action.

Finance

In two years we will have achieved our initial goals, and our investment will be generating profit from which other opportunities will arise for further investment in the real estate market.

Gross revenue projected for the first 12 months of operation (January 1, 2007, through January 1, 2008), without external funding, is expected to be $234,000. Gross margin (company dollars) for the same period of time is projected to be $124,500. Annual growth is projected to be 10 percent per year through 2007.

Present Situation

Market Environment

The real estate marketplace is undergoing rapid changes in the Raleigh metropolitan area. Due to the strengthening of the economy in the Raleigh area, more home buyer today are looking to purchase homes. These changes in attitudes of home buyer are a tremendous boost to real estate firms.

We are poised to take advantage of these changes, and expect to become a recognized name and profitable entity in the Raleigh real estate market.

Current prices of residential homes in Metropolitan Raleigh are increasing, and revenue to real estate companies is also increasing. With the average home price up 6 percent during the past two years, prices have increased from an average of $76,500 to $80,851. We are seeing the marketplace turn around, as the value of homes begins to increase.

We chose to locate our office in the area of most revenue potential. Our targeted market area, the DiamondBack corridor, shows stability and growth. The average selling price for homes in our area for the past 15 months is $187,400. The average price is considerably higher than the rest of the Metropolitan Raleigh area. (Please refer to the Market Analysis Section for a more comprehensive analysis.)

The present situation of our organization is very exciting. We have a beautiful 4500-square-foot office, centered in the DiamondBack corridor of Raleigh. This location will enable our sales associates to work in an area that will allow them to make more money in a shorter period of time.

Management

Our management is in place and each manager has his or her specific responsibilities outlined. (Please refer to the Management Section.)

Objectives

The primary objectives of our organization are to:

1. Become a profitable enterprise to allow us the freedom of taking advantage of other real estate investment opportunities as they become available.

2. Recruit and hire self-motivated, success-oriented, and hardworking sales agents.

3. Maintain an office of at least 25 sales agents who meet the previous requirements.

4. Develop a solid, corporate identity in our specified targeted market area.

5. Become one of the Top Ten Regional Worldwide offices by our fourth year of operation, or before.

6. Realize a positive return on investment within the first 12 months of operation.

Rationale

We believe the above-mentioned objectives are obtainable because of the professionalism of our managers and sales associates. Our management team is highly skilled in the critical areas that are required to develop a successful real estate office. Each comes from an environment where he or she experienced managing large organizations, rapid growth, development of quality control, and building a strong, client-centered team of sales professionals.

Financial Objectives

Item	Year One	Year Five
Gross revenue	$234,000	$356,000
Gross margin (company dollars)	124,500	189,000

Broker Objectives

We have set the following objectives for our broker to accomplish. The broker will be responsible for:

1. Recruiting and maintaining a level of at least 25 sales associates.

2. Retaining successful sales professionals.

3   Motivating the sales associates to produce quality listings.

4. Developing checks and balances to evaluate the productivity of the sales associates.

5. Ensuring the highest possible level of penetration into our targeted market by number of listings and closings.

6. Maintaining the highest possible profile within appropriate real estate organizations and associations.

7. Ensuring the highest possible quality of service to our clients.

Management

How We Started

Residential Realty, Inc., was founded in early 2006 by Tom and Randy Jones. The Joneses invested a great deal of time and energy looking for a business development opportunity in North Carolina. Since they came from service industries, they concentrated their investigations in this sector. They came to believe that a niche existed for a real estate company with an extraordinarily high commitment to customer service.

The legal form of Residential Realty, Inc., is a Subchapter S Corporation, incorporated in the State of North Carolina.

The founders have been issued 100 percent of the original stock issue. Tom Jones holds 50 percent of the stock and Randy holds 50 percent.

Management Team

Three people make up the development staff:

> Tom Jones, President
> Randy Jones, Vice-President and Marketing Director
> Bill Thomas, Vice-President of Sales and Designated Broker

The founders and key managers of Residential Realty, Inc., have combined experiences exceeding 15 years in the real estate industry, and combined experiences exceeding 50 years in general business management.

The strength of the Residential Realty management team stems from the combined expertise in management, real estate, and sales areas. Those years of experience and successful operations in other companies will produce outstanding results.

The leadership qualities and characteristics of our management team have resulted in broad and flexible goal setting to meet the everchanging demands of the quickly moving marketplace requiring our services. This is evident when the team responds to situations requiring new and innovative capabilities.

Responsibilities

Tom Jones, President
Management of working capital, including receivables, inventory, cash and marketable securities; financial forecasting, including capital budget, cash budget, pro forma financial statements, external financing requirements, financial condition requirements, and facilitating staff services.

Randy Jones, Vice-President, and Marketing Director
Manage market planning, advertising, public relations, sales promotions, identify new markets, develop marketing strategies, and direct market research and analysis.

Bill Thomas—Vice-President of Sales and Designated Broker
Manage field sales organization, territories and quotas; manage sales activities, including customer support service; develop and maintain a high industry profile, and be signatory to all company contracts.

Outside Support

An outside team of highly qualified business and industry professionals will assist our management team to make productive decisions and take the most effective actions to generate the greatest possible profits for our enterprise. However, they will not be responsible for final management decisions.

> Legal—Jack Anderson, Attorney
> Accounting—Emily Smith, Certified Public Accountant
> Management Consulting—Trico Business Solutions, Inc.
> Quality Control—Worldwide Real Estate Corp.

Management Team

Following their participation in the North Carolina real estate market, the Joneses turned their attention to the Raleigh market. They have purchased three dozen separate real estate properties in North Carolina for investment purposes, and they plan to pursue other real estate investments in the North Carolina market.

Tom Jones
After several years of learning the real estate business, Tom opened his own agency in Charlotte, North Carolina. He developed the company into a successful enterprise, and in 2006 sold the agency to Banner and Banner, Ltd.

Tom's successful sales and promotion experience covers the spectrum of all types of real estate properties, including residential, commercial, and industrial. He has also participated in the promotion of the oil and gas industry.

Randy Jones
Randy's career path has been a distinguished one in sales and communication as a corporate vice-president and executive. He was the vice-president of the Fortune 100 Company, Southern Bell Telephone Co. Prior to Southern Bell he was with ATT&R, one of the world's best known International Telecommunications companies.

Randy has developed successful sales and marketing campaigns for these companies that have produced outstanding results. He was awarded the prestigious Malcolm Smith sales award while at ATT&R.

Bill Thomas
Bill has been successfully involved in the North Carolina real estate industry for 25 years. He is the designated broker to Residential Realty, Inc., and oversees the development of the entire sales force.

Bill is a graduate of the Realty Institute, and has received the GRI designation for his real estate educational training. He is also a member of several industry associations and committees.

Outside Support
Finance and Accounting—Emily Smith, CPA
Emily holds professional designations as Certified Public Accountant in both North Carolina and Kentucky. She is a member of the American Institute of Certified Public Accountants and the North Carolina Society of Certified Public Accountants.

Her original contribution to Residential Realty, Inc., was in the incorporation and original setup of the company and its accounting procedures. Her ongoing contribution is in the role of accounting services and as a tax and financial consultant.

Legal—Jack Anderson, Attorney
Mr. Anderson is a graduate of the Harvard School of Finance & Commerce and Stanford University School of Law.

Jack was admitted to the North Carolina State Bar in 1990. His areas of preferred practice are estate planning, real estate, and business law. He has extensive experience as an instructor and lecturer at the college and university level, as well as for a variety of businesses, industry organizations, and community groups.

Jack is a member of the American, North Carolina, and Raleigh Bar Associations.

His original contribution to Residential Realty, Inc., was in the incorporation of the company. His ongoing role is in all matters of business law, as they arise, concerning the company.

Management Consulting—Trico Business Solutions, Inc.
Trico Business Solutions, Inc., is a professional management consulting firm located in Raleigh, North Carolina. Its diverse client base includes businesses in manufacturing, wholesale, retail, and service industries. The senior management team of Trico consists of executives with more than 40 years of combined management, marketing, and sales experience.

Joseph A. Thomas, MBA (Finance), is a graduate of Fairleigh Dickinson University. He has 15 years' experience in accounting and upper management. He has been vice-president of finance and general manager in large manufacturing and distribution corporations. Joe is also an instructor for business and human relations courses at Raleigh College.

Brian J. Hanson, BA (Marketing), is a graduate of Western International University. Brian has been a top sales representative and regional sales manager in large service and distribution companies. He is also a licensed REALTOR in North Carolina.

Brian has appeared as a guest on several radio and television talk shows regarding business plan development and marketing strategies.

Quality Control—Worldwide Regional Headquarters
A team of professional managers with direct, hands-on experience within the real estate industry is always available to assist Residential Realty, Inc. These professionals are constantly in touch with our senior managers to assist and make suggestions for the overall benefit of our business in the areas of sales and marketing support and training.

Functional Organization Chart of
Residential Realty, Inc., as of January 1, 2007

President	**Vice-President/Marketing Director**
Tom Jones	Randy Jones
Financial, Administrative,	Marketing, Advertising,
Long Range Planning	Public Relations

Designated Broker/Sales Manager	**Outside Support**
Bill Thomas	**Finance/Accounting**
Sales Associate Training	Emily Smith, CPA

Sales Associates	**Legal**
M. Wicks	Jack Anderson, Attorney
G. Steppon	
C. Stevens	**Management Consultants**
R. Rich	Trico Business Solutions
H. Pachoe	
D. Rutan	**Secretarial**
L. Walker	S. Haymond
L. Benson	
L. Holtman	**Quality Control/Operations**
G. Wright	Worldwide Regional Headqtrs.

Service Description

At Residential Realty, Inc., our principal service consists of selling residential real estate in a targeted market area. Our target market is located in the DiamondBack corridor of Raleigh. This particular area covers from 10th Street to Amazon Road, and from Washington Drive to Stenson Road. (Please refer to the Market Analysis Section.)

Residential Realty, Inc., is a full service residential sales agency. The development of three other services is already in progress. These additional services will allow us to satisfy several different needs of our clients. These services are:

1. Property Management,

2. Commercial Real Estate Sales, and

3. Business Brokerage Services.

Useful Purpose and Benefits

Our services provide our clients with an international network of buyers and sellers through the Worldwide International System, as well as the local multiple listing service (MLS). Because of our capabilities to network with other brokers, we will sell homes faster than our clients could if they tried to market their home without the assistance of a licensed real estate agent.

In addition, our customers will list their homes with our agency because of our aggressive and highly-skilled professionals. We will continuously have an above-average sales force to generate and close residential listings.

The owners and management team of Residential Realty, Inc., are committed to success in the real estate market. Our high level of commitment will enable the company to attract top professionals as sales associates and clients looking to buy and sell residential real estate.

Benefits of Belonging to the Worldwide System

As part of the Worldwide System, Residential Realty, Inc., is able to offer detailed services that help make the sales and purchases of residential homes much easier for our clients. Residential Realty, Inc., is a full-service real estate office. The following categories of services help make up this dynamic format of customer service.

Residential Real Estate Sales

Residential real estate is the foundation of the Worldwide and Residential Realty, Inc., systems. While continuing to strengthen its position in the residential real estate market, Worldwide Real Estate Corp. has also renewed its commitment to additional services, which allows Residential Realty, Inc., to become more influential with our clients.

Broker-to-Broker Referrals

Broker-to-broker referrals continue to be one of the hallmarks of the Worldwide System. In an increasingly mobile society, the referral opportunities available to Residential Realty, Inc., and other Worldwide brokers are a lucrative income source. And with approximately 12,000 offices worldwide, referral capabilities are a valuable benefit to our buyers and sellers.

Worldwide Military Program

The Worldwide Military Program has been in operation since 1992. This system was developed in cooperation with U.S. Military officials. The military program features substantial savings to military transferees on fees required to purchase a home, plus a variety of other specialized services. The Worldwide System is officially endorsed by the military to provide this service.

Corporate Real Estate Services Department

The corporate Real Estate Services Department at Worldwide conducts a national corporate calling program and administers real estate services to corporate clients. Through this program, corporate clients have access to services such as:

1. Home purchase assistance,

2. Home search assistance,

3. Early sales program assistance,

4. Mortgage and insurance assistance, and

5. Household goods transportation assistance.

Residential Realty, Inc., will utilize the vast library of knowledge provided to us as a Worldwide franchise owner. As our sales associates use the successful tools also provided by Worldwide, our firm will generate more revenues in a relatively short period of time.

Sales Support Materials

The sales materials used by our sales associates are developed by the Worldwide organization. Our sales materials reflect the enormous success of the Worldwide network. These materials are easy to understand and follow. Their purpose is to assist our sales associates when giving presentations to clients. We feel that our sales materials will help our agents list and sell more properties.

Key Benefits of all Services

The combination of all services provided by Worldwide enabled the Joneses to make an intelligent decision of which franchise to purchase. To illustrate this point even further, a national survey and a local Metropolitan Raleigh survey was performed by The Thomlinson Group, a leading survey research organization. The results of the surveys clearly indicate why Worldwide enjoys the rating of "Number One" in the world. (Please refer to the Market Analysis Section.)

Market Analysis

Market Definition

Key points in defining the market segment for our service are our geographical location and the lifestyle of our targeted customers. Currently, the market distribution is shared by several participants due to overlapping segments of the targeted market.

We will show where our targeted markets are in the Raleigh area and provide figures for the number of homes presently listed, as well as the number of homes that have sold during the past 15 months.

For our market analysis, we will provide facts and figures from the following areas listed in the Multiple Listing Service (MLS) for the Raleigh area:

1. MURRAY (Area 105 on the map);

2. DIAMONDBACK MOUNTAIN (Area 104);

3. LAMBSON VALLEY (Area 106);

4. WASHINGTON DRIVE TO SOUTHERN AVENUE (Area 103);

5. AMAZON ROAD TO 10TH STREET, AND STENSON ROAD TO 20TH STREET (Area 406);

6. DIAMONDBACK ROAD TO THOMASSON DRIVE (Area 410).

Market research (as of December 15, 2006) indicates that there are currently 987 to 1,003 active listings in these areas. This is our targeted market area, and gives our office a tremendous boost, because all the homes listed are in medium- to upper-income areas.

Like most of the northeastern region of the United States, this market segment has been unstable in the past few years. However, the trend is swinging upward for the number of listings and number of sold homes, particularly in our target area.

During the past 15 months, our area has produced approximately 1,009 sales of middle- to upper-income homes. The approximate average selling price for these homes in all the combined areas of our target market is $187,400. The average selling price in the Metropolitan Raleigh area is $80,851.

Based on the real estate market performance over the past 24 months, the average selling Raleigh area has increased almost 6 percent. The trend is expected to continue for the next five years as our market begins to rebound from a slow period from 2000 to 2005.

Figures from the North Carolina Regional Multiple Listing Service show that 1,908 buyers and sellers connected in December 2006. That is the highest figure recorded in the five years the organization has kept monthly statistics.

In November 2005, the average home sale price increased $2,500 more than posted increases in October 2005. Homes are moving quickly in Raleigh. The North Carolina Regional MLS figures show that nearly half of all homes sold in December 2006 had been on the market for 60 days or less (*The Raleigh Business Journal*, December 29, 2006).

The following list illustrates what the average selling prices are for our specific areas during the past 15 months.

Area	Average Selling Price
106	$ 87,000
105	215,000
103	120,000
410	108,000
104	407,000

The overall target market for the DiamondBack Corridor is presently generating about $217 million. It is projected to be $266 million by the end of 2006. (This is based on a 4 percent increase of sales over the next five years.) (North Carolina Regional Multiple Listing Service.)

The major competitors in our market are:
Red Canyon
Jack Holmes and Associates
Realty People
Connors
Other Worldwide offices

Strengths

In terms of our service strengths, we will recruit sales associates who live within our target market to gain even greater influence. It is very important for sales associates to live in the area where they will generate most of their leads and, consequently, their sales.

The physical location of our office is a definite strength. We are located in the heart of our target market at 10th Street and DiamondBack in Raleigh. This is only a few minutes from four of the most influential and high-income residential areas of the immediate area.

In the corporate arena, Residential Realty, Inc., is supported by Worldwide System. Our market strengths are the recognized symbols of quality, success, and professionalism. These several advantages have already been outlined in the Service Description Section.

Opportunities

The upside potential for a real estate agency like Residential Realty, Inc., backed by the Number One real estate organization in the world is tremendous.

Based on existing conditions, we are poised to take full advantage of the current market in Raleigh. As we follow the detailed educational process provided by Worldwide Real Estate Corp., there really is no way for our firm to fail.

We will succeed in becoming one of the major competitors in the Raleigh real estate market, because of our management team, the superior service that we provide, the powerful training provided by Worldwide, and our focused market segment, located a few miles from our office.

National and Local Survey Results

The following surveys, conducted by The Thomlinson Group (referred to in the Service Description Section), offer further positive references for our decision of owning and operating a Worldwide franchise.

The national survey included 1,500 telephone interviews with a random sample of homeowner's from across the United States, and was conducted during August 5–9, 2006. No coaching or preferences were provided by the survey company to persuade the homeowners to state any specific answers.

The local survey included 300 telephone interviews, and was conducted during August 15–19, 2006.

National Survey

QUESTION: Which company would you say is the company you would want to join if you were going to work in real estate?

WORLDWIDE	33%
Connors	6
E.S.S.A.	3
Bigger Homes	2
Maximum	2
Presidential	2

QUESTION: Supposing you were going to sell your home, which one of the following types of agencies would you most likely select to list your home?

An agency associated with a national organization	58%
An agency not associated with a national organization	16
An agency owned and operated by a national organization	14
Does not matter/Would not use a real estate agency	12

QUESTION: Which real estate company would you say can do the most to help someone like you sell a home?

WORLDWIDE	22%
Connors	4
E.S.S.A.	2
Bigger Homes	2
Maximum	1
Presidential	1

Metropolitan Raleigh Survey

QUESTION: Which real estate sales organization would you most likely use to sell your home?

WORLDWIDE	13%
Realty People	7
Red Canyon	3
Connors	3
E.S.S.A.	2
Realty Professionals	2
Jack Holmes	1
South USA	1
Southern Bell	1

QUESTION: Which company would you want to join if you were going to work in real estate?

WORLDWIDE	15%
Realty People	7
Connors	4
Red Canyon	3
E.S.S.A.	2
Bigger Homes	1
Help Us Sell	1
Jack Holmes	1

QUESTION: Which one of the following types of agencies would you most likely select to list your home?

An agency associated with a national organization, but which is independently owned and operated by local business people	55%
An agency owned and operated by a national organization	21
An agency not associated with a national organization	11
The type of agency doesn't matter/Would not use a real estate agency/ Don't know	14

Customers

Our customer service philosophy is unique. In a philosophic sense, Residential Realty, Inc., has three distinct customer groups: *sellers*, *buyers*, and *agents*.

Sellers of real property are our *first* customers. Listers of properties {sellers} pay commissions from the sale of their property and are the direct clients of the real estate brokers. We will never lose our focus that clients who have retained Residential Realty, Inc., to list and sell their properties are our first obligation.

Our second real customer is the buyer of residential real estate. We will provide superior personal service to buyers.

Our *third* real customer is the licensed real estate sales *agent*. It is the agent's job to provide a professional service to both sellers and buyers, specifically in this order. Therefore, it is the direct responsibility of Residential Realty, Inc., to provide service to our sales agents.

Typical Customer

We have identified the most typical buyer for our office. The purpose of the following information is to illustrate the age, income level, and emotional biases of our targeted clientele base. This information is also intended to assist our sales associates in understanding who our typical clients are.

Corporate Executive

Title:	President, VP Finance, VP Manufacturing, Office Manager, Advertising Manager, etc.
Power:	Permitter, decision-maker, influencer, initiator
Viewpoint:	Big picture, financial, personal
Emotional Influences:	Status, power, nice neighborhood, low crime area
Practical Influences:	Saving money, efficiency
Education:	Ph.D., MBA, college graduate
Limitations:	Geographical, purchasing approval from spouse

Housewife

Age:	35–55
Household Income:	$50,000 +
Sex:	Female
Family:	Full nest
Geographic:	Suburban
Occupation:	White-collar family
Emotional Influences:	Comfort, safe surroundings, close to schools, church, and shopping

Young Professionals

Age:	25–45
Income:	Medium to high
Sex:	Male or female
Family:	Bachelor or married
Geographic:	Suburban
Occupation:	White-collar
Emotional Influences:	Status, power, close to work

Young Married Couples

Age:	35–45
Income:	Medium to high
Sex:	Male or female
Family:	Married, with or without children
Geographic:	Suburban
Occupation:	White-collar
Emotional Influences:	Comfort; safe surroundings; close to schools, church, and shopping

Wealthy Rural Families

Age:	35–55
Income:	High
Sex:	Male or female
Family:	Full nest
Geographic:	Rural
Occupation:	White-collar
Emotional Influences:	Status; power; close to work; comfort; safe surroundings; close to schools, church, and shopping

Older Couple

Age:	55–70
Income:	High or fixed
Sex:	Male or female
Family:	Empty nest
Geographic:	Suburban
Occupation:	White-collar or retired
Emotional Influences:	Comfort; safe surroundings, close to church and shopping

Selling Agent

Recruiting Guidelines

The typical selling agent that we will constantly recruit will fall under the following categories:

- Middle Management personnel, earning approximately $60,000 a year.

- Retired persons in search of a second career.

- Persons who have a burning desire to earn a good living.

- Spouses who can contribute an above-average income to a family unit as a second income.

During the recruiting process and once the sales associate is hired, we will emphasize three key areas that are important attributes for all of our sales associates to maintain. They are

- Commitment to individual success and to the success of Residential Realty, Inc.

- Attitude and direction

- Knowledge and skills

Recruiting Goals

As part of our ongoing recruiting process, we have established recruiting goals to project our profit potential. These goals are based on the following important parameters:

1. What our monthly expenses are to keep the doors open.

2. The number of sales each month needed to meet the budget.

3. The amount of profit we should be earning each month on our investment in the company.

4. Minimum number of salespeople needed.

5. The average number of sales per sales associate per month.

Marketing and Advertising Strategies

Residential Realty, Inc., is committed to an extensive promotional campaign. This must be done aggressively and on a wide scale. To accomplish our initial sales goals, we require an extremely effective promotional campaign to accomplish two primary objectives:

1. Attract quality sales personnel that have a burning desire to be successful, and

2. Attract sellers and buyers that we will represent as their broker.

Residential Realty, Inc., plans to advertise in trade magazines and newspapers in the Raleigh area. *Raleigh Executive* is one publication that our ads have been placed in for recruiting quality female sales associates.

The Raleigh Times has a wide distribution network that allows us to advertise for sales associates as well as to list properties.

The Raleigh Guide is one of the more influential magazines for newcomers to the Raleigh area. This publication gives us some very good exposure to potential home buyers.

Unique Homes is distributed nationally. We will be advertising homes that list for $500,000 and above in this publication.

Due to the high Jewish population in our target area, we will be advertising for sales associates and listing homes in two prominent Jewish publications: *Jewish News* and *Jewish Living in Raleigh.*

Old Times is a tabloid newspaper, which covers a diverse psychographic audience. We will use this publication for recruiting.

On the DiamondBack Corridor is a business tabloid read by persons who work in the area, and may wish to move or relocate to the area. We will advertise in this publication for home sales.

We will also take advantage of the promotional opportunities provided by our memberships in both the Raleigh and the Durham Chambers of Commerce.

Advertising will be done independently and cooperatively with Worldwide of The South Eastern Region, Inc. A fixed amount of sales revenues will go toward the national Worldwide advertising campaign. The amount will be a minimum of $230 and a maximum of $690 per sale. These figures are a part of the agreement between Residential Realty, Inc., and Worldwide Inc.

Media Strategy

It is the practice of Residential Realty, Inc., to position the company in a compatible editorial environment consistent with communication objectives. We have selected primary publications with specific and tactical market penetration.

Promotion

In addition to standard local advertising practices, we will gain considerable recognition through the national advertising campaign from Worldwide Real Estate Corp. Worldwide ranks in the top 100 advertisers and enjoys an awareness factor of 90 percent with the American public. It is the only real estate organization to do so.

This is very important to our recruiting process, as well as to the buyers and sellers who may consider working with Residential Realty, Inc. People naturally want to be associated with successful organizations.

As a benefit of membership in the Worldwide System, we have available to us the services of the professional public relations firm, Jorgan & Haas, which has undertaken a promotional campaign on our behalf. Jorgan & Haas is located in Manhattan, NY.

Incentives

As an extra incentive for customers and recruits to remember Residential Realty's name, we plan to distribute coffee mugs, t-shirts, and other advertising specialties with the company logo. This will be an ongoing program to promote the company, when appropriate and where it is identified as beneficial.

Corporate Capabilities Brochure

Objective: To portray Residential Realty, Inc., as a leader in the Raleigh real estate market.

Recommended Contents: Utilize the powerful messages already created by Worldwide that have been proven successful. We will develop three separate brochures initially: one to use for recruiting, one to be used to promote sales, and another to promote referrals within the Worldwide Network.

Investment in Advertising and Promotion

For the first 12 months of operations, advertising and promotion is budgeted at approximately $12,000. On an ongoing basis, we feel that we can budget our advertising investment as 10 percent of revenues to Residential Realty, Inc.

Financial Projections

Assumptions, Definitions, and Notes

Revenues

1. Gross Revenues—Three percent has been used to determine the amount per side (a side may either be a listing or sale of a home) to be applied against the selling price of homes. The following has been used in the time periods indicated:

	Avg. Sale Price per Home	Gross Revenue per Side
January 2005-December 2005	$100,000	$3,000
January 2006-December 2006	120,000	3,600
January 2007-December 2007	140,000	4,200
January 2008-December 2008	150,000	4,500

The increase in the average sale price per home is a result of having a greater number of experienced and knowledgeable sales associates on staff.

Annual gross revenue is projected to increase by 25 percent for year three and 10 percent for years four and five.

Cost of Services

1. *Agent Commission*—Sales associates are paid on a commission only basis. The average commission rates used were as follows:

	Avg. Comm. Rate
January 2004-December 2004	50%
January 2005-March 2005	55
April 2005-December 2006	60

The average commission rate was applied against the net of gross revenues less Worldwide service fees and cooperative advertising costs.

2. *Worldwide Service Fee*—Six percent of monthly gross revenue is paid to Worldwide of The Southern Region, Inc., as a service fee per the franchise agreement.

3. *Cooperative Advertising*—Two percent of monthly gross revenue is also paid to Worldwide of The Southeastern Region, Inc., for advertising media per the franchise agreement, with the following limitation:

On an aggregate monthly basis, the amount to Worldwide of The Southeastern Region, Inc., must be at least $230 but must not exceed $690.

General and Administrative Expenses

1. *Advertising*—For year one advertising expenditures are estimated to be 15 percent of company dollars. This amount will be needed to gain immediate market recognition. Advertising amounts for years two through five have been reduced to approximately 11 percent of company dollars.

2. *Rent*—Has been recorded per the actual signed lease, including rental sales tax. The lease is a gross lease.

3. *Wages, Clerical*—One clerical support staff member has been hired for 2007. Another support staff member will be added at the beginning of 2008. No additional support staff will be needed through 2009.

4. *Wages, Broker, and Brokers Commission*—Base wages to be paid to one broker as a monthly fixed salary. The Broker will also receive as commission 5 percent of all company dollars.

5. *Wages, Officers*—Officers will not receive wages until loan to officers has been fully repaid. Wages are anticipated to begin January 2006.

6. *All Other Expenses*—Have been recorded on estimated usage for each category for all years. Anticipated inflation of 6 percent has been included.

Assets

1. *Cash*—Reflects limited amount of cash on hand at any balance sheet date. Positive generation of cash is to be applied against loan payable officer until fully repaid and then distributed to stockholders.

2. *Fixed Assets*—Projected purchase of all furniture and fixtures and office equipment for years 2007 through 2009 is recorded in January of each year. Depreciation will be calculated per Modified Accelerated Cost Recovery System (MACRS).

3. *Franchise Fee*—The actual cost to purchase a Worldwide franchise has been recorded. Straight-line amortization will be used systematically over a ten-year period.

4. *Rent Deposit*—Actual rent deposit required by landlord upon execution of the rental lease has been recorded.

Liabilities

1. *Accounts Payable*—Represents balances due vendors for items such as supplies, telephone, legal and accounting, travel, and entertainment.

2. *Accrued Liabilities*—Include unpaid Federal, State, FICA, FUTA, and SUI, withholding taxes payable, as well as other miscellaneous items not recorded through accounts payable.

The Financials

Authors' Note

As suggested earlier, the financial presentation portion of the business plan needs to be well prepared. If assistance is needed, contact a reputable accounting or other business firm that will be able to provide accurate, reasonable, and meaningful information.

As a general guide, the financial section may include the following data:

- *Notes, definitions, and assumptions used in preparing the financial data*

- *Profit and loss forecasts: years one and two by month, years three through five by year*

- *Balance sheet forecasts: years one and two by quarter, years three through five by year*

- *Cash flow forecasts: years one and two by quarter, years three through five by year*

Appendix

Authors' Note:

List all supporting documentation in the Appendix; section as noted and referenced throughout your business plan. Remember, this information should be clearly and neatly presented so the reader of your business plan can easily reference and understand the data provided.

Blank Forms

appendix c

This page intentionally left blank

State of North Carolina
Department of the Secretary of State

APPLICATION TO RESERVE A BUSINESS ENTITY NAME

Pursuant to §55D-23 of the General Statutes of North Carolina, the undersigned hereby applies to the Secretary of State to reserve the following business entity name:

1. The business entity name to be reserved is:

    _____

2. The name of the applicant is: _____

3. The address of the applicant is:

    Street Address _____

    City, State, Zip Code _____

4. The above entity name is to be reserved for a nonrenewable period of 120 days from the date of the filing of this application.

    This the _____ day of _____ , 20_____.

    _____
    Entity Name

    _____
    Signature

    _____
    Type or Print Name and Title

NOTES:
1. **Filing fee is $30. This document must be filed with the Secretary of State.**

CORPORATIONS DIVISION   P. O. BOX 29622   RALEIGH, NC 27626-0622
(Revised October 2002)   *(Form BE-03)*

This page intentionally left blank

STATE OF SOUTH CAROLINA
SECRETARY OF STATE

APPLICATION TO RESERVE
CORPORATE NAME

TYPE OR PRINT CLEARLY WITH BLACK INK

1. Pursuant to Section 33-4-102 (a) of the 1976 South Carolina Code of Laws, as amended, the undersigned hereby applies to the Secretary of State to reserve the following corporate name

_____

for a period of one hundred twenty days from the date of filing this application.

2. Name, address and signature of the applicant_____
Name

_____
Street

_____
City   State   Zip Code

Date_____

_____
Name Reserved

_____
Signature

_____
Print Name

FILING INSTRUCTIONS

1. Two copies of this form, the original and either a duplicate original or a conformed copy, must by filed. Include a self-addressed envelope for quicker return.

2. Filing Fee (payable to the Secretary of State at the time of filing this document) - $10.00

   Return to: Secretary of State
               P.O. Box 11350
               Columbia, SC 29211

NOTE

THIS RESERVATION EXPIRES 120 DAYS FROM THE DATE OF FILING.

REGISTERING YOUR CORPORATE NAME DOES NOT, IN AND OF ITSELF, PROVIDE AN EXCLUSIVE RIGHT TO USE THAT NAME ON OR IN CONNECTION WITH ANY PRODUCT OR SERVICE. USE OF A NAME AS A TRADEMARK OR SERVICE MARK WILL REQUIRE FURTHER CLEARANCE AND REGISTRATION AND BE AFFECTED BY PRIOR USE OF THE MARK. FOR MORE INFORMATION, CONTACT THE TRADEMARKS DIVISION OF THE SECRETARY OF STATE'S OFFICE AT (803) 734-1728.

Form Revised by South Carolina
Secretary of State, January 2000

This page intentionally left blank

STATE OF SOUTH CAROLINA
SECRETARY OF STATE

APPLICATION TO RESERVE
A LIMITED LIABILITY COMPANY NAME

TYPE OR PRINT CLEARLY IN BLACK INK

The applicant applies to reserve the exclusive use of a Limited Liability Company name (including in accordance with Section 33-44-1005 of the 1976 South Carolina Code of Laws, as amended a fictitious name for a foreign Limited Liability Company whose name is not available), for a non-renewable one hundred and twenty (120) day period as provided in Section 33-44-106 of the 1976 South Carolina Code of Laws, as amended.

1. The Limited Liability Company name to be reserved which complies with the requirements of Section 33-44-105 or Section 33-43-1005 of the 1976 South Carolina Code of Laws, as amended, is _____

2. The name and address of the applicant is

    _____
    Name

    _____
    Street Address

    _____
    City   State   Zip Code

Date _____   _____
                                        Signature of Applicant

FILING INSTRUCTIONS

1. File two copies of this application, the original and either a duplicate original or a conformed copy.

2. If space on this form is insufficient, please attach additional sheets containing a reference to the appropriate paragraph in this form, or prepare this using a computer disk, which will allow additional space to be included in the form.

3. This application must be accompanied by the filing fee of $25.00, payable to the Secretary of State.

    Return to: Secretary of State
                PO Box 11350
                Columbia SC 29211

NOTE

RESERVING THIS CORPORATE NAME DOES NOT, IN AND OF ITSELF, PROVIDE AN EXCLUSIVE RIGHT TO USE THIS CORPORATE NAME ON OR IN CONNECTION WITH ANY PRODUCT OR SERVICE. USE OF A NAME AS A TRADEMARK OR SERVICE MARK WILL REQUIRE FURTHER CLEARANCE AND REGISTRATION AND BE AFFECTED BY PRIOR USE OF THE MARK. FOR MORE INFORMATION, CONTACT THE TRADEMARKS DIVISION OF THE SECRETARY OF STATE'S OFFICE AT (803) 734-1728.

Form Revised by South Carolina
Secretary of State, January 2000

This page intentionally left blank

form 4   161

STATE OF NORTH CAROLINA
DEPARTMENT OF THE SECRETARY OF STATE

NOTICE OF TRANSFER OF RESERVED ENTITY NAME

Pursuant to §55D-23 of the General Statutes of North Carolina, notice is hereby given that the undersigned has transferred the following reserved business entity name.

1. The reserved entity name is:_____

2. The reserved entity name is hereby transferred to:_____

    Name_____

    Address_____

    City, State, Zip Code_____

3. The date of filing of the original application to reserve this entity name was:_____

This the_____day of _____, 20_____

_____
Name of Original Applicant/Transferor

_____
Signature

_____
Type or Print Name and Title

NOTES:
1. **Filing fee is $10. One executed original must be filed with the Secretary of State.**

CORPORATIONS DIVISION   P. O. BOX 29622   RALEIGH, NC 27626-0622
(Revised January 2002)   *(Form BE-04)*

NOTICE OF TRANSFER OF RESERVED ENTITY NAME
Instructions for Filing

Item 1   Enter the complete name exactly as it appears on the reservation.

Item 2   Enter the name and complete address of the person to whom the reserved name is being transferred.

Item 3   Enter the date the original reservation was filed.

Date and Execution
Enter the date the document was executed.
In the blanks provided enter:
- The name of the entity or individual that is the transferor or owner of the reserved name.
- The signature of the transferor or of the representative of the entity transferring the name.
- The name and title of the above-signed representative (only if an entity is the transferor).

STATE OF SOUTH CAROLINA
SECRETARY OF STATE

NOTICE OF TRANSFER OF
RESERVED CORPORATE NAME

<u>TYPE OR PRINT CLEARLY IN BLACK INK</u>

Pursuant to Section 33-4-102(b) of the 1976 South Carolina Code, as amended, notice is hereby given that the undersigned has transferred to:

_____

whose address is_____
                      Street   City   State

the following reserved corporate name_____

which name was reserved in the Office of the Secretary of State for the exclusive use of the undersigned

on_____ for a period of one hundred twenty days after such filing date.

Date_____

                                                _____
                                                Name of original applicant

                                                _____
                                                Signature

FILING INSTRUCTIONS

1.   Two copies of this form, the original and either a duplicate original or a conformed copy, must be filed.

2.   Filing Fee (payable to the Secretary of State at the time of filing this document) - $10.00

       Return to: Secretary of State
                  PO Box 11350
                  Columbia, SC 29211

This page intentionally left blank

STATE OF SOUTH CAROLINA
SECRETARY OF STATE

NOTICE OF TRANSFER OF A RESERVED
LIMITED LIABILITY COMPANY NAME

<u>TYPE OR PRINT CLEARLY IN BLACK INK</u>

Pursuant to Section 33-44-106(b) of 1976 South Carolina Code of Laws, as amended, notice is hereby given that the undersigned has transferred to

_____

whose address is _____
                              Street Address

_____
City   State   Zip Code

the following reserved Limited Liability Company name

_____

which name was reserved in the Office of the Secretary of State for the exclusive use of the undersigned

on _____
                              Date of filing

for a period of one hundred twenty days after such filing date.

Date _____   _____
                                       Name of Original Applicant

                                       _____
                                       Signature

                                       _____
                                       Type or Print Name

FILING INSTRUCTIONS

1.   File two copies of this application, the original and either a duplicate original or a conformed copy.

2.   If space on this form is insufficient, please attach additional sheets containing a reference to the appropriate paragraph in this form, or prepare this using a computer disk, which will allow additional space to be included in the form.

3.   This application must be accompanied by the filing fee of $10.00, payable to the Secretary of State.

     Return to: Secretary of State
                 PO Box 11350
                 Columbia SC 29211

Form Revised by South Carolina
Secretary of State, January 2000

This page intentionally left blank

State of North Carolina
Department of the Secretary of State

APPLICATION FOR CERTIFICATE OF AUTHORITY

Pursuant to §55-15-03 of the General Statutes of North Carolina, the undersigned corporation hereby applies for a Certificate of Authority to transact business in the State of North Carolina, and for that purpose submits the following:

1. The name of the corporation is _____ ; and if the corporate name is unavailable for use in the State of North Carolina, the name the corporation wishes to use is:

   _____.

2. The state or country under whose laws the corporation was organized is: _____.

3. The date of incorporation was _____ ; its period of duration is: _____.

4. Principal office information: *(Select either a or b.)*

   a. ☐ The corporation has a principal office.

      The street address and county of the principal office of the corporation is:

      Number and Street_____

      City, State, Zip Code_____County_____

      The mailing address, *if different from the street address*, of the principal office of the corporation is:

      _____

   b. ☐ The corporation does not have a principal office.

5. The street address and county of the registered office in the State of North Carolina is:

   Number and Street _____

   City, State, Zip Code _____County_____

6. The mailing address, *if different from the street address,* of the registered office in the State of North Carolina is:

   _____

7. The name of the registered agent in the State of North Carolina is: _____

8. The names, titles, and usual business addresses of the current officers of the corporation are (attach if necessary):

Name	*Title*	*Business Address*

9. Attached is a Certificate of Existence (or document of similar import) duly authenticated by the Secretary of State or other official having custody of corporate records in the state or country of incorporation. ***The Certificate of Existence must be an original and less than six months old.***

APPLICATION FOR CERTIFICATE OF AUTHORITY
Page 2

10. If the corporation is required to use a fictitious name in order to transact business in this State, a copy of the resolution of its board of directors, certified by its secretary, adopting the fictitious name is attached.

11. This application will be effective upon filing, unless a delayed date and/or time is specified:

This is the _____ day of _____ , 20____

_____
Name of Corporation

_____
Signature

_____
Type or Print Name and Title

NOTES:
1.   Filing fee is $250. This document must be filed with the Secretary of State.

Instructions for Filing

APPLICATION FOR CERTIFICATE OF AUTHORITY
(Form B-09)

Item 1 Enter the complete name of the corporation exactly as it appears in the records of the appropriate official in the state or country of incorporation. If the name cannot be used in North Carolina, enter the name (including a corporate ending) that it wishes to use in North Carolina.

Item 2 Enter the state or country of incorporation.

Item 3 Enter the date of incorporation and the period of duration.

Item 4 Select item "a" if the corporation has a principal office. Enter the complete street address of the principal office and the county in which it is located. If mail is not delivered to the street address of the principal office or if you prefer to receive mail at a P.O. Box or Drawer, enter the complete mailing address of the principal office.
Select item "b" if the corporation does not have a principal office.

Item 5 Enter the complete street address of the corporation's registered office and the county in which it is located.

Item 6 Enter the complete mailing address of the corporation's registered agent, only if mail is not delivered to the street address above or if you prefer to receive mail at a P. O. Box or Drawer.

Item 7 Enter the name of the registered agent. The registered agent must be a North Carolina resident, an existing domestic business corporation, nonprofit corporation or limited liability company, or a foreign business corporation, nonprofit corporation or limited liability company authorized to transact business or conduct affairs in North Carolina.

Item 8 Enter the names, titles, and usual business address of the current officers of the corporation.

Item 9 See Form

Item 10 See Form

Item 11 The document will be effective on the date and at the time of filing, unless a delayed date or an effective time (on the date of filing) is specified. If a delayed effective date is specified without a time, it will be effective at 11:59:59 p.m. A delayed effective date may be specified up to and including the 90th day after the day of filing.

Date and Execution

Enter the date the document was executed.

In the blanks provided enter:

- The name of the corporation as it appears in Item 1
- The signature of the representative of the corporation executing the document (may be the chairman of the board of directors or any officer of the corporation).
- The name and title of the above-signed representative.

This page intentionally left blank

State of North Carolina
Department of the Secretary of State

APPLICATION FOR CERTIFICATE OF AUTHORITY
FOR LIMITED LIABILITY COMPANY

Pursuant to §57C-7-04 of the General Statutes of North Carolina, the undersigned limited liability company hereby applies for a Certificate of Authority to transact business in the State of North Carolina, and for that purpose submits the following:

1. The name of the limited liability company is _____;

   and if the limited liability company name is unavailable for use in the State of North Carolina, the name the limited

   liability company wishes to use is _____

2. The state or country under whose laws the limited liability company was formed is: _____

3. The date of formation was _____; its period of duration is: _____

4. Principal office information: *(Select either a or b.)*

   a. ☐ The limited liability company has a principal office.

      The street address and county of the principal office of the limited liability company is:

      Number and Street_____
      City, State, Zip Code_____County_____

      The mailing address, *if different from the street address*, of the principal office of the corporation is:

      _____

   b. ☐ The limited liability company does not have a principal office.

5. The street address and county of the registered office in the State of North Carolina is:

   Number and Street _____

   City, State, Zip Code _____ County _____

6. The mailing address, *if different from the street address,* of the registered office in the State of North Carolina is:

   _____

7. The name of the registered agent in the State of North Carolina is: _____

APPLICATION FOR CERTIFICATE OF AUTHORITY
Page 2

8. The names, titles, and usual business addresses of the current managers of the limited liability company are:
   (use attachment if necessary)

   <u>**Name**</u>   <u>**Business Address**</u>

   _____   _____

   _____   _____

   _____   _____

   _____   _____

   _____   _____

9. Attached is a certificate of existence (or document of similar import), duly authenticated by the secretary of state or other official having custody of limited liability company records in the state or country of formation. **The Certificate of Existence must be less than six months old. A photocopy of the certification cannot be accepted.**

10. If the limited liability company is required to use a fictitious name in order to transact business in this State, a copy of the resolution of its managers adopting the fictitious name is attached.

11. This application will be effective upon filing, unless a delayed date and/or time is specified: _____

This the _____ day of _____, 20____

                                        _____
                                            Name of Limited Liability Company

                                        _____
                                            Signature of Manager

                                        _____
                                            Type or Print Name

Notes:
1. **Filing fee is $250**. This document must be filed with the Secretary of State.

CORPORATIONS DIVISION   P. O. BOX 29622   RALEIGH, NC 27626-0622

(Revised January 2002)   *(Form L-09)*

**STATE OF SOUTH CAROLINA
SECRETARY OF STATE**

**APPLICATION BY A FOREIGN CORPORATION
FOR A CERTIFICATE OF AUTHORITY
TO TRANSACT BUSINESS
IN THE STATE OF SOUTH CAROLINA**

<u>TYPE OR PRINT CLEARLY WITH BLACK INK</u>

Pursuant to Section 33-15-103 of the 1976 South Carolina Code of Laws, as amended, the undersigned corporation hereby applies for authority to transact business in the State of South Carolina, and for that purpose, hereby submits the following statement:

1. The name of the corporation is (see Sections 33-4-101 and 33-15-106 and Section 33-19-500(b)(1) if the corporation is a professional corporation) _____.

2. It is incorporated as (check applicable item) [   ] a general business corporation, [   ] a professional corporation, under the laws of the state of _____.

3. The date of its incorporation is _____ and the period of its duration is

    _____.

4. The address of the principal office of the corporation is _____ in the
    Street Address

    city of _____ and the state of _____.
    Zip Code

5. The address of the proposed registered office the state of South Carolina is

    _____ in the city of _____ in
    Street Address

    South Carolina _____.
    Zip Code

6. The name of the proposed registered agent in this state at such address is

    _____
    Print Name

    I hereby consent to the appointment as registered agent of the corporation.

    _____
    Signature of the Registered Agent

Name of Corporation

7. The name and usual business address of the corporation's directors (if the corporation has no directors, then the name and address of the persons who are exercising the statutory authority of the directors on behalf of the corporation) and principal officers:

a)   Name of Directors   Business Address

_____   _____

_____   _____

_____   _____

_____   _____

b)   Name and Office
of Principal Officers   Business Address

_____   _____

_____   _____

_____   _____

_____   _____

8. The aggregate number of shares which the corporation has authority to issue, itemized by classes and series, if any, within a class:

Class of Shares (and Series, if any)   Authorized Number of Each Class (and Series)

_____   _____

_____   _____

_____   _____

_____   _____

9. Unless a delayed date is specified, this application shall be effective when accepted for filing by the Secretary of State (See Section 33-1-230):_____

Date _____   _____
Name of Corporation

_____
Signature

_____
Type or Print Name and Office

_____

Name of Corporation

FILING INSTRUCTIONS

1. Two copies of this form, the original and either a duplicate original or a conformed copy, must by filed.

2. If the space in this form is insufficient, please attach additional sheets containing a reference to the appropriate paragraph in this form.

3. Schedule of Fees (Payable at the time of filing this document):

Fee for filing Application	$10.00
Filing Tax	$100.00
Annual Report	$25.00
Total	**$135.00**

4. This form must be accompanied by the initial annual report of corporations and an original certificate of existence no more than 30 days old from the official state of jurisdiction where the corporation is incorporated.

5. If the applicant corporation's domestic name is unavailable in South Carolina, then it must file a certified copy of the board of directors resolution approving the fictitious name along with this application pursuant to Section 33-15-106(a)(2). (additional $10 filing fee)

6. If the applicant is a foreign professional corporation, then in addition to satisfying the name requirements in Sections 33-19-150 and 33-19-500(b)(1), the following information must be included in the application:

   a) A statement that the corporation's sole business purpose is to engage in a specified form of professional services (e.g. Law firm).
   b) A statement that all of its shareholders, not less than one-half of its directors, and all of its officers other than its secretary or treasurer, if any, are licensed in one or more states to render a professional service described in its articles of incorporation.

   Return to: Secretary of State
                P.O. Box 11350
                Columbia, SC 29211

NOTE

THE FILING OF THIS DOCUMENT DOES NOT, IN AND OF ITSELF, PROVIDE AN EXCLUSIVE RIGHT TO USE THIS CORPORATE NAME ON OR IN CONNECTION WITH ANY PRODUCT OR SERVICE. USE OF A NAME AS A TRADEMARK OR SERVICE MARK WILL REQUIRE FURTHER CLEARANCE AND REGISTRATION AND BE AFFECTED BY PRIOR USE OF THE MARK. FOR MORE INFORMATION, CONTACT THE TRADEMARKS DIVISION OF THE SECRETARY OF STATE'S OFFICE AT (803) 734-1728.

This page intentionally left blank

STATE OF SOUTH CAROLINA
SECRETARY OF STATE

APPLICATION FOR A CERTIFICATE OF AUTHORITY
BY A FOREIGN LIMITED LIABILITY COMPANY
TO TRANSACT BUSINESS IN SOUTH CAROLINA

<u>TYPE OR PRINT CLEARLY WITH BLACK INK</u>

The following Foreign Limited Liability Company applies for a Certificate of Authority to Transact Business in South Carolina in accordance with Section 33-44-1002 of the 1976 South Carolina Code of Laws, as amended.

1.   The name of the foreign limited liability which complies with Section 33-44-1005 of the 1976 South Carolina Code as amended is _____

2.   The name of the State or Country under whose law the company is organized is
       _____

3.   The street address of the Limited Liability Company's principal office is

       _____
                                          Street Address

       _____
               City   State   Zip Code

4.   The address of the Limited Liability Company's current designated office in South Carolina is

       _____
                                          Street Address

       _____
               City   State   Zip Code

5.   The street address of the Limited Liability Company's initial agent for service of process in South Carolina is

       _____
                                          Street Address

       _____
               City   State   Zip Code

       and the name of the Limited Liability Company's agent for service of process at the address is

       _____   _____
       Name   Signature

6. [ ] Check this box if the duration of the company is for a specified term, and if so, the period
         specified_____

Name of Limited Liability Company

7. [ ] Check this box if the company is manager-managed. If so, list the names and business addresses of each manager

a. _____
Name

_____
Business Address

_____
City   State   Zip Code

b. _____
Name

_____
Business Address

_____
City   State   Zip Code

8. [ ] Check this box if one or more members of the foreign limited liability company are to be liable for the company's debt and obligation under a provision similar to Section 33-44-303(c) of the 1976 South Carolina Code of Laws, as amended.

Date _____   _____
                                            Signature

                                            _____
                                            Name   Capacity

FILING INSTRUCTIONS

1.   This application must be accompanied by an original certificate of existence not more than 30 days old (or a record of similar import) authenticated by the Secretary of State or other official having custody of the Limited Liability Company records in the state or country under which it is organized.

2.   File two copies of these articles, the original and either a duplicate original or a conformed copy.

3.   If management of a limited liability company is vested in managers, a manager shall execute this form. If management of a limited liability company is reserved to the members, a member shall execute this form. Specify whether a member or manager is executing this form.

4.   This form must be accompanied by the filing fee of $110.00 payable to the Secretary of State.

        Return to: Secretary of State
                    P.O. Box 11350
                    Columbia, SC 29211

5.   The first annual report for limited liability company must be delivered to the Secretary of State between January first and April first of the calendar year after which the limited liability company was organized or the foreign company was first authorized to transact business in South Carolina. Subsequent annual reports must be delivered to the Secretary of State on or before the fifteenth day of the fourth month following the close of the limited liability company's taxable year.

For Office Use Only
Registration Number

APPLICATION FOR
REGISTRATION AND RENEWAL OF TRADEMARK/SERVICE MARK
STATE OF NORTH CAROLINA

Pursuant to N.C.G.S. §80-3 and §80-5 the undersigned hereby makes application for the registration or renewal of a Trademark or Service Mark and submits the following information:

1. The application is for: _____ Initial Registration - $75.00 (Fees are non-refundable)
_____ Renewal - $35.00 (Fees are non-refundable)
Registration Number T-_____(See instructions)

OWNER/APPLICANT INFORMATION
2. Name of Owner/Applicant of the Mark (Individual or Business Entity):_____
_____

3. The undersigned Owner/Applicant is: **(Must check one box only & must match #2)**

☐ an individual   ☐ a sole proprietorship   ☐ an association   ☐ a government

☐ a union

☐ a corporation or limited liability company (LLC), indicate the state of incorporation or organization:
_____

☐ a partnership, indicate the state of organization: _____
List the names of the general partners: _____
(Attach a continuation sheet, if necessary)

4. Owner/Applicant Business Address: _____

City _____ State _____ Zip Code_____

Contact Name: (if business Entity)_____Telephone:_____

E-mail: _____

MARK INFORMATION
5. Describe the mark in words. If the mark is only a word or phrase, insert that word or phrase in the space provided. If a specific design is part of the mark to be registered, you must describe that design. Do not tape or draw a design on this application. Any design features must have a written description. **The design must match the specimens submitted.** You may attach additional pages if extra space is needed for the written description.

_____

_____

_____

_____

_____

APPLICATION FOR TRADEMARK/SERVICE MARK REGISTRATION & RENEWAL   Page 2

Complete item #6 or #7 not both in a single application

6. For Trademarks Only (if producing a good)	**7. For Service Marks Only (if providing a service)**
The principal place of business or distribution in this State.	The physical location where services are being rendered or offered in this State.

6. (left column)

_____
Address

_____
City   State   Zip

Check as many as apply
The Trademark is applied:
_____ Directly to the goods;
_____ Directly to containers for the goods;
_____ To tags/labels affixed to the goods; or
_____ By displaying it in physical association with
 the goods in sale or distribution thereof

7. (right column)

_____
Address

_____
City   State   Zip

Check as many as apply
The Service Mark is applied:
_____ In advertisements of the service;
_____ On documents, wrappers or articles
 delivered in connection with the services
 rendered; or
_____ In the following specified manner:

 _____

 _____

8. Identify the specific goods or services in connection with which the mark is used. [Example of goods (Item #6): "This Trademark is used in connection with the production of BBQ sauce". Example of Services (Item #7): "This Service Mark is used in connection with restaurant services."] **Refer to instructions.**

_____
_____
_____

9. You may apply for one classification of goods and services per application (refer to class listing on page 5 of the instructions).

Class Number: _____   Subclass: _____(Required for Service Classes 100 or 101, pages 2 and 7 of the instructions)

Class Title: _____

10. SPECIMENS: Three Specimens of the Mark in use are required.

I have attached **THREE (3)** original specimens of the mark as required with each initial application **AND** renewal as used in North Carolina. Examples of original specimens: for **Trademarks (Goods):** the item itself, actual labels, tags, containers; for **Service Marks (Services):** business cards, letterhead, newspaper advertisements (complete page which features the ad). **See instructions for more examples.** Please note that we will accept THREE (3) IDENTICAL specimens.

Please note: Specimens must be complete (not cut from a larger item), original (no photocopies or "camera ready art") and current (within six months). Specimens must also be consistent with the description in #5.

11. Required for Initial Registration Only:

Date of first use of the mark by applicant, predecessor or licensee. If you are using the mark for the first time in the month of mark application, please specify the specific date of use (Month/Day/Year).

_____ In North Carolina (Month/Year)

_____ Anywhere (Month/Year)

APPLICATION FOR TRADEMARK/SERVICE MARK REGISTRATION & RENEWAL   Page 3

CERTIFICATION (Application must be Acknowledged by a Notary Public)

For all applicants: The applicant is the owner of the mark, that the mark is in use, and to the best knowledge of the person verifying the application, no other person has registered in this State, or has the right to use the mark in this State either in the identical form thereof or in such near resemblance thereto as to be likely, when applied to the goods or services of the other person, to cause confusion, or to cause mistake, or to deceive.

For Renewals only: The mark described above is still in use in North Carolina for the goods or services for which registration was initially granted and these goods or services are described above in this application.

For Corporations and Limited Liability Companies only: I certify that the applying corporation or limited liability company is in good standing in the above-named state.

Name (Please Print):_____

Signature: _____

Official Capacity: _____ Date:_____

NORTH CAROLINA
_____ COUNTY

I, _____, a Notary Public for _____
County, North Carolina, do hereby certify that _____
personally appeared before me this day and acknowledged to me that he or she voluntarily signed the foregoing document for the purpose stated therein and in the capacity indicated. That I either posses personal knowledge of the identity of the principal or was provided with satisfactory evidence of the principal's identity.

Witness my hand and official seal, this the _____ day of _____, 20____

_____(Official Seal)
                 Notary Public

My Commission Expires: _____, 20____
                            Month/Day

DID YOU REMEMBER TO INCLUDE:

_____   The complete original signed and notarized application

_____   Three original specimens showing actual use of the mark.

_____   Application Processing fee of either $75.00 Initial Application or $35.00 Renewal Application.

Please make check or money order payable to NC Secretary of State.

INSTRUCTIONS

REGISTRATION AND RENEWAL OF TRADEMARK/SERVICE MARK
STATE OF NORTH CAROLINA

Application must be completed, including the notary section.
Application must be verified and executed by the Applicant or authorized agent of the Applicant.

1. **Identify** whether this form is submitted for the purpose of an Initial Registration or Renewal of an existing registration. The filing fee for an initial registration is $75.00. The filing fee for a renewal is $35.00. These fees are non-refundable. Please do not send cash. Make checks and money orders payable to the NC Secretary of State.

   For renewals only, insert the registration number for the North Carolina Trademark or Service Mark. The registration number is located on the renewal notice and on the upper right corner of the registration certificate.

2. **The Owner/Applicant** is the owner of the Mark (Individual or Business Entity) who controls the product or services. State the name of the individual or Business Entity who will own the mark.

3. **Identify** whether the Applicant is a person, sole proprietor or other form of business entity. If a corporation or limited liability company, please indicate the state of incorporation or organization. If a partnership, indicate the state of organization and list only the names of the general partners. If you need additional lines, it is appropriate to attach a continuation sheet.

4. **Owner/Applicant Business Address**: State the business address of the applicant in terms of street and number, city, state, and zip code. Include a contact name if different from the applicant and include the telephone number and e-mail address of the contact person. The contact person is someone authorized to answer any questions regarding the application.

5. **Describe the mark in words**. If the mark is only a word or phrase, insert that word or phrase in the space provided. If a specific design is part of the mark to be registered, you must describe that design. **Do not tape or draw a design on this application. Any design features must have a written description. The design must match the specimens submitted.** You may attach additional pages if extra space is needed for the description.

   A single application may not be used to seek registration of multiple variations of a phrase or design. An applicant seeking to register more than one version of the mark would need to make separate applications for each version.

   Example of description when mark is only comprised of words: "Pink Cat Restaurant"

   Example of description of design features: "The mark is a circle containing a pink cat sitting next to a green and white ball with a willow tree in the background."

The term **Trademark** means any word, name, symbol, or device or any combination thereof adopted and used by a person to identify goods made, sold, or distributed by him and to distinguish them from the goods made, sold, or distributed by others.

The term **Service Mark** means a mark is used in the sale or advertising of services to identify the services of one person and distinguish them from the services of others.

For Items 6 and 7: Complete the Trademark Section OR the Service Mark Section – Not Both

6. **For Trademarks**: If this application relates to a mark used in connection with goods, list either the address of the applicant's principal place of business in North Carolina or a place of distribution and usage of the goods in this State. Check the appropriate box(es) as necessary to relate how the trademark is applied to the good.

7. **For Service Marks**: If this application relates to a mark used in connection with services, list a physical location at which the services are being rendered or offered in this State. Check the appropriate box(es) as necessary to relate how the service mark is applied in connection with services.

8. **Identify** the specific good or services in connection with which the mark is used. [Example of goods (Item #9): "This Trademark is used in connection with the production of BBQ sauce or a brand name of clothing." Example of Services (Item #10): "This Service Mark is used in connection with restaurant services," or " This Service Mark is used in connection with landscaping services."]

    If the goods or services fall into more than one classification, a separate application must be made for each classification.

    The identification of the specific good or service must fall within the guidelines of the Class and Title indicated in Item #12 of the application.

9. **Insert** the class number, subclass (if applicable), and title of the mark to be registered. Class numbers, subclasses, and titles for goods and services begin on page five of these instructions, and can be found in the North Carolina Department of the Secretary of State publication, How to Register a Trademark or Service Mark in North Carolina, or on the Internet at the following address: http://www.sosnc.com, then click on the Trademarks hyperlink, then click on download forms.

    Do not list more than one class per application. If the mark is used in multiple classes, a separate and complete application must be made for each class.

Examples	
Trademark (goods)	Class _2_ Title: Receptacles
Service Mark (services)	Class: 100 Subclass: A Title: Miscellaneous Services

For Service Marks only, please list only one subclass if the class is either 100 or 101. If there are multiple subclasses as in a variety store or a general merchandise retail store, please choose 101M for miscellaneous.

10. **Specimens: Three specimens of the mark in use are required.** Attach **THREE (3)** original and complete specimens as currently used. Three (3) original and complete specimens of use must be filed along with this application for both initial registrations **AND** renewals. See North Carolina General Statute §80-1(g) for further definition of use in this State. Specimens must support use of the classification sought in Item #12 of the application. **Photocopies, drawings, blueprints, faxes, voided checks, deposit slips, or camera-ready layouts are NOT accepted as specimens.**

Acceptable specimens: Please note that we will accept THREE (3) IDENTICAL specimens. **Trademark Applications (Goods):** Submit specimens of use that show the mark affixed to the goods, such as actual labels or tags as affixed to the goods, mark stamping affixed to the goods, or containers for the goods. IF the specimen is too bulky to be mailed, a clear, color photo showing use of the mark on the goods themselves maybe acceptable when both the mark and the complete product are clearly visible. When the mark as affixed to the bulky product cannot be shown in a color photo that also clearly shows the entire product, a color photo accompanied by point-of-sale information such as provided in a catalog may also be acceptable. Letterheads and business cards are NOT acceptable specimens for Trademark goods.

Service Mark Applications (Services): Submit material used in selling or advertising services, such as menus for restaurants, business cards, letterhead, newspaper advertisements (complete page that features the ad), or the like. Color computer screen printout of the mark in use on the applicant's web page is also acceptable. Letterheads and business cards must contain at least some general understandable reference to the services provided in connection with the mark. (If these services are also referenced in the mark itself, that reference is sufficient.)

Note: Specimens must be original (no photocopies of "camera ready art"), complete (not cut from a larger item), and current (within six months).

11. **A mark** must be in use in the State of North Carolina prior to filing an application for trademark or service mark registration. Indicate the date the mark was first used (1) in North Carolina, and (2) anywhere. If you are using the mark for the first time in the month of mark application, please specify the specific date of use (Month/Day/Year).

Certification & Notary Acknowledgment: State the name and title of the person signing this application. The owner/applicant must sign the application if the applicant is an individual or sole proprietor. If the owner/applicant is not an individual or sole proprietor, a partner, manager of a limited liability company, or officer of a corporation who is authorized to execute this application on behalf of the applicant must sign the application. If a person acting under a power of attorney from the applicant signs the application, an original power of attorney or a certified copy of the power of attorney must accompany this application.

A Notary Public, who must properly execute the verification and affix his/her seal in the space provided, must verify the application. Please make sure that all spaces in the verification and Notary Acknowledgment have been filled in.

APPLICATION FOR TRADEMARK/SERVICE MARK REGISTRATION & RENEWAL   Page 7

Examination Process

Upon filing an application for registration and payment of the application fee, the Secretary may cause the

application to be examined for conformity with Article 80 of the North Carolina General Statutes.

The applicant shall provide any additional relevant information requested by the Secretary, including a description of a design mark, and may make, or authorize the Secretary to make, any amendments to the application reasonably requested by the Secretary or deemed by the applicant to be advisable to respond to a rejection or objection.

The Secretary may require the applicant to disclaim an unregisterable component of a mark otherwise registerable, and an applicant may voluntarily disclaim a component of a mark requested to be registered. No disclaimer shall prejudice or affect the applicant's or registrant's rights then existing or thereafter arising in the disclaimed matter, or the applicant's or registrant's rights of registration on another application if the disclaimed matter is distinctive of the applicant's or registrant's goods or services.

The Secretary may (i) amend the application submitted by the applicant, if the applicant consents, or (ii) require a new application to be submitted.

If the Secretary of State finds that the applicant is not entitled to registration, the Secretary of State shall advise the applicant of the reasons the applicant is not entitled to registration. The applicant shall have a reasonable period of time, specified by the Secretary, in which to reply or to amend the application. If the applicant replies and amends the application, the Secretary shall reexamine the application. This procedure may be repeated until (i) the Secretary finally refuses registration of the mark, or (ii) the applicant fails to reply or to amend the application within the specified period. If the applicant fails to reply or to amend the application, the application shall be deemed to have been abandoned. **Should the applicant still desire to register the Trademark or Service Mark in North Carolina after abandonment, a new application and fee is required.**

If you have questions regarding the completion of this application, you may contact a Trademark Registrar at the below addresses and telephone numbers.

Please Note: The Trademark Registrars act in an administrative capacity only and cannot give legal advice.

North Carolina Department of the Secretary of State
Trademark Section
PO Box 29622
Raleigh, North Carolina 27626-0622

Trademark Phone: 919-807-2162
Trademark Fax: 919-807-2215
E-mail: trademark@sosnc.com

APPLICATION FOR TRADEMARK/SERVICE MARK REGISTRATION & RENEWAL   Page 8
North Carolina Classification of Goods

1. **Raw or partly-prepared materials**: Items such as animal pelts, hides, leather and imitation leather; live animals including insects, live fowl and hatching eggs; ore, clay, gravel, sand and rock; packing material for forming seals or packing padding of plastic or rubber for shipping containers, hair, excelsior, etc.; plastic sheets, synthetic or natural resins; synthetic or natural rubber; seeds; straw or hay, sawdust, shavings, etc.; charcoal and solid fuels including logs; natural and synthetic fibers and textile filaments.

2. **Receptacles**: Items such as baskets, buckets, jugs, boxes, trays, canisters and cans; gas cylinders; and non-glass jars.

3. **Baggage, animal equipment, portfolios and pocketbooks**: Items such as duffel bags and knitting bags; harnesses, saddles, leashes, collars and animal blankets; horseshoes; luggage of all kinds including briefcases and trunks; wallets, purses and handbags.

4. **Abrasives and polishing materials**: Items such as abrasive cleaners, sandpaper, belts; floor and furniture oils, floor waxes; metal polishes, natural and artificial abrasives, polishing and buffing compounds, polishing and cleaning preparation combined, polishing waxes, powders, shoe polish, and steel wool.

5. **Adhesives**: Items such as adhesive sides; asphalt tile cement; any combination of adhesive with a backing or reinforcement tape or strip of paper, cloth; gasket cement; glues and mucilages; pastes and rubber cement.

6. **Chemicals and chemical compositions**: Items such as air fresheners and air deodorants; carbons (absorbing); electrocardiograph electrodes (chemical conductors for use with); brake fluid; rust inhibitors (automobile cooling system); sizing compounds; emulsifiers for us in the manufacture of goods and in the manufacture of leather and textiles; photographic chemicals; dyes for use in the manufacture of leather, fur, wood, pigment (color); preservatives for flowers or masonry; chemical additives; oxidants; preparations and chemically treated papers; agricultural pesticides; catalysts; antifreeze; fire extinguishers using chemical compounds.

7. **Cordage**: Items such as clothesline cord; rope (macramé); wire; cargo strings of metal); string; twine; baling twine; wire rope and wire rope slings.

8. **Smoker's articles**: Items such as ash trays of all forms; cigarette cases, cigar cutters; pouches; cigarette papers; lighters, flints; pipes, pipe cleaners and cigarette holders.

9. **Explosives, firearms, equipment and projectiles**: Items such as blasting caps; compounds; explosives; gelatin; paper and powder; detonators; bombs; explosive caps; fog signals; fuses used in mining; powders, primers, shells, torpedoes; fireworks; and dynamite.

10. **Fertilizers**: Items such as compost, manure; lime (agricultural); plant food and plant growth regulators, fertilizers for agricultural or domestic use; soil conditioners; potting soil.

11. **Inks and inking materials**: Items such as carbon paper; ribbons for typewriter, printers, computers, inking, label printing, and office machines; ink of all forms; inking pads; and stamp pads.

12. **Construction materials**: Items such as cement mixes; posts, cement roofing; ceramic enamel fiber insulation; concrete, concrete beams; building materials; patching compound; plaster; doors; non-metal guard rails; forms for use in casting; windows, window casements; frames, shutters; sills and frames; glass windows; insulating material; glazes; jalousies; caulking and caulking compounds; lumber; plywood; fiberboard; bricks; stones and paving stones; panels; prefabricated homes and houses; roofing materials; flashing; gutters; louvers.

13. **Hardware, plumbing and steam-fitting supplies**: Items such as cabinet hardware and store fixture parts; key rings and metal plugs; nails, screws, nuts and bolts; pipe, conduit, hose and pipe couplings, pipe and hose fittings; valves; sinks, lavatories, tubs, toilets and parts; wire, barbed wire; fencing panels; stays; posts.

14. **Metal, metal casings and forgings**: Items such as aluminum, brass, bronze, copper and nickel products in strip, sheet, wire, rods for brazing and welding; die steel; metal tubing; rails and railroad ties (metal); sheet steel; casting alloys; metal castings.

15. **Oils and greases**: Items such as gasoline, kerosene and penetrating oils; lubricants and greases; naphtha and fuel oils.

16. **Protective and decorative coatings**: Items such as paint, paint thinners, paint primer; sealer coatings; paint sealers; leather and wood stains; shellac as a surface coating; varnish; undercoatings.

17. **Tobacco products**: Items such as tobacco in general as well as chewing, smokeless and flavorings for; snuffs; cigarettes, cigars and cigarillos.

18. **Medicines and pharmaceutical preparations**: Items such as antiseptics, antibiotic creams, tablets and ointments; fungicides for agricultural and domestic use; hormones; vitamin and mineral supplements; food, herbal, nutritional and dietary supplements; medicated lotions; medicated skin-care preparations; analgesic or medicated lip balm; acne treatment or medications; pharmaceutical preparations.

19. **Vehicles**: Items such as airplanes, boats, automobiles. trucks, buses, bicycles, motorcycles and parts therefore; baby carriages; personal watercraft; strollers; parachutes; hang gliders; railroad cars; trailers; dollies; wagons; and mobile homes.

20. **Linoleum and oiled cloth**: Items such as linoleum flooring, vinyl and plastic tiles; vinyl and plastic wall coverings; oilcloths; carpet padding.

21. **Electrical apparatus, machines, supplies and consumer electronic goods**: Items such as electric motors for machines; capacitors; ceramic insulators; insulating tape; cathode ray tubes; batteries and battery chargers; light switches; light bulbs; light dimmers; lighting fixtures; florescence; electric track lighting units; computer cables; computer chips; electrical cables; flashlights; lamps and lamp shades; warning lights; generators; alternators; circuit boards, circuit breakers; telephones and telephone receivers; cellular telephones; television sets and antennas; radios; electric stoves; blenders; vacuum cleaners; microscopes; video tapes; video recorders; voltage surge protectors and suppressors; switches and switch plates; facsimile machines; receivers; satellites; laser scanners and lasers not used for medial use; UPC scanners and other bar-code scanners .

22. **Games, toys and sporting goods**: Items such as amusement park equipment, coin-operated machines and games of skill; bowling equipment, billiard and pool tables; children's toy furniture; dolls, balls, rubber and plastic toys, skates, skis, skate boards, snow boards and surf boards; fishing tackle and artificial bait; exercise equipment; mechanical toys; playing cards, games and parts; puzzles; tents; inflatable swimming pools.

23. **Cutlery, machinery tools and parts**: Items such as centrifuges and centrifugal pumps; grinders, grinding wheels and grindstones; lathes; mills and milling machines; earth moving machines, namely graders, loaders, sarifiers and scrapers; electric pencil sharpeners; fire extinguishers; garbage disposals; garden hoses; gardening tools, namely trowels, weeding forks, spades, and hoes; lawn mowers; blowers for lawn debris; tractors; milking machines; die-cutting or stamping machines; diesel engines for machines; cookie paper or pizza cutters; staples and staple removers; pumps; pocket knives; shears and shearing machines; shredders; pulleys; chucks for power drills; sewing machines; power tools; spreaders; sprayers; dishwashers.

24. **Laundry appliances and machines**: Items such as ironing boards; electric, flat or steam irons; washing machines for clothes; washing boards; clothes pins.

25. **Locks and safes**: Items such as lockboxes; metal locks and keys therefore; ash or money boxes; safes; door chains; padlocks; key chains; key blanks; key and key cylinders (door hardware, namely).

26. **Measuring and scientific equipment**: Items such as video monitors; video camcorders; camera cases, film, tripods, filters and photographic cameras; radar and radar detectors; sonars; calipers; measuring cups and spoons; adding machines and cash registers; gas and water meters; microfiche; metal detectors; microscopes; microwave ovens for laboratory use; computer discs or diskettes; computer hardware including mouse, keyboard, modem, interface boards; film projectors and projection screens; laboratory glassware; scales; levels; gasoline pumps; recorders; optical cables; mirrors; filters and scanners; eyeglass lenses and frames; safety markers, harnesses and goggles; safety cones.

27. **Horological instruments**: Items such as watches and watch fobs, chains, movements, stop watches and parts therefore; clocks, clock radios, alarm clocks and parts therefore; sundials, chronometers and chronographs.

28. **Jewelry and precious metalware**: Items such as jewelry, costume jewelry and jewelry boxes; lapel pins, brooches; cuff links; ID bracelets; trophies of precious metal; sterling silver tableware; and other items fashioned from precious metals.

29. **Brooms, brushes and dusters**: Items such as brushes; brooms; mops; window and furniture dusters; paint roller covers; paint trays; paint stirrers and applicators; polishing cloths and gloves; toothbrushes.

30. **Crockery, earthenware and porcelain**: Items such as china ornaments; pottery, vases; porcelain eggs.

31. **Filters and refrigerators**: Items such as ice chip machines; freezers and walk-in freezers, refrigerators and refrigerator cabinets; water filters; water coolers.

32. **Furniture and upholstery**: Items such as bedroom furniture; box springs and mattresses; children's furniture; cushions, sofas and hassocks; file cabinets, storage files and racks for storage; living room furniture; mirrors and easels; office furniture; outdoor furniture; reclining chairs and sofa beds; tables, desks and office chairs.

33. **Glassware**: Items such as cut, blown and cast glass; crystal prisms; plate glass for cars or vehicle windows; glass granules; glass rods, panes or panels; glass bowls; bulbs and beverageware.

34. **Heating, lighting and ventilation apparatus**: Items such as air conditioning equipment; kilns; fireplace equipment; heat transfer apparatus; heat treating equipment; heaters and heat pumps; clothes dryers; light sticks; non-electric lights; radiation-type furnaces and room heaters; steam appliances; wood-burning stoves; oil lanterns; radiators (electric and steam); steam generators; stoves; solar collectors and solar heating panels.

35. **Belting, hoses, machinery packing and non-metallic tires**: Items such as clutch and brake facings; conveyer and transmission belting; rubber hoses, packings, gaskets and washers; tires, tire patches and inner tubes; rubber bands; joint, graphite, plastic and asbestos packing for pipes, gaskets, plumps, valves, shipping containers and for forming seals; rubber and fiber washers.

36. **Musical instruments and supplies**: Items such as harmonicas; percussion, wind and stringed instruments; phonographs, records and record players; pianos and organs; synthesizers; audio cassettes; digital audio tapes and tape players; compact discs; dictation machines.

37. **Paper and stationery**: Items such as binders and ledger books; mimeograph and copier paper; continuous-feed and laser printer computer papers; unprinted labels; paper wrappers, paper towels and scratch pads; pens, crayons, pencils, erasers, chalk and magic markers; wallpaper, cleaning and toilet tissue paper; waxed paper, printing paper and sketch paper.

38. **Prints and publications**: Items such as dictionaries, booklets; exposed photo prints and transparencies; greeting cards; decals; pamphlets, books and manuals; art and graphic reproductions; news columns and cartoons, newspaper supplements; newsletters; printed labels; reports and advertising material; publications fixed in electronic media; software; wall calendars; medical ID cards.

39. **Clothing**: Items such as blouses, skirts and sweaters; dresses, suits, skirts, coats, topcoats, overcoats and vests; earmuffs; fur coats, capes, stoles and hats; hosiery; insulated garments, gloves, aprons and jackets; raincoats, swimwear and diapers; shoes, slippers, suspenders, garters and belts; sleepwear, lingerie, underwear, etc.

40. **Fancy goods, furnishings and notions**: Items such as braids, shoe laces; buttons, buckles and snap fasteners; elastic tape; hair pins and clips; hand-sewing needles, pins, crochet and knitting needles; sewing kits; shoe horns; clothing hooks as well as hooks and eyes.

41. **Canes, parasols and umbrellas**: Items such as umbrellas and parts therefore; canes and cane handles; walking sticks.

42. **Knitted, netted and textile fabrics and substitutes**: Items such as bedsheets, blankets, comforters and pillow cases; fabrics such as cottons, polyester, nylon, gauze, woolens, rayon, acetate; curtains; rugs and carpets; upholstery fabrics, draperies and slip covers.

43. **Threads and yarns**: Items such as threads of all kinds, including silk, cotton and synthetic sewing threads; yarns of all kinds.

44. **Dental, medical and surgical appliances**: Items such as dentures; bridges and crowns; dental instruments; pacifiers; diagnostic apparatus; medical x-ray equipment; eye droppers and eye patches; hospital beds and invalid lifts; prosthetic and orthopedic devices; orthodontic appliances; respirators and resuscitators; stretchers and crutches; surgical instruments and devices; computer-aided tomography (CAT) scanners, magnetic resonance imaging (MRI) scanners; lasers used for medical purposes.

45. **Soft drinks and carbonated waters**: Items such as non-alcoholic carbonated beverages; spring waters; soda water; soft drinks; lemonades and lemonade syrup; and other fruit-based or artificially-flavored beverages.

46. **Foods and food ingredients**: Items such as animal feeds; breads, cookies, pies, rolls, cakes and other baked goods; cake, bread, biscuit and roll mixes; four and corn meal; candies, fruits, confections and chewing gum; canned fruits, vegetables, sauces, meats and meat substitutes; cereals and hominy grits; cider and grape juice; coffee, tea and dried milk; dehydrated soups, sauces, puddings and gelatin; fish, shrimp and lobster; food colors and preservatives; frozen fruits, juices, meats, vegetables, etc.; honey, syrup, jams and jellies; peanut butter; pet foods; salad dressings, spices, seasonings and yeast shortenings and vegetable oils; seafood.

47. **Wines**: Items such as wines used for cooking and aperitif, wine cocktails, wine coolers and wine in general. Other items are hard cider, sherry, vermouth, champagne and port wines.

48. **Malt beverages and liquors**: Items such as ale and porter; beer; stout; and malt liquors.

49. **Distilled alcoholic liquors**: Items such as cordials and rum; alcoholic cocktails; gin, vodka; brandy and brandy spirits; whiskey; specialty liqueurs.

50. **Merchandise not otherwise classified**: Items such as artificial plants, Christmas trees and ornaments; sculptures; tarpaulins; dressmaker dummies; hangers; shoe trees and mannequins; miscellaneous kits; plaques; pennants and flags.

51. **Cosmetics and toiletries**: Items such as bath salts, oils, etc.; tooth pastes, powders and creams; mouthwashes; personal deodorants; hair spray and preparations, tints, dressings, creams and lotions; lipstick, eye makeup; perfumes, colognes and toilet waters; shave creams and depilatories; skin creams, lotions, face and body powders.

52. **Detergents and soaps**: Items such as cleaner preparations; cleaning concentrates; floor cleaners; soaps and shampoos; detergent solvents; skin soaps.

APPLICATION FOR TRADEMARK/SERVICE MARK REGISTRATION & RENEWAL   Page 10

North Carolina Classification of Services

100. Miscellaneous
A. Hotels and motels
B. Convenience stores
C. Child care services
D. Dental services
E. Employment services, data processing and printing
F. Flowers, balloons, gifts, telegrams, musical dancers, etc.
G. Government services; promotions of cities and towns
H. Health care services and facilities; Emergency Medical Technician certification
I. Interior design and decorating
J. Cosmetology, hair, nails, etc.
K. Charitable organizations
L. Landscaping
M. Miscellaneous services not otherwise classified
N. Night clubs and entertainment services
O. Consulting services and hypnosis clinics
P. Photographic and camera services; art sales
Q. Framing services
R. Restaurants
S. Spa, tanning and diet services
T. Real estate, building, surveying, etc.
U. Union labels; membership services
V. Veterinary services; animal-related services and boarding
W. Recreation
X. Janitorial
Y. Religious; funeral, burial and cremation

101. Advertising and business services:
A. Computer sales, service, supplies and consulting
B. Convenience stores, grocery stores, gourmet food stores, etc.
D. Clothing sales and dry cleaning
E. Employment services, data processing and printing
F. Flowers, balloons, gifts, telegrams, musical dancers and crafts
G. Auto sales and repairs, rentals, supplies and oil jobbers
H. Health care, drug stores and medical supplies
I. Interior design, carpet sales and installation, furniture, etc.
J. Cosmetology, makeup, nails, hair, etc.
L. Landscaping, plant sales, etc.
M. Miscellaneous services not otherwise classified
N. Advertising agencies, promotion agencies, sign rentals
P. Photo, camera and art sales
Q. Jewelry sales
R. Video rentals and sales; book, music and electronic consumer goods sales
S. Spa, tanning, diet services and modeling
T. Real estate, building, surveying, mobile home sales
U. Membership service for clubs and associations; funeral, burial and cremation services
V. Veterinary, animal-related and pet board services
W. Recreational equipment sales, sporting goods and recreational vehicle sales.
X. Janitorial, chimney sweeps
Z. Credit card discount buying services; insurance and financial services

102. Financial and insurance:
Services such as banking and credit agencies; pawn brokers and bonding agents; security and commodity brokerage; insurance sales agents; insurance underwriting.

103. Construction and repair:
Services such as highway construction and repair; building construction; construction machinery, tools and materials sales and rental; custom tailoring and fabric reweaving; dry cleaning and laundry; electrical services; construction inspection; interior decoration; maintenance of tools and equipment; auto sales and maintenance; auto service stations; painting, including automotive painting; pest control in buildings; jewelry and watch repairs; chimney sweeps; drain and sewer cleaning services; window washing; janitorial building care; servicing and refueling of building and heating equipment.

104. Communications:
Services such as cable television and broadcasting; radio broadcasting; cellular telephone and paging services; telephone, telegraph, teleprinter and leased-line communications services; World Wide Web information and Web site maintenance services; commercial e-mail services.

105. Transportation and storage:
Services such as messenger services; packing and storing goods; air, rail, road or water transport of goods; trailer, auto and truck rentals; taxicab service for disabled persons; bus, rail, air or water transport of passengers; oil, gas and petrochemical transport and storage; travel agencies and travel guide services.

106. Material treatment:
Services such as dyeing; lens grinding; metal machining and casting; metal plating and soldering; photofinishing; textile fabric finishing; weed control by chemical treatment.

107. Education and entertainment:
Services such as historic material collection; genealogical research; study and correspondence courses; music, dance, martial arts, sports and theatrical instruction; equitation and riding instruction; museum displays, lectures and demonstrations; drill team organizations; play, concert, operatic and other live performances and production; radio and television programs; book and videotape rentals; Internet access and content provision; amusement center rides; athletic, academic and band booster organizations.

STATE OF SOUTH CAROLINA

APPLICATION FOR REGISTRATION
OF A TRADEMARK OR SERVICE MARK

Original: $15 per mark, per class
Renewal: $5
Assignment: $3

Check one:
[ ] Trademark or [ ] Service Mark

1. Name of Applicant: _____

2. Applicant's principal place of business address: _____

_____

3. Applicant's place of business address in South Carolina, if any:_____

_____

4. Applicant is:

[ ] an individual or sole proprietor

[ ] a corporation duly organized under the laws of the State of _____

[ ] a partnership duly organized under the laws of the State of _____

Names of General Partners:_____

[ ] a Limited Liability Company duly organized under the laws of the State of _____

[ ] other _____

5. Describe the mark, including any literal and/or design elements if claimed:_____

_____

_____

6. The actual goods or services in connection with which the mark is used (i.e., shoe laces, cat food, heating repair services, baby-sitting services, etc.):_____

_____

7. The mode or manner in which the mark is used (i.e., labels, advertisements, brochures, etc.): _____

_____

_____

8. The class(es) in which the goods or services fall (see attached):_____

_____

9. The mark, with respect to the goods or services identified above, was first used by applicant or predecessor in interest as follows (include month, day, and year):

Date of first use anywhere:_____Date of first use in South Carolina: _____

10. Has the applicant, or any predecessor in interest, ever filed an application to register the mark or portions of the mark or a composite of the mark with the United States Patent and Trademark Office?

[ ] YES   [ ] NO

If you answered "YES", please provide the full particulars including the filing date, serial number and status of each application. If an application was finally refused registration or has otherwise not resulted in registration, please state the reason for this:

_____

_____

11. Please enclose three (3) original, identical specimens showing the mark as actually used.

DECLARATION OF OWNERSHIP

Applicant herewith declares that he/she has read the above and foregoing application and knows the contents thereof and that the facts set out herein are true and correct, that the three specimens of the mark submitted are true and correct, that the applicant is the owner of the mark, and that the mark is in use. Additionally, to knowledge of the person verifying this application, no other person has registered this mark either federally or in this State, or has the right to use this mark in its identical form or in near resemblance as to be likely, when applied to the goods or services of another person, to cause confusion or to cause mistake or to deceive.

Sworn to and subscribed before me

this _____ day of _____, _____.

_____
Signature

_____
Notary Public of South Carolina

My Commission Expires: _____

_____
Name

_____
Title

_____
Telephone Number

_____
Date

<u>NOTE</u>

THE ACCEPTANCE OF A TRADEMARK OR SERVICE MARK FOR REGISTRATION BY THE OFFICE OF THE SECRETARY OF STATE PROVIDES THE OWNER WITH A RIGHT TO USE SUCH MARK IN THE STATE OF SOUTH CAROLINA ON THE GOODS AND SERVICES IDENTIFIED IN THE REGISTRATION APPLICATION. HOWEVER, THE OFFICE OF THE SECRETARY OF STATE DOES NOT SEARCH OTHER STATE OR FEDERAL REGISTRATIONS, INTERNET DOMAIN NAMES OR OTHER COMMON LAW (UNREGISTERED) USERS, THEREFORE, RIGHTS GRANTED BY THIS REGISTRATION MAY BE AFFECTED OR PREEMPTED BY PRIOR USE OR OTHER REGISTRATION OF THE MARK.

MAIL TO:
Secretary of State
P.O. Box 11350
Columbia, SC 29211

NOTES

The term "mark" includes a trademark or service mark entitled to registration. The term "trademark" means any word, name, symbol, or device or any combination of these used by a person to identify and distinguish goods of that person, including a unique product, from those manufactured and sold by others and to indicate the source of the goods, even if that source is unknown. The term "service mark" means a word, name, symbol, or device or any combination of these used by a person to identify and distinguish the services of one person, including a unique service, from the services of others and to indicate the source of the services, even if the source is unknown. Titles, character names used by a person, and other distinctive features of radio or television programs, motion picture(s), newspapers, or magazines may be registered as service marks notwithstanding that they or the programs, may advertise the goods of the sponsor.

CLASSES OF GOODS AND SERVICES

Section 39-15-1150 of the 1976 South Carolina Code of Laws: The general classification of goods and services provided for in subsections (B) and (C) are established for convenience of administration of this article but does not limit or extend the applicant's or registrant's rights, and a single application for registration of a mark may include goods upon which or services with which the mark is actually being used indicating the appropriate class or classes of goods or services. When a single application includes goods or services which fall within multiple classes, the secretary may require payment of a fee for each class. To the extent practical, the classification of goods and services shall conform to the classification adopted by the United State Patent and Trademark Office.

(B) The following is the international schedule of classes of goods:

(1) chemical products used in industry, science, photography, agriculture, horticulture, forestry; artificial and synthetic resins; plastics in the form of powders, liquids, or pastes for industrial use; manure (natural and artificial); fire extinguishing composition; tempering substances for preserving foodstuffs, tanning substances, adhesive substances used in industry;

(2) paints, varnishes, lacquers; preservatives against rust and against deterioration of wood, coloring matters, dyestuffs, mordant, natural resins; metals in foil powder form for painters and decorators;

(3) bleaching preparations and other substances for laundry use, cleaning, polishing, scouring and abrasive preparations, soaps, perfumery, essential oils, cosmetics, hair lotions; dentifrice;

(4) industrial oils and greases (other than oils and fats and essential oils); lubricants; dust laying and absorbing compositions; fuels (including motor spirit) and illuminants; candles, tapers, night lights, and wicks;

(5) pharmaceutical, veterinary, and sanitary substances; infants' and invalids' foods; plasters, material for bandaging; material for stopping teeth, dental wax, disinfectants; preparations for killing weeds and destroying vermin;

(6) unwrought and partly wrought common metals and their alloys, anchors, anvils, bells, rolled and cast building materials, rails and other metallic materials for railway tracks, chains (except driving chains for vehicles), cables and wires (nonelectric), locksmiths' work; metallic pipes and tubes; safes and cash boxes, steel balls; horseshoes; nails and screws; other goods in nonprecious metal not included in other classes; ores;

(7) machines and machine tools; motors (except for land vehicles); machine couplings and belting (except for land vehicles); large size agricultural implements, incubators;

(8) hand tools and instruments; cutlery, forks, and spoons, side arms;

(9) scientific, nautical, surveying and electrical apparatus and instruments (including wireless), photographic, cinematographic, optical, weighing, measuring, signaling, checking (supervision), life-saving and teaching apparatus and instruments; coin or counterfreed apparatus; talking machines; cash registers; calculating machines; fire extinguishing apparatus;

(10) surgical, medical, dental, and veterinary instruments and apparatus (including artificial limbs, eyes and teeth);

(11) installations for lighting, heating, steam generating, cooking, refrigerating, drying, ventilating, water supply, and sanitary purposes;

(12) vehicles; apparatus for locomotion by land, air, or water;

(13) firearms; ammunition and projectiles; explosive substances; fireworks;

(14) precious metals and their alloys and goods in precious metals or coated therewith (except cutlery, forks, and spoons); jewelry, precious stones, horological and other chronometric instruments;

(15) musical instruments (other than talking machines and wireless apparatus);

(16) paper and paper articles, cardboard and cardboard articles; printed matter, newspaper and periodicals, books; bookbinding material; photographs; stationery, adhesive materials (stationery); artists' materials; paint brushes; typewriters and office requisites (other than furniture); instructional and teaching material (other than apparatus); playing cards; printers' type and cliches (stereotype);

(17) gutta percha, india rubber, balata and substitutes, articles made from these substances and not included in other classes; plastics in the form of sheets, blocks and rods, being for use in manufacture, materials for packing, stopping or insulating; asbestos, mica and their products; hose pipes (nonmetallic);

(18) leather and imitations of leather, and articles made from these materials and not included in other classes; skins, hides; trunks and traveling bags; umbrellas, parasols and walking sticks; whips, harness and saddlery;

(19) building materials, natural and artificial stone, cement, lime mortar, plaster and gravel; pipes of earthenware or cement; roadmaking materials; asphalt, pitch and bitumen, portable buildings; stone monuments; chimney pots;

(20) furniture, mirrors, picture frames; articles (not included in other classes) of wood, cork, reeds, cane, wicker, horn, bone, ivory, whalebone, shell, amber, mother-or-pearl, meerschaum, celluloid, substitutes for all these materials, or of plastics;

(21) small domestic utensils and containers (not of precious metals, or coated therewith); combs and sponges, brushes (other than paint brushes); brushmaking materials, instruments and material for cleaning purposes, steel wool; unworked or semi-worked glass (excluding glass used in building); glassware, porcelain and earthenware, not included in other classes;

(22) ropes, string, nets, tents, awnings, tarpaulins sails, sacks, padding and stuffing materials (hair, kapok, feathers, seaweed, etc.); raw fibrous textile materials;

(23) yarns, threads;

(24) tissues (piece goods); bed and table covers; textile articles not included in other classes;

(25) clothing (including boots, shoes, and slippers);

(26) lace and embroidery, ribands, and braid; buttons, press buttons, hooks, dyes, pins and needles; artificial flowers;

(27) carpets, rugs, mats, and matting; linoleum and other materials for covering existing floors; wall hangings (nontextile);

(28) games and playthings; gymnastic and sporting articles (except clothing); ornaments and decorations for Christmas tree:

(29) meats, fish, poultry, and games; meat extracts; preserved, dried, and cooked fruits and vegetables; jellies, jams; eggs, milk, and other diary products; edible oils and fats; preserves, pickles;

(30) coffee, tea, cocoa, sugar, rice, tapioca, sago, coffee substitutes; flour and preparaton made from cereal; bread, biscuits, cakes, pastry, and confectionery, ices; honey, treacle; yeast, baking powder; salt, mustard, pepper, vinegar, sauces, spices; ice;

(31) agricultural, horticultural, and forestry products and grains not included in other classes; living animals; fresh fruits and vegetables; seeds; live plants and flowers; foodstuffs for animals, malt;

(32) beer, ale, and porter; mineral and aerated waters and other nonalcoholic drinks; syrups and other preparations for making beverages;

(33) wines, spirits, and liqueurs;

(34) tobacco, raw, or manufactures; smokers' articles; matches.

(C) The following is the international schedule of classes of services:

   (1) advertising and business;
   (2) insurance and financial;
   (3) construction and repair;
   (4) communication;

(5) transportation and storage;
(6) material treatment;
(7) education and entertainment;
(8) miscellaneous.

Form Revised by South Carolina
Secretary of State, January 2000

This page intentionally left blank

State of North Carolina
Department of the Secretary of State

ARTICLES OF INCORPORATION

Pursuant to §55-2-02 of the General Statutes of North Carolina, the undersigned does hereby submit these Articles of Incorporation for the purpose of forming a business corporation.

1. The name of the corporation is: _____

2. The number of shares the corporation is authorized to issue is: _____

3. These shares shall be: *(check either a or b)*

   a. ☐ all of one class, designated as common stock; or

   b. ☐ divided into classes or series within a class as provided in the attached schedule, with the information required by N.C.G.S. Section 55-6-01.

4. The street address and county of the initial registered office of the corporation is:

   Number and Street _____

   City _____ State _____ Zip Code _____ County _____

5. The mailing address, *if different from the street address,* of the initial registered office is:

   Number and Street _____

   City _____ State _____ Zip Code _____ County _____

6. The name of the initial registered agent is: _____

7. Principal office information: (*must select either a or b.*)

   a.   ☐ The corporation has a principal office.

   The street address and county of the principal office of the corporation is:

   Number and Street _____

   City _____ State _____ Zip Code _____ County _____

   The mailing address, *if different from the street address*, of the principal office of the corporation is:

   Number and Street _____

   City _____ State _____ Zip Code _____ County _____

   b.   ☐ The corporation does not have a principal office.

8. Any other provisions, which the corporation elects to include, are attached.

9. The name and address of each incorporator is as follows:

_____

_____

_____

_____

_____

10. These articles will be effective upon filing, unless a date and/or time is specified:

_____

_____

_____

This the _____ day of _____, 200_____

_____

_____
Signature

_____
Type or Print Name and Title

NOTES:
1. **Filing fee is $125. This document must be filed with the Secretary of State.**
    Instructions for Filing

ARTICLES OF INCORPORATION
(Form B-01)

Item 1   Enter the complete corporate name which must include a corporate ending required by N.C.G.S. §55D-20-01(a) (corporation, company, limited, incorporated, corp., co., ltd., or inc.).

Item 2   Enter the number of shares the corporation will have the authority to issue.

           Check (a) or (b), whichever is applicable. If (b) is checked, add an attachment that includes the description of the designations, preferences, limitations, and relative rights of the shares.

Item 3   Enter the complete street address of the registered office and the county in which it is located.

Item 4   Enter the complete mailing address of the registered agent only if mail is not delivered to the street address stated in Item 3 or if you prefer to receive mail at a P. O. Box or Drawer.

Item 5   Enter the name of the registered agent. The registered agent must be either an individual who resides in North Carolina; a domestic business corporation, nonprofit corporation, or limited liability company whose business office is identical with the registered office; or a foreign corporation, nonprofit corporation or limited liability company authorized to transact business in North Carolina whose business office is identical with the registered office.

Item 6   Select item "a" if the corporation has a principal office. Enter the complete street address of the principal office and the county in which it is located. If mail is not delivered to the street address of the principal office or if you prefer to receive mail at a P.O. Box or Drawer, enter the complete mailing address of the principal office.

           Select item "b" if the corporation does not have a principal office.

Item 7   See form.

Item 8   Enter the name and address of each incorporator. Only one incorporator is required in order to file.

Item 9   The document will be effective on the date and at the time of filing, unless a delayed date or an effective time (on the day of filing) is specified. If a delayed effective date is specified without a time, the document will be effective at 11:59:59 p.m. on the day specified. If a delayed effective date is specified with a time, the document will be effective on the day and time so specified. A delayed effective date may be specified up to and including the 90th day after the day of filing.

Date and Execution
Enter the date the document was executed.
In the blanks provided enter:
- The name of the entity executing the Articles of Incorporation; if an individual, leave blank.
- The signature of the incorporator or representative of the incorporating entity.
- The name of the incorporator or name and title of the above signed representative

ATTENTION: Corporations wishing to render a professional service as defined in N.C.G.S. §55b-2(6) shall contact the appropriate North Carolina licensing board to determine whether compliance with additional licensing requirements may be mandated by law.

This page intentionally left blank

STATE OF SOUTH CAROLINA
SECRETARY OF STATE

ARTICLES OF INCORPORATION

<u>TYPE OR PRINT CLEARLY IN BLACK INK</u>

1.   The name of the proposed corporation is _____

2.   The initial registered office of the corporation is _____
                                                            Street Address

_____
City   County   State   Zip Code

and the initial registered agent at such address is _____
                                                        Print Name

        I hereby consent to the appointment as registered agent of the corporation:

                            _____
                                        Agent's Signature

3.   The corporation is authorized to issue shares of stock as follows. Complete "a" or "b", whichever
      is applicable:

      a.   [ ]   The corporation is authorized to issue a single class of shares, the total number
                   of shares authorized is _____.

      b.   [ ]   The corporation is authorized to issue more that one class of shares:

                   Class of Shares   Authorized No. of Each Class

                   _____   _____

                   _____   _____

                   _____   _____

      The relative right, preference, and limitations of the shares of each class, and of each series
      within a class, are as follows:

4.   The existence of the corporation shall begin as of the filing date with the Secretary of State unless
      a delayed date is indicated (See Section 33-1-230(b) of the 1976 South Carolina Code of Laws,
      as amended) _____

Name of Corporation

5. The optional provisions, which the corporation elects to include in the articles of incorporation, are as follows (See the applicable provisions of Sections 33-2-102, 35-2-105, and 35-2-221 of the 1976 South Carolina Code of Laws, as amended).

6. The name, address, and signature of each incorporator is as follows (only one is required):

    a. _____
        Name

        _____
        Address

        _____
        Signature

    b. _____
        Name

        _____
        Address

        _____
        Signature

    c. _____
        Name

        _____
        Address

        _____
        Signature

7. I, _____, an attorney licensed to practice in the state of South Carolina, certify that the corporation, to whose articles of incorporation this certificate is attached, has complied with the requirements of Chapter 2, Title 33 of the 1976 South Carolina Code of Laws, as amended, relating to the articles of incorporation.

Date _____

_____
Signature

_____
Type or Print Name

_____
Address

_____

_____
Telephone Number

_____
Name of Corporation

FILING INSTRUCTIONS

1.   Two copies of this form, the original and either a duplicate original or a conformed copy, must be filed.

2.   If the space in this form is insufficient, please attach additional sheets containing a reference to the appropriate paragraph in this form.

3.   Enclose the fee of $135.00 payable to the Secretary of State.

4.   THIS FORM MUST BE ACCOMPANIED BY THE FIRST REPORT TO CORPORATIONS (SEE SECTION 12-19-20 OF THE 1976 SOUTH CAROLINA CODE OF LAWS, AS AMENDED).

      Return to: Secretary of State
                       PO Box 11350
                       Columbia, SC 29211

SPECIAL NOTE

THE FILING OF THIS DOCUMENT DOES NOT, IN AND OF ITSELF, PROVIDE AN EXCLUSIVE RIGHT TO USE THIS CORPORATE NAME ON OR IN CONNECTION WITH ANY PRODUCT OR SERVICE. USE OF A NAME AS A TRADEMARK OR SERVICE MARK WILL REQUIRE FURTHER CLEARANCE AND REGISTRATION AND BE AFFECTED BY PRIOR USE OF THE MARK. FOR MORE INFORMATION, CONTACT THE TRADEMARKS DIVISION OF THE SECRETARY OF STATE'S OFFICE AT (803) 734-1728.

This page intentionally left blank

State of North Carolina
Department of the Secretary of State

Limited Liability Company
ARTICLES OF ORGANIZATION

Pursuant to §57C-2-20 of the General Statutes of North Carolina, the undersigned does hereby submit these Articles of Organization for the purpose of forming a limited liability company.

1.   The name of the limited liability company is: _____

2.   If the limited liability company is to dissolve by a specific date, the latest date on which the limited liability company is to dissolve: (*If no date for dissolution is specified, there shall be no limit on the duration of the limited liability company.*)_____

3.   The name and address of each person executing these articles of organization is as follows: (*State whether each person is executing these articles of organization in the capacity of a member, organizer or both*).

      _____

      _____

      _____

      _____

4.   The street address and county of the initial registered office of the limited liability company is:

      Number and Street _____

      City, State, Zip Code _____County _____

5.   The mailing address, *if different from the street address,* of the initial registered office is:

      _____

6.   The name of the initial registered agent is: _____

7.   Principal office information: (*Select either a or b.*)

      a. ☐ The limited liability company has a principal office.

      The street address and county of the principal office of the limited liability company is:

      Number and Street_____
      City, State, Zip Code_____County_____

      The mailing address, *if different from the street address*, of the principal office of the corporation is:

      _____

      b. ☐ The limited liability company does not have a principal office.

8.   Check one of the following:

_____(i) **Member-managed LLC**: all members by virtue of their status as members shall be managers of this limited liability company.

_____(ii) **Manager-managed LLC**: except as provided by N.C.G.S. Section 57C-3-20(a), the members of this limited liability company shall not be managers by virtue of their status as members.

9.   Any other provisions which the limited liability company elects to include are attached.

10.   These articles will be effective upon filing, unless a date and/or time is specified:

_____

This is the____ day of _____, 20_____.

_____

_____
Signature

_____
Type or Print Name and Title

NOTES:

1.   **Filing fee is $125. This document must be filed with the Secretary of State.**

Instructions for Filing
LIMITED LIABILITY COMPANY
ARTICLES OF ORGANIZATION
(Form L-01)

Item 1   Enter the complete company name, which must include a limited liability company ending required by N.C.G.S. § 55D-20 (limited liability company, L.L.C., ltd. liability co., limited liability co., or ltd. liability company).

Item 2   Enter the latest date on which the limited liability company may dissolve. If no date for dissolution is specified, there shall be no limit on the duration of the limited liability company. (See N.C.G.S §57C-2-30)

Item 3   Enter the name and address of each person who executes the articles of organization and whether they are executing them in the capacity of a member or of an organizer or both. Unless the articles of organization provide otherwise, each person executing the articles of organization in the capacity of a member of the limited liability company becomes a member at the time that the filing by the Secretary of State of the articles of organization of the limited liability company becomes effective. (See N.C.G.S. § 57C-3-01)

Item 4   Enter the complete street address of the registered office and the county in which it is located.

Item 5   Enter the complete mailing address of the registered office only if mail is not delivered to the street address shown in Item 4 or if the registered agent prefers to have mail delivered to a P.O. Box or Drawer.

Item 6   Enter the name of the registered agent. The registered agent must be either an individual who resides in North Carolina; a domestic business corporation, nonprofit corporation, or limited liability company whose business office is identical with the registered office; or a foreign corporation, nonprofit corporation or limited liability company authorized to transact business or conduct affairs in North Carolina whose business office is identical with the registered office.

Item 7   Select item "a" if the limited liability company has a principal office. Enter the complete street address of the principal office and the county in which it is located. If mail is not delivered to the street address of the principal office or if you prefer to receive mail at a P.O. Box or Drawer, enter the complete mailing address of the principal office.
Select item "b" if the limited liability company does not have a principal office.

Item 8   Unless the articles of organization provide otherwise, all members shall be managers of the LLC, together with any other persons designated as managers in, or in accordance with, the articles of organization or the LLC's written operating agreement. If the articles of organization provide that all members are not necessarily managers by virtue of their status as members, then those persons designated as managers in, or in accordance with, the articles of organization or a operating agreement shall manage the LLC, except for such period during which no designation has been made or is in effect, in which case all members shall be managers.

Item 9   N.C.G.S. §57C-2-21(b) states that the articles of organization may contain any provision not inconsistent with law, including any matter that under Chapter 57C is permitted to be set forth in a limited liability company's operating agreement. The name and address of each of the initial members of the limited liability company may be stated as an attachment. Unless the articles of organization provide otherwise, each person who is named in the articles of organization as a member of the limited liability company becomes a member at the time that the filing by the Secretary of State of the articles of organization of the limited liability company becomes effective. (See N.C.G.S. § 57C-3-01)

Item 10   The document will be effective on the date and at the time of filing, unless a delayed date or an effective time (on the day of filing) is specified. If a delayed effective date is specified without a time, the document will be effective at 11:59:59 p.m. Raleigh, North Carolina time on the day specified. If a delayed effective date is specified, the document will be effective on the day and at the time specified. A delayed effective date may be specified up to and including the 90th day after the day of filing.

Date and Execution

Enter the date the document was executed.
In the blanks provided enter:

- The name of the entity executing the Articles of Organization; if an individual, leave blank.
- The signature of the member and/or organizer or representative of the organizing entity.
- The name of the member and/or organizer or name of the above-signed representative.
- The title of the individual or entity executing the Articles of Organization (i.e. Organizer, Member or both)
- The document may, but need not, contain an acknowledgment, verification, or proof.

ATTENTION: Limited liability companies wishing to render a professional service as defined in N.C.G.S. §55B-2(6) shall contact the appropriate North Carolina licensing board to determine whether compliance with additional licensing requirements may be mandated by law. Such limited liability companies should consult N.C.G.S. §57C-2-01 for further details.

This page intentionally left blank

STATE OF SOUTH CAROLINA
SECRETARY OF STATE

ARTICLES OF ORGANIZATION
LIMITED LIABILITY COMPANY

<u>TYPE OR PRINT CLEARLY IN BLACK INK</u>

The undersigned delivers the following articles of organization to form a South Carolina limited liability company pursuant to Sections 33-44-202 and 33-44-203 of the 1976 South Carolina Code of Laws, as amended.

1.   The name of the limited liability company which complies with Section 33-44-105 of the South Carolina Code of 1976, as amended is _____

2.   The address of the initial designated office of the Limited Liability Company in South Carolina is

_____
Street Address

_____
City   Zip Code

3.   The initial agent for service of process of the Limited Liability Company is

_____   _____
Name   Signature

and the street address in South Carolina for this initial agent for service of process is

_____
Street Address

_____
City   Zip Code

4.   The name and address of each organizer is

(a)   _____
        Name

       _____   _____
        Street Address   City

       _____   _____
        State   Zip Code

(b)   _____
        Name

       _____   _____
        Street Address   City

       _____   _____
        State   Zip Code

       (Add additional lines if necessary)

5.   [ ]   Check this box only if the company is to be a term company. If so, provide the term specified:

_____

6.   [ ]   Check this box only if management of the limited liability company is vested in a manager or managers. If this company is to be managed by managers, specify the name and address of each initial manager:

(a)   _____
    Name

    _____
    Street Address   City

    _____
    State   Zip Code

(b)   _____
    Name

    _____
    Street Address   City

    _____
    State   Zip Code

(c)   _____
    Name

    _____
    Street Address   City

    _____
    State   Zip Code

(d)   _____
    Name

    _____
    Street Address   City

    _____
    State   Zip Code

(Add additional lines if necessary)

7.   [ ]   Check this box only if one or more of the members of the company are to be liable for its debts and obligations under section 33-44-303(c). If one or more members are so liable, specify which members, and for which debts, obligations or liabilities such members are liable in their capacity as members.

_____

_____

_____

Name of Limited Liability Company

8.   Unless a delayed effective date is specified, these articles will be effective when endorsed for filing by the Secretary of State. Specify any delayed effective date and time:

_____

9.   Set forth any other provisions not inconsistent with law which the organizers determine to include, including any provisions that are required or are permitted to be set forth in the limited liability company operating agreement.

10.   Signature of each organizer

_____

_____   Date _____
(Add Additional lines if necessary)

FILING INSTRUCTIONS

1.   File two copies of this form, the original and either a duplicate original or a conformed copy.

2.   If space on this form is not sufficient, please attach additional sheets containing a reference to the appropriate paragraph in this form, or prepare this using a computer disk which will allow for expansion of the space on the form.

3.   This form must be accompanied by the filing fee of $110.00 payable to the Secretary of State.

      Return to: Secretary of State
                  P.O. Box 11350
                  Columbia, SC 29211

4.   The first annual report for a Limited Liability Company must be delivered to the Secretary of State between January first and April first of the calendar year after which the Limited Liability Company was organized or the foreign company was first authorized to transact business in South Carolina. Subsequent annual reports must be delivered to the Secretary of State on or before the fifteenth day of the fourth month following the close of the limited liability company's taxable year.

NOTE

THE FILING OF THIS DOCUMENT DOES NOT, IN AND OF ITSELF, PROVIDE AN EXCLUSIVE RIGHT TO USE THIS CORPORATE NAME ON OR IN CONNECTION WITH ANY PRODUCT OR SERVICE. USE OF A NAME AS A TRADEMARK OR SERVICE MARK WILL REQUIRE FURTHER CLEARANCE AND REGISTRATION AND BE AFFECTED BY PRIOR USE OF THE MARK. FOR MORE INFORMATION, CONTACT THE TRADEMARKS DIVISION OF THE SECRETARY OF STATE'S OFFICE AT (803) 734-1728.

Form Revised by South Carolina
Secretary of State, January 2000

This page intentionally left blank

Form SS-4

(Rev. February 2006)

Department of the Treasury
Internal Revenue Service

Application for Employer Identification Number

(For use by employers, corporations, partnerships, trusts, estates, churches, government agencies, Indian tribal entities, certain individuals, and others.)

▶ See separate instructions for each line.   ▶ Keep a copy for your records.

OMB No. 1545-0003

EIN

Type or print clearly.

1 Legal name of entity (or individual) for whom the EIN is being requested

2 Trade name of business (if different from name on line 1)

3 Executor, administrator, trustee, "care of" name

4a Mailing address (room, apt., suite no. and street, or P.O. box)

5a Street address (if different) (Do not enter a P.O. box.)

4b City, state, and ZIP code

5b City, state, and ZIP code

6 County and state where principal business is located

7a Name of principal officer, general partner, grantor, owner, or trustor

7b SSN, ITIN, or EIN

8a **Type of entity** (check only one box)

☐ Sole proprietor (SSN) _____
☐ Partnership
☐ Corporation (enter form number to be filed) ▶ _____
☐ Personal service corporation
☐ Church or church-controlled organization
☐ Other nonprofit organization (specify) ▶ _____
☐ Other (specify) ▶

☐ Estate (SSN of decedent) _____
☐ Plan administrator (SSN) _____
☐ Trust (SSN of grantor) _____
☐ National Guard   ☐ State/local government
☐ Farmers' cooperative   ☐ Federal government/military
☐ REMIC   ☐ Indian tribal governments/enterprises
Group Exemption Number (GEN) ▶ _____

8b If a corporation, name the state or foreign country (if applicable) where incorporated

State

Foreign country

9 **Reason for applying** (check only one box)

☐ Started new business (specify type) ▶_____
_____
☐ Hired employees (Check the box and see line 12.)
☐ Compliance with IRS withholding regulations
☐ Other (specify) ▶

☐ Banking purpose (specify purpose) ▶ _____
☐ Changed type of organization (specify new type) ▶ _____
☐ Purchased going business
☐ Created a trust (specify type) ▶ _____
☐ Created a pension plan (specify type) ▶ _____

10 Date business started or acquired (month, day, year). See instructions.

11 Closing month of accounting year

12 First date wages or annuities were paid (month, day, year). **Note.** If applicant is a withholding agent, enter date income will first be paid to nonresident alien. (month, day, year) . . . . ▶

13 Highest number of employees expected in the next 12 months (enter -0- if none).

Do you expect to have $1,000 or less in employment tax liability for the calendar year? ☐ **Yes** ☐ **No.** (If you expect to pay $4,000 or less in wages, you can mark yes.)

Agricultural	Household	Other

14 Check **one** box that best describes the principal activity of your business.
☐ Construction ☐ Rental & leasing ☐ Transportation & warehousing ☐ Health care & social assistance ☐ Wholesale–agent/broker
☐ Real estate ☐ Manufacturing ☐ Finance & insurance ☐ Accommodation & food service ☐ Wholesale–other ☐ Retail
☐ Other (specify)

15 Indicate principal line of merchandise sold, specific construction work done, products produced, or services provided.

16a Has the applicant ever applied for an employer identification number for this or any other business? . . . . ☐ **Yes** ☐ **No**
Note. If "Yes," please complete lines 16b and 16c.

16b If you checked "Yes" on line 16a, give applicant's legal name and trade name shown on prior application if different from line 1 or 2 above.
Legal name ▶   Trade name ▶

16c Approximate date when, and city and state where, the application was filed. Enter previous employer identification number if known.

Approximate date when filed (mo., day, year) | City and state where filed | Previous EIN

Third Party Designee

Complete this section **only** if you want to authorize the named individual to receive the entity's EIN and answer questions about the completion of this form.

Designee's name

Designee's telephone number (include area code)
( )

Address and ZIP code

Designee's fax number (include area code)
( )

Under penalties of perjury, I declare that I have examined this application. and to the best of my knowledge and belief, it is true, correct, and complete.

Applicant's telephone number (include area code)
( )

Name and title (type or print clearly) ▶

Applicant's fax number (include area code)
( )

Signature ▶   Date ▶

For Privacy Act and Paperwork Reduction Act Notice, see separate instructions.   Cat. No. 16055N   Form **SS-4** (Rev. 2-2006)

212

Do I Need an EIN?

File Form SS-4 if the applicant entity does not already have an EIN but is required to show an EIN on any return, statement, or other document.[1] See also the separate instructions for each line on Form SS-4.

IF the applicant...	AND...	THEN...
Started a new business	Does not currently have (nor expect to have) employees	Complete lines 1, 2, 4a–8a, 8b (if applicable), and 9–16c.
Hired (or will hire) employees, including household employees	Does not already have an EIN	Complete lines 1, 2, 4a–6, 7a–b (if applicable), 8a, 8b (if applicable), and 9–16c.
Opened a bank account	Needs an EIN for banking purposes only	Complete lines 1–5b, 7a–b (if applicable), 8a, 9, and 16a–c.
Changed type of organization	Either the legal character of the organization or its ownership changed (for example, you incorporate a sole proprietorship or form a partnership)[2]	Complete lines 1–16c (as applicable).
Purchased a going business[3]	Does not already have an EIN	Complete lines 1–16c (as applicable).
Created a trust	The trust is other than a grantor trust or an IRA trust[4]	Complete lines 1–16c (as applicable).
Created a pension plan as a plan administrator[5]	Needs an EIN for reporting purposes	Complete lines 1, 3, 4a–b, 8a, 9, and 16a–c.
Is a foreign person needing an EIN to comply with IRS withholding regulations	Needs an EIN to complete a Form W-8 (other than Form W-8ECI), avoid withholding on portfolio assets, or claim tax treaty benefits[6]	Complete lines 1–5b, 7a–b (SSN or ITIN optional), 8a–9, and 16a–c.
Is administering an estate	Needs an EIN to report estate income on Form 1041	Complete lines 1, 2, 3, 4a–6, 8a, 9-11, 12-15 (if applicable), and 16a–c.
Is a withholding agent for taxes on non-wage income paid to an alien (i.e., individual, corporation, or partnership, etc.)	Is an agent, broker, fiduciary, manager, tenant, or spouse who is required to file Form 1042, Annual Withholding Tax Return for U.S. Source Income of Foreign Persons	Complete lines 1, 2, 3 (if applicable), 4a–5b, 7a–b (if applicable), 8a, 9, and 16a–c.
Is a state or local agency	Serves as a tax reporting agent for public assistance recipients under Rev. Proc. 80-4, 1980-1 C.B. 581[7]	Complete lines 1, 2, 4a–5b, 8a, 9, and 16a–c.
Is a single-member LLC	Needs an EIN to file Form 8832, Entity Classification Election, for filing employment tax returns, **or** for state reporting purposes[8]	Complete lines 1–16c (as applicable).
Is an S corporation	Needs an EIN to file Form 2553, Election by a Small Business Corporation[9]	Complete lines 1–16c (as applicable).

[1] For example, a sole proprietorship or self-employed farmer who establishes a qualified retirement plan, or is required to file excise, employment, alcohol, tobacco, or firearms returns, must have an EIN. A partnership, corporation, REMIC (real estate mortgage investment conduit), nonprofit organization (church, club, etc.), or farmers' cooperative must use an EIN for any tax-related purpose even if the entity does not have employees.

[2] However, do not apply for a new EIN if the existing entity only (a) changed its business name, (b) elected on Form 8832 to change the way it is taxed (or is covered by the default rules), or (c) terminated its partnership status because at least 50% of the total interests in partnership capital and profits were sold or exchanged within a 12-month period. The EIN of the terminated partnership should continue to be used. See Regulations section 301.6109-1(d)(2)(iii).

[3] Do not use the EIN of the prior business unless you became the "owner" of a corporation by acquiring its stock.

[4] However, grantor trusts that do not file using Optional Method 1 and IRA trusts that are required to file Form 990-T, Exempt Organization Business Income Tax Return, must have an EIN. For more information on grantor trusts, see the Instructions for Form 1041.

[5] A plan administrator is the person or group of persons specified as the administrator by the instrument under which the plan is operated.

[6] Entities applying to be a Qualified Intermediary (QI) need a QI-EIN even if they already have an EIN. See Rev. Proc. 2000-12.

[7] See also Household employer on page 3. **Note.** State or local agencies may need an EIN for other reasons, for example, hired employees.

[8] Most LLCs do not need to file Form 8832. See Limited liability company (LLC) on page 4 for details on completing Form SS-4 for an LLC.

[9] An existing corporation that is electing or revoking S corporation status should use its previously-assigned EIN.

Instructions for Form SS-4

Department of the Treasury
Internal Revenue Service

(Rev. February 2006)

Application for Employer Identification Number

Section references are to the Internal Revenue Code unless otherwise noted.

General Instructions

Use these instructions to complete Form SS-4, Application for Employer Identification Number. Also see *Do I Need an EIN?* on page 2 of Form SS-4.

Purpose of Form

Use Form SS-4 to apply for an employer identification number (EIN). An EIN is a nine-digit number (for example, 12-3456789) assigned to sole proprietors, corporations, partnerships, estates, trusts, and other entities for tax filing and reporting purposes. The information you provide on this form will establish your business tax account.

 An EIN is for use in connection with your business activities only. Do not use your EIN in place of your social security number (SSN).

Reminders

Apply online. Generally, you can apply for and receive an EIN online using the Internet. See *How To Apply* below.

File only one Form SS-4. Generally, a sole proprietor should file only one Form SS-4 and needs only one EIN, regardless of the number of businesses operated as a sole proprietorship or trade names under which a business operates. However, if the proprietorship incorporates or enters into a partnership, a new EIN is required. Also, each corporation in an affiliated group must have its own EIN.

EIN applied for, but not received. If you do not have an EIN by the time a return is due, write "Applied For" and the date you applied in the space shown for the number. Do not show your SSN as an EIN on returns.

If you do not have an EIN by the time a tax deposit is due, send your payment to the Internal Revenue Service Center for your filing area as shown in the instructions for the form that you are filing. Make your check or money order payable to the "United States Treasury" and show your name (as shown on Form SS-4), address, type of tax, period covered, and date you applied for an EIN.

Federal tax deposits. New employers that have a federal tax obligation will be pre-enrolled in the Electronic Federal Tax Payment System (EFTPS). EFTPS allows you to make all of your federal tax payments online at *www.eftps.gov* or by telephone. Shortly after we have assigned you your EIN, you will receive instructions by mail for activating your EFTPS enrollment. You will also receive an EFTPS Personal Identification Number (PIN) that you will use to make your payments, as well as instructions for obtaining an Internet password you will need to make payments online.

If you are not required to make deposits by EFTPS, you can use Form 8109, Federal Tax Deposit (FTD) Coupon, to make deposits at an authorized depositary. If you would like to receive Form 8109, call 1-800-829-4933. Allow 5 to 6 weeks for delivery. For more information on federal tax deposits, see Pub. 15 (Circular E).

How To Apply

You can apply for an EIN online, by telephone, by fax, or by mail depending on how soon you need to use the EIN. Use only one method for each entity so you do not receive more than one EIN for an entity.

Online. Generally, you can receive your EIN by Internet and use it immediately to file a return or make a payment. Go to the IRS website at *www.irs.gov/businesses* and click on Employer ID Numbers.

Applicants that may not apply online. The online application process is not yet available to:
• Applicants with foreign addresses (including Puerto Rico),
• Limited Liability Companies (LLCs) that have not yet determined their entity classification for federal tax purposes (see *Limited liability company (LLC)* on page 4),
• Real Estate Investment Conduits (REMICs),
• State and local governments,
• Federal Government/Military, and
• Indian Tribal Governments/Enterprises.

Telephone. You can receive your EIN by telephone and use it immediately to file a return or make a payment. Call the IRS at 1-800-829-4933. (International applicants must call 215-516-6999.) The hours of operation are 7:00 a.m. to 10:00 p.m. local time (Pacific time for Alaska and Hawaii). The person making the call must be authorized to sign the form or be an authorized designee. See *Signature* and *Third Party Designee* on page 6. Also see the *TIP* below.

If you are applying by telephone, it will be helpful to complete Form SS-4 before contacting the IRS. An IRS representative will use the information from the Form SS-4 to establish your account and assign you an EIN. Write the number you are given on the upper right corner of the form and sign and date it. Keep this copy for your records.

If requested by an IRS representative, mail or fax (facsimile) the signed Form SS-4 (including any Third Party Designee authorization) within 24 hours to the IRS address provided by the IRS representative.

 *Taxpayer representatives can apply for an EIN on behalf of their client and request that the EIN be faxed to their client on the same day. **Note.** By using this procedure, you are authorizing the IRS to fax the EIN without a cover sheet.*

Fax. Under the Fax-TIN program, you can receive your EIN by fax within 4 business days. Complete and fax Form SS-4 to the IRS using the Fax-TIN number listed on page 2 for your state. A long-distance charge to callers outside of the local calling area will apply. Fax-TIN

Cat. No. 62736F

numbers can only be used to apply for an EIN. The numbers may change without notice. Fax-TIN is available 24 hours a day, 7 days a week.

Be sure to provide your fax number so the IRS can fax the EIN back to you.

Note. By using this procedure, you are authorizing the IRS to fax the EIN without a cover sheet.

Mail. Complete Form SS-4 at least 4 to 5 weeks before you will need an EIN. Sign and date the application and mail it to the service center address for your state. You will receive your EIN in the mail in approximately 4 weeks. See also *Third Party Designee* on page 6.

Call 1-800-829-4933 to verify a number or to ask about the status of an application by mail.

Where to Fax or File

If your principal business, office or agency, or legal residence in the case of an individual, is located in:	Fax or file with the "Internal Revenue Service Center" at:
Connecticut, Delaware, District of Columbia, Florida, Georgia, Maine, Maryland, Massachusetts, New Hampshire, New Jersey, New York, North Carolina, Ohio, Pennsylvania, Rhode Island, South Carolina, Vermont, Virginia, West Virginia	Attn: EIN Operation Holtsville, NY 11742 Fax-TIN: 631-447-8960
Illinois, Indiana, Kentucky, Michigan	Attn: EIN Operation Cincinnati, OH 45999 Fax-TIN: 859-669-5760
Alabama, Alaska, Arizona, Arkansas, California, Colorado, Hawaii, Idaho, Iowa, Kansas, Louisiana, Minnesota, Mississippi, Missouri, Montana, Nebraska, Nevada, New Mexico, North Dakota, Oklahoma, Oregon, South Dakota, Tennessee, Texas, Utah, Washington, Wisconsin, Wyoming	Attn: EIN Operation Philadelphia, PA 19255 Fax-TIN: 859-669-5760
If you have no legal residence, principal place of business, or principal office or agency in any state:	Attn: EIN Operation Philadelphia, PA 19255 Fax-TIN: 215-516-1040

How To Get Forms and Publications

Phone. Call 1-800-TAX-FORM (1-800-829-3676) to order forms, instructions, and publications. You should receive your order or notification of its status within 10 workdays.

Internet. You can access the IRS website 24 hours a day, 7 days a week at *www.irs.gov* to download forms, instructions, and publications.

CD-ROM. For small businesses, return preparers, or others who may frequently need tax forms or publications, a CD-ROM containing over 2,000 tax products (including many prior year forms) can be purchased from the National Technical Information Service (NTIS).

To order Pub. 1796, IRS Tax Products CD, call 1-877-CDFORMS (1-877-233-6767) toll free or connect to *www.irs.gov/cdorders.*

Tax Help for Your Business

IRS-sponsored Small Business Workshops provide information about your federal and state tax obligations. For information about workshops in your area, call 1-800-829-4933.

Related Forms and Publications

The following forms and instructions may be useful to filers of Form SS-4.
- Form 990-T, Exempt Organization Business Income Tax Return.
- Instructions for Form 990-T.
- Schedule C (Form 1040), Profit or Loss From Business.
- Schedule F (Form 1040), Profit or Loss From Farming.
- Instructions for Form 1041 and Schedules A, B, D, G, I, J, and K-1, U.S. Income Tax Return for Estates and Trusts.
- Form 1042, Annual Withholding Tax Return for U.S. Source Income of Foreign Persons.
- Instructions for Form 1065, U.S. Return of Partnership Income.
- Instructions for Form 1066, U.S. Real Estate Mortgage Investment Conduit (REMIC) Income Tax Return.
- Instructions for Forms 1120 and 1120-A.
- Form 2553, Election by a Small Business Corporation.
- Form 2848, Power of Attorney and Declaration of Representative.
- Form 8821, Tax Information Authorization.
- Form 8832, Entity Classification Election.

For more information about filing Form SS-4 and related issues, see:
- Pub. 51 (Circular A), Agricultural Employer's Tax Guide;
- Pub. 15 (Circular E), Employer's Tax Guide;
- Pub. 538, Accounting Periods and Methods;
- Pub. 542, Corporations;
- Pub. 557, Tax-Exempt Status for Your Organization;
- Pub. 583, Starting a Business and Keeping Records;
- Pub. 966, The Secure Way to Pay Your Federal Taxes for Business and Individual Taxpayers;
- Pub. 1635, Understanding Your EIN;
- Package 1023, Application for Recognition of Exemption Under Section 501(c)(3) of the Internal Revenue Code; and
- Package 1024, Application for Recognition of Exemption Under Section 501(a).

Specific Instructions

Print or type all entries on Form SS-4. Follow the instructions for each line to expedite processing and to avoid unnecessary IRS requests for additional information. Enter "N/A" (nonapplicable) on the lines that do not apply.

Line 1 — Legal name of entity (or individual) for whom the EIN is being requested. Enter the legal name of the entity (or individual) applying for the EIN exactly as it appears on the social security card, charter, or other applicable legal document. An entry is required.

Individuals. Enter your first name, middle initial, and last name. If you are a sole proprietor, enter your individual name, not your business name. Enter your business name on line 2. Do not use abbreviations or nicknames on line 1.

Trusts. Enter the name of the trust.

Estate of a decedent. Enter the name of the estate. For an estate that has no legal name, enter the name of the decedent followed by "Estate."

Partnerships. Enter the legal name of the partnership as it appears in the partnership agreement.

Corporations. Enter the corporate name as it appears in the corporate charter or other legal document creating it.

Plan administrators. Enter the name of the plan administrator. A plan administrator who already has an EIN should use that number.

Line 2 — Trade name of business. Enter the trade name of the business if different from the legal name. The trade name is the "doing business as " (DBA) name.

 Use the full legal name shown on line 1 on all tax returns filed for the entity. (However, if you enter a trade name on line 2 and choose to use the trade name instead of the legal name, enter the trade name on all returns you file.) To prevent processing delays and errors, always use the legal name only (or the trade name only) on all tax returns.

Line 3 — Executor, administrator, trustee, "care of" name. Trusts enter the name of the trustee. Estates enter the name of the executor, administrator, or other fiduciary. If the entity applying has a designated person to receive tax information, enter that person's name as the "care of" person. Enter the individual's first name, middle initial, and last name.

Lines 4a-b — Mailing address. Enter the mailing address for the entity's correspondence. If line 3 is completed, enter the address for the executor, trustee or "care of" person. Generally, this address will be used on all tax returns.

 File Form 8822, Change of Address, to report any subsequent changes to the entity's mailing address.

Lines 5a-b — Street address. Provide the entity's physical address only if different from its mailing address shown in lines 4a-b. Do not enter a P.O. box number here.

Line 6 — County and state where principal business is located. Enter the entity's primary physical location.

Lines 7a-b — Name of principal officer, general partner, grantor, owner, or trustor. Enter the first name, middle initial, last name, and SSN of (a) the principal officer if the business is a corporation, (b) a general partner if a partnership, (c) the owner of an entity that is disregarded as separate from its owner (disregarded entities owned by a corporation enter the corporation's name and EIN), or (d) a grantor, owner, or trustor if a trust.

If the person in question is an alien individual with a previously assigned individual taxpayer identification number (ITIN), enter the ITIN in the space provided and submit a copy of an official identifying document. If necessary, complete Form W-7, Application for IRS Individual Taxpayer Identification Number, to obtain an ITIN.

You must enter an SSN, ITIN, or EIN unless the only reason you are applying for an EIN is to make an entity classification election (see Regulations sections 301.7701-1 through 301.7701-3) and you are a nonresident alien or other foreign entity with no effectively connected income from sources within the United States.

Line 8a — Type of entity. Check the box that best describes the type of entity applying for the EIN. If you are an alien individual with an ITIN previously assigned to you, enter the ITIN in place of a requested SSN.

 This is not an election for a tax classification of an entity. See Limited liability company (LLC) on page 4.

Other. If not specifically listed, check the "Other" box, enter the type of entity and the type of return, if any, that will be filed (for example, "Common Trust Fund, Form 1065" or "Created a Pension Plan"). Do not enter "N/A." If you are an alien individual applying for an EIN, see the *Lines 7a-b* instructions above.

● **Household employer.** If you are an individual, check the "Other" box and enter "Household Employer" and your SSN. If you are a state or local agency serving as a tax reporting agent for public assistance recipients who become household employers, check the "Other" box and enter "Household Employer Agent." If you are a trust that qualifies as a household employer, you do not need a separate EIN for reporting tax information relating to household employees; use the EIN of the trust.

● **QSub.** For a qualified subchapter S subsidiary (QSub) check the "Other" box and specify "QSub."

● **Withholding agent.** If you are a withholding agent required to file Form 1042, check the "Other" box and enter "Withholding Agent."

Sole proprietor. Check this box if you file Schedule C, C-EZ, or F (Form 1040) and have a qualified plan, or are required to file excise, employment, alcohol, tobacco, or firearms returns, or are a payer of gambling winnings. Enter your SSN (or ITIN) in the space provided. If you are a nonresident alien with no effectively connected income from sources within the United States, you do not need to enter an SSN or ITIN.

Corporation. This box is for any corporation other than a personal service corporation. If you check this box, enter the income tax form number to be filed by the entity in the space provided.

 If you entered "1120S" after the "Corporation" checkbox, the corporation must file Form 2553 no later than the 15th day of the 3rd month of the tax year the election is to take effect. Until Form 2553 has been received and approved, you will be considered a Form 1120 filer. See the Instructions for Form 2553.

Personal service corporation. Check this box if the entity is a personal service corporation. An entity is a personal service corporation for a tax year only if:

● The principal activity of the entity during the testing period (prior tax year) for the tax year is the performance of personal services substantially by employee-owners, and

● The employee-owners own at least 10% of the fair market value of the outstanding stock in the entity on the last day of the testing period.

Personal services include performance of services in such fields as health, law, accounting, or consulting. For more information about personal service corporations, see the Instructions for Forms 1120 and 1120-A and Pub. 542.

Other nonprofit organization. Check this box if the nonprofit organization is other than a church or church-controlled organization and specify the type of nonprofit organization (for example, an educational organization).

 If the organization also seeks tax-exempt status, you must file either Package 1023 or Package 1024. See Pub. 557 for more information.

If the organization is covered by a group exemption letter, enter the four-digit group exemption number (GEN). (Do not confuse the GEN with the nine-digit EIN.) If you do not know the GEN, contact the parent organization. Get Pub. 557 for more information about group exemption numbers.

If the organization is a section 527 political organization, check the box for *Other nonprofit organization* and specify "section 527 organization" in the space to the right. To be recognized as exempt from tax, a section 527 political organization must electronically file Form 8871, Political Organization Notice of Section 527 Status, within 24 hours of the date on which the organization was established. The organization may also have to file Form 8872, Political Organization Report of Contributions and Expenditures. See *www.irs.gov/polorgs* for more information.

Plan administrator. If the plan administrator is an individual, enter the plan administrator's SSN in the space provided.

REMIC. Check this box if the entity has elected to be treated as a real estate mortgage investment conduit (REMIC). See the Instructions for Form 1066 for more information.

State/local government. If you are a government employer and you are not sure of your social security and Medicare coverage options, go to *www.ncsssa.org/ssaframes.html* to obtain the contact information for your state's Social Security Administrator.

Limited liability company (LLC). An LLC is an entity organized under the laws of a state or foreign country as a limited liability company. For federal tax purposes, an LLC may be treated as a partnership or corporation or be disregarded as an entity separate from its owner.

By default, a domestic LLC with only one member is disregarded as an entity separate from its owner and must include all of its income and expenses on the owner's tax return (for example, Schedule C (Form 1040)). Also by default, a domestic LLC with two or more members is treated as a partnership. A domestic LLC may file Form 8832 to avoid either default classification and elect to be classified as an association taxable as a corporation. For more information on entity classifications (including the rules for foreign entities), see the instructions for Form 8832.

 Do not file Form 8832 if the LLC accepts the default classifications above. If the LLC is eligible to be treated as a corporation that meets certain tests and it will be electing S corporation status, it must timely file Form 2553. The LLC will be treated as a corporation as of the effective date of the S corporation election and does not need to file Form 8832. See the Instructions for Form 2553.

Complete Form SS-4 for LLCs as follows.

• A single-member domestic LLC that accepts the default classification (above) does not need an EIN and generally should not file Form SS-4. Generally, the LLC should use the name and EIN of its owner for all federal tax purposes. However, the reporting and payment of employment taxes for employees of the LLC may be made using the name and EIN of either the owner or the LLC as explained in Notice 99-6. You can find Notice 99-6 on page 12 of Internal Revenue Bulletin 1999-3 at *www.irs.gov/pub/irs-irbs/irb99-03.pdf.* (**Note.** If the LLC applicant indicates in box 13 that it has employees or expects to have employees, the owner (whether an individual or other entity) of a single-member domestic LLC will also be assigned its own EIN (if it does not already have one) even if the LLC will be filing the employment tax returns.)

• A single-member, domestic LLC that accepts the default classification (above) and wants an EIN for filing employment tax returns (see above) or non-federal purposes, such as a state requirement, must check the "Other" box and write "Disregarded Entity" or, when applicable, "Disregarded Entity — Sole Proprietorship" in the space provided.

• A multi-member, domestic LLC that accepts the default classification (above) must check the "Partnership" box.

• A domestic LLC that will be filing Form 8832 to elect corporate status must check the "Corporation" box and write in "Single-Member" or "Multi-Member" immediately below the "form number" entry line.

Line 9 — Reason for applying. Check only one box. Do not enter "N/A."

Started new business. Check this box if you are starting a new business that requires an EIN. If you check this box, enter the type of business being started. Do not apply if you already have an EIN and are only adding another place of business.

Hired employees. Check this box if the existing business is requesting an EIN because it has hired or is hiring employees and is therefore required to file employment tax returns. Do not apply if you already have an EIN and are only hiring employees. For information on employment taxes (for example, for family members), see Pub. 15 (Circular E).

 You may have to make electronic deposits of all depository taxes (such as employment tax, excise tax, and corporate income tax) using the Electronic Federal Tax Payment System (EFTPS). See Federal tax deposits on page 1; section 11, Depositing Taxes, of Pub. 15 (Circular E); and Pub. 966.

Created a pension plan. Check this box if you have created a pension plan and need an EIN for reporting purposes. Also, enter the type of plan in the space provided.

 Check this box if you are applying for a trust EIN when a new pension plan is established. In addition, check the "Other" box in line 8a and write "Created a Pension Plan" in the space provided.

Banking purpose. Check this box if you are requesting an EIN for banking purposes only, and enter the banking purpose (for example, a bowling league for depositing dues or an investment club for dividend and interest reporting).

Changed type of organization. Check this box if the business is changing its type of organization. For example, the business was a sole proprietorship and has been incorporated or has become a partnership. If you check this box, specify in the space provided (including available space immediately below) the type of change made. For example, "From Sole Proprietorship to Partnership."

Purchased going business. Check this box if you purchased an existing business. Do not use the former owner's EIN unless you became the "owner" of a corporation by acquiring its stock.

Created a trust. Check this box if you created a trust, and enter the type of trust created. For example, indicate if the trust is a nonexempt charitable trust or a split-interest trust.

Exception. Do not file this form for certain grantor-type trusts. The trustee does not need an EIN for the trust if the trustee furnishes the name and TIN of the grantor/owner and the address of the trust to all payors. However, grantor trusts that do not file using Optional Method 1 and IRA trusts that are required to file Form 990-T, Exempt Organization Business Income Tax Return, must have an EIN. For more information on grantor trusts, see the Instructions for Form 1041.

 Do not check this box if you are applying for a trust EIN when a new pension plan is established. Check "Created a pension plan."

Other. Check this box if you are requesting an EIN for any other reason; and enter the reason. For example, a newly-formed state government entity should enter "Newly-Formed State Government Entity" in the space provided.

Line 10 — Date business started or acquired. If you are starting a new business, enter the starting date of the business. If the business you acquired is already operating, enter the date you acquired the business. If you are changing the form of ownership of your business, enter the date the new ownership entity began. Trusts should enter the date the trust was funded. Estates should enter the date of death of the decedent whose name appears on line 1 or the date when the estate was legally funded.

Line 11 — Closing month of accounting year. Enter the last month of your accounting year or tax year. An accounting or tax year is usually 12 consecutive months, either a calendar year or a fiscal year (including a period of 52 or 53 weeks). A calendar year is 12 consecutive months ending on December 31. A fiscal year is either 12 consecutive months ending on the last day of any month other than December or a 52-53 week year. For more information on accounting periods, see Pub. 538.

Individuals. Your tax year generally will be a calendar year.

Partnerships. Partnerships must adopt one of the following tax years.
• The tax year of the majority of its partners.
• The tax year common to all of its principal partners.
• The tax year that results in the least aggregate deferral of income.
• In certain cases, some other tax year.

See the Instructions for Form 1065 for more information.

REMICs. REMICs must have a calendar year as their tax year.

Personal service corporations. A personal service corporation generally must adopt a calendar year unless it meets one of the following requirements.
• It can establish a business purpose for having a different tax year.
• It elects under section 444 to have a tax year other than a calendar year.

Trusts. Generally, a trust must adopt a calendar year except for the following trusts.
• Tax-exempt trusts.
• Charitable trusts.
• Grantor-owned trusts.

Line 12 — First date wages or annuities were paid. If the business has employees, enter the date on which the business began to pay wages. If the business does not plan to have employees, enter "N/A."

Withholding agent. Enter the date you began or will begin to pay income (including annuities) to a nonresident alien. This also applies to individuals who are required to file Form 1042 to report alimony paid to a nonresident alien.

Line 13 — Highest number of employees expected in the next 12 months. Complete each box by entering the number (including zero ("-0-")) of "Agricultural," "Household," or "Other" employees expected by the applicant in the next 12 months. Check the appropriate box to indicate if you expect your annual employment tax liability to be $1,000 or less. Generally, if you pay $4,000 or less in wages subject to social security and Medicare taxes and federal income tax withholding, you are likely to pay $1,000 or less in employment taxes.

For more information on employment taxes, see Pub. 15 (Circular E); or Pub. 51 (Circular A) if you have agricultural employees (farmworkers).

Lines 14 and 15. Check the one box in line 14 that best describes the principal activity of the applicant's business. Check the "Other" box (and specify the applicant's principal activity) if none of the listed boxes applies. You must check a box.

Use line 15 to describe the applicant's principal line of business in more detail. For example, if you checked the "Construction" box in line 14, enter additional detail such as "General contractor for residential buildings" in line 15. An entry is required.

Construction. Check this box if the applicant is engaged in erecting buildings or engineering projects, (for example, streets, highways, bridges, tunnels). The term "Construction" also includes special trade contractors, (for example, plumbing, HVAC, electrical, carpentry, concrete, excavation, etc. contractors).

Real estate. Check this box if the applicant is engaged in renting or leasing real estate to others; managing, selling, buying or renting real estate for others; or providing related real estate services (for example, appraisal services).

Rental and leasing. Check this box if the applicant is engaged in providing tangible goods such as autos, computers, consumer goods, or industrial machinery and equipment to customers in return for a periodic rental or lease payment.

Manufacturing. Check this box if the applicant is engaged in the mechanical, physical, or chemical transformation of materials, substances, or components into new products. The assembling of component parts of manufactured products is also considered to be manufacturing.

Transportation & warehousing. Check this box if the applicant provides transportation of passengers or cargo; warehousing or storage of goods; scenic or sight-seeing transportation; or support activities related to transportation.

Finance & insurance. Check this box if the applicant is engaged in transactions involving the creation, liquidation, or change of ownership of financial assets and/or facilitating such financial transactions; underwriting annuities/insurance policies; facilitating such underwriting by selling insurance policies; or by providing other insurance or employee-benefit related services.

Health care and social assistance. Check this box if the applicant is engaged in providing physical, medical, or psychiatric care or providing social assistance activities such as youth centers, adoption agencies, individual/family services, temporary shelters, daycare, etc.

Accommodation & food services. Check this box if the applicant is engaged in providing customers with lodging, meal preparation, snacks, or beverages for immediate consumption.

Wholesale–agent/broker. Check this box if the applicant is engaged in arranging for the purchase or sale of goods owned by others or purchasing goods on a commission basis for goods traded in the wholesale market, usually between businesses.

Wholesale–other. Check this box if the applicant is engaged in selling goods in the wholesale market generally to other businesses for resale on their own account, goods used in production, or capital or durable nonconsumer goods.

Retail. Check this box if the applicant is engaged in selling merchandise to the general public from a fixed store; by direct, mail-order, or electronic sales; or by using vending machines.

Other. Check this box if the applicant is engaged in an activity not described above. Describe the applicant's principal business activity in the space provided.

Lines 16a-c. Check the applicable box in line 16a to indicate whether or not the entity (or individual) applying for an EIN was issued one previously. Complete lines 16b and 16c only if the "Yes" box in line 16a is checked. If the applicant previously applied for more than one EIN, write "See Attached" in the empty space in line 16a and attach a separate sheet providing the line 16b and 16c information for each EIN previously requested.

Third Party Designee. Complete this section only if you want to authorize the named individual to receive the entity's EIN and answer questions about the completion of Form SS-4. The designee's authority terminates at the time the EIN is assigned and released to the designee. You must complete the signature area for the authorization to be valid.

Signature. When required, the application must be signed by (a) the individual, if the applicant is an individual, (b) the president, vice president, or other principal officer, if the applicant is a corporation, (c) a responsible and duly authorized member or officer having

knowledge of its affairs, if the applicant is a partnership, government entity, or other unincorporated organization, or (d) the fiduciary, if the applicant is a trust or an estate. Foreign applicants may have any duly-authorized person, (for example, division manager), sign Form SS-4.

Privacy Act and Paperwork Reduction Act Notice. We ask for the information on this form to carry out the Internal Revenue laws of the United States. We need it to comply with section 6109 and the regulations thereunder, which generally require the inclusion of an employer identification number (EIN) on certain returns, statements, or other documents filed with the Internal Revenue Service. If your entity is required to obtain an EIN, you are required to provide all of the information requested on this form. Information on this form may be used to determine which federal tax returns you are required to file and to provide you with related forms and publications.

We disclose this form to the Social Security Administration (SSA) for their use in determining compliance with applicable laws. We may give this information to the Department of Justice for use in civil and criminal litigation, and to the cities, states, and the District of Columbia for use in administering their tax laws. We may also disclose this information to other countries under a tax treaty, to federal and state agencies to enforce federal nontax criminal laws, and to federal law enforcement and intelligence agencies to combat terrorism.

We will be unable to issue an EIN to you unless you provide all of the requested information that applies to your entity. Providing false information could subject you to penalties.

You are not required to provide the information requested on a form that is subject to the Paperwork Reduction Act unless the form displays a valid OMB control number. Books or records relating to a form or its instructions must be retained as long as their contents may become material in the administration of any Internal Revenue law. Generally, tax returns and return information are confidential, as required by section 6103.

The time needed to complete and file this form will vary depending on individual circumstances. The estimated average time is:

Recordkeeping	8 hrs., 22 min.
Learning about the law or the form	42 min.
Preparing the form	52 min.
Copying, assembling, and sending the form to the IRS	- - - - -

If you have comments concerning the accuracy of these time estimates or suggestions for making this form simpler, we would be happy to hear from you. You can write to Internal Revenue Service, Tax Products Coordinating Committee, SE:W:CAR:MP:T:T:SP, IR-6406, 1111 Constitution Avenue, NW, Washington, DC 20224. Do not send the form to this address. Instead, see *Where to Fax or File* on page 2.

Department of Homeland Security
U.S. Citizenship and Immigration Services

OMB No. 1615-0047; Expires 03/31/07

Employment Eligibility Verification

INSTRUCTIONS
PLEASE READ ALL INSTRUCTIONS CAREFULLY BEFORE COMPLETING THIS FORM.

Anti-Discrimination Notice. It is illegal to discriminate against any individual (other than an alien not authorized to work in the U.S.) in hiring, discharging, or recruiting or referring for a fee because of that individual's national origin or citizenship status. It is illegal to discriminate against work eligible individuals. Employers **CANNOT** specify which document(s) they will accept from an employee. The refusal to hire an individual because of a future expiration date may also constitute illegal discrimination.

Section 1- Employee.
All employees, citizens and noncitizens, hired after November 6, 1986, must complete Section 1 of this form at the time of hire, which is the actual beginning of employment. **The employer is responsible for ensuring that Section 1 is timely and properly completed.**

Preparer/Translator Certification. The Preparer/Translator Certification must be completed if Section 1 is prepared by a person other than the employee. A preparer/translator may be used only when the employee is unable to complete Section 1 on his/her own. However, the employee must still sign Section 1 personally.

Section 2 - Employer.
For the purpose of completing this form, the term "employer" includes those recruiters and referrers for a fee who are agricultural associations, agricultural employers or farm labor contractors.

Employers must complete Section 2 by examining evidence of identity and employment eligibility within three (3) business days of the date employment begins. If employees are authorized to work, but are unable to present the required document(s) within three business days, they must present a receipt for the application of the document(s) within three business days and the actual document(s) within ninety (90) days. However, if employers hire individuals for a duration of less than three business days, Section 2 must be completed at the time employment begins. **Employers must record: 1)** document title; **2)** issuing authority; **3)** document number, **4)** expiration date, if any; and **5)** the date employment begins. Employers must sign and date the certification. Employees must present original documents. Employers may, but are not required to, photocopy the document(s) presented. These photocopies may only be used for the verification process and must be retained with the I-9. **However, employers are still responsible for completing the I-9.**

Section 3 - Updating and Reverification.
Employers must complete Section 3 when updating and/or reverifying the I-9. Employers must reverify employment eligibility of their employees on or before the expiration date recorded in Section 1. Employers **CANNOT** specify which document(s) they will accept from an employee.

- If an employee's name has changed at the time this form is being updated/reverified, complete Block A.

- If an employee is rehired within three (3) years of the date this form was originally completed and the employee is still eligible to be employed on the same basis as previously indicated on this form (updating), complete Block B and the signature block.

- If an employee is rehired within three (3) years of the date this form was originally completed and the employee's work authorization has expired **or** if a current employee's work authorization is about to expire (reverification), complete Block B and:

- examine any document that reflects that the employee is authorized to work in the U.S. (see List A **or** C),

- record the document title, document number and expiration date (if any) in Block C, and

- complete the signature block.

Photocopying and Retaining Form I-9. A blank I-9 may be reproduced, provided both sides are copied. The Instructions must be available to all employees completing this form. Employers must retain completed I-9s for three (3) years after the date of hire or one (1) year after the date employment ends, whichever is later.

For more detailed information, you may refer to the Department of Homeland Security (DHS) Handbook for Employers, (Form M-274). You may obtain the handbook at your local U.S. Citizenship and Immigration Services (USCIS) office.

Privacy Act Notice. The authority for collecting this information is the Immigration Reform and Control Act of 1986, Pub. L. 99-603 (8 USC 1324a).

This information is for employers to verify the eligibility of individuals for employment to preclude the unlawful hiring, or recruiting or referring for a fee, of aliens who are not authorized to work in the United States.

This information will be used by employers as a record of their basis for determining eligibility of an employee to work in the United States. The form will be kept by the employer and made available for inspection by officials of the U.S. Immigration and Customs Enforcement, Department of Labor and Office of Special Counsel for Immigration Related Unfair Employment Practices.

Submission of the information required in this form is voluntary. However, an individual may not begin employment unless this form is completed, since employers are subject to civil or criminal penalties if they do not comply with the Immigration Reform and Control Act of 1986.

Reporting Burden. We try to create forms and instructions that are accurate, can be easily understood and which impose the least possible burden on you to provide us with information. Often this is difficult because some immigration laws are very complex. Accordingly, the reporting burden for this collection of information is computed as follows: **1)** learning about this form, 5 minutes; **2)** completing the form, 5 minutes; and **3)** assembling and filing (recordkeeping) the form, 5 minutes, for an average of 15 minutes per response. If you have comments regarding the accuracy of this burden estimate, or suggestions for making this form simpler, you can write to U.S. Citizenship and Immigration Services, Regulatory Management Division, 111 Massachuetts Avenue, N.W., Washington, DC 20529. OMB No. 1615-0047.

NOTE: This is the 1991 edition of the Form I-9 that has been rebranded with a current printing date to reflect the recent transition from the INS to DHS and its components.

EMPLOYERS MUST RETAIN COMPLETED FORM I-9
PLEASE DO NOT MAIL COMPLETED FORM I-9 TO ICE OR USCIS

Form I-9 (Rev. 05/31/05)Y

Department of Homeland Security
U.S. Citizenship and Immigration Services

OMB No. 1615-0047; Expires 03/31/07

Employment Eligibility Verification

Please read instructions carefully before completing this form. The instructions must be available during completion of this form. ANTI-DISCRIMINATION NOTICE: It is illegal to discriminate against work eligible individuals. Employers CANNOT specify which document(s) they will accept from an employee. The refusal to hire an individual because of a future expiration date may also constitute illegal discrimination.

Section 1. Employee Information and Verification. To be completed and signed by employee at the time employment begins.

Print Name: Last	First	Middle Initial	Maiden Name

Address (Street Name and Number)	Apt. #	Date of Birth (month/day/year)

City	State	Zip Code	Social Security #

I am aware that federal law provides for imprisonment and/or fines for false statements or use of false documents in connection with the completion of this form.

I attest, under penalty of perjury, that I am (check one of the following):

☐ A citizen or national of the United States
☐ A Lawful Permanent Resident (Alien #) A _____
☐ An alien authorized to work until _____
(Alien # or Admission #) _____

Employee's Signature	Date (month/day/year)

Preparer and/or Translator Certification. *(To be completed and signed if Section 1 is prepared by a person other than the employee.) I attest, under penalty of perjury, that I have assisted in the completion of this form and that to the best of my knowledge the information is true and correct.*

Preparer's/Translator's Signature	Print Name

Address (Street Name and Number, City, State, Zip Code)	Date (month/day/year)

Section 2. Employer Review and Verification. To be completed and signed by employer. Examine one document from List A OR examine one document from List B and one from List C, as listed on the reverse of this form, and record the title, number and expiration date, if any, of the document(s).

List A	OR	List B	AND	List C
Document title:				
Issuing authority:				
Document #:				
Expiration Date (if any):				
Document #:				
Expiration Date (if any):				

CERTIFICATION - I attest, under penalty of perjury, that I have examined the document(s) presented by the above-named employee, that the above-listed document(s) appear to be genuine and to relate to the employee named, that the employee began employment on *(month/day/year)* _____ **and that to the best of my knowledge the employee is eligible to work in the United States. (State employment agencies may omit the date the employee began employment.)**

Signature of Employer or Authorized Representative	Print Name	Title

Business or Organization Name	Address (Street Name and Number, City, State, Zip Code)	Date (month/day/year)

Section 3. Updating and Reverification. To be completed and signed by employer.

A. New Name (if applicable)	B. Date of Rehire (month/day/year) (if applicable)

C. If employee's previous grant of work authorization has expired, provide the information below for the document that establishes current employment eligibility.

Document Title: _____   Document #: _____   Expiration Date (if any): _____

I attest, under penalty of perjury, that to the best of my knowledge, this employee is eligible to work in the United States, and if the employee presented document(s), the document(s) I have examined appear to be genuine and to relate to the individual.

Signature of Employer or Authorized Representative	Date (month/day/year)

NOTE: This is the 1991 edition of the Form I-9 that has been rebranded with a current printing date to reflect the recent transition from the INS to DHS and its components.

Form I-9 (Rev. 05/31/05)Y Page 2

LISTS OF ACCEPTABLE DOCUMENTS

LIST A		LIST B		LIST C
Documents that Establish Both Identity and Employment Eligibility	**OR**	**Documents that Establish Identity**	**AND**	**Documents that Establish Employment Eligibility**

LIST A — Documents that Establish Both Identity and Employment Eligibility

1. U.S. Passport (unexpired or expired)

2. Certificate of U.S. Citizenship *(Form N-560 or N-561)*

3. Certificate of Naturalization *(Form N-550 or N-570)*

4. Unexpired foreign passport, with *I-551 stamp or* attached *Form I-94* indicating unexpired employment authorization

5. Permanent Resident Card or Alien Registration Receipt Card with photograph *(Form I-151 or I-551)*

6. Unexpired Temporary Resident Card *(Form I-688)*

7. Unexpired Employment Authorization Card *(Form I-688A)*

8. Unexpired Reentry Permit *(Form I-327)*

9. Unexpired Refugee Travel Document *(Form 1-571)*

10. Unexpired Employment Authorization Document issued by DHS that contains a photograph *(Form I-688B)*

OR

LIST B — Documents that Establish Identity

1. Driver's license or ID card issued by a state or outlying possession of the United States provided it contains a photograph or information such as name, date of birth, gender, height, eye color and address

2. ID card issued by federal, state or local government agencies or entities, provided it contains a photograph or information such as name, date of birth, gender, height, eye color and address

3. School ID card with a photograph

4. Voter's registration card

5. U.S. Military card or draft record

6. Military dependent's ID card

7. U.S. Coast Guard Merchant Mariner Card

8. Native American tribal document

9. Driver's license issued by a Canadian government authority

For persons under age 18 who are unable to present a document listed above:

10. School record or report card

11. Clinic, doctor or hospital record

12. Day-care or nursery school record

AND

LIST C — Documents that Establish Employment Eligibility

1. U.S. social security card issued by the Social Security Administration *(other than a card stating it is not valid for employment)*

2. Certification of Birth Abroad issued by the Department of State *(Form FS-545 or Form DS-1350)*

3. Original or certified copy of a birth certificate issued by a state, county, municipal authority or outlying possession of the United States bearing an official seal

4. Native American tribal document

5. U.S. Citizen ID Card *(Form I-197)*

6. ID Card for use of Resident Citizen in the United States *(Form I-179)*

7. Unexpired employment authorization document issued by DHS *(other than those listed under List A)*

Illustrations of many of these documents appear in Part 8 of the Handbook for Employers (M-274)

This page intentionally left blank

Form **2553**
(Rev. March 2005)

Department of the Treasury
Internal Revenue Service

Election by a Small Business Corporation
(Under section 1362 of the Internal Revenue Code)
▶ See Parts II and III on back and the separate instructions.
▶ The corporation may either send or fax this form to the IRS. See page 2 of the instructions.

OMB No. 1545-0146

Notes: 1. *Do not file **Form 1120S,** U.S. Income Tax Return for an S Corporation, for any tax year before the year the election takes effect.*

2. *This election to be an S corporation can be accepted only if all the tests are met under **Who May Elect** on page 1 of the instructions; all shareholders have signed the consent statement; an officer has signed this form; and the exact name and address of the corporation and other required form information are provided.*

Part I	**Election Information**	

Please Type or Print

Name (see instructions)	**A** Employer identification number
Number, street, and room or suite no. (If a P.O. box, see instructions.)	**B** Date incorporated
City or town, state, and ZIP code	**C** State of incorporation

D Check the applicable box(es) if the corporation, after applying for the EIN shown in **A** above, changed its name ☐ or address ☐

E Election is to be effective for tax year beginning (month, day, year) . . . . ▶ ___ / ___ / ___

F Name and title of officer or legal representative who the IRS may call for more information

G Telephone number of officer or legal representative

(   )

H If this election takes effect for the first tax year the corporation exists, enter month, day, and year of the **earliest** of the following: (1) date the corporation first had shareholders, (2) date the corporation first had assets, or (3) date the corporation began doing business . . . . ▶ ___ / ___ / ___

I Selected tax year: Annual return will be filed for tax year ending (month and day) ▶ --------------------------------

If the tax year ends on any date other than December 31, except for a 52-53-week tax year ending with reference to the month of December, complete Part II on the back. If the date you enter is the ending date of a 52-53-week tax year, write "52-53-week year" to the right of the date.

J Name and address of each shareholder or former shareholder required to consent to the election. (See the instructions for column K)	**K** Shareholders' Consent Statement. Under penalties of perjury, we declare that we consent to the election of the above-named corporation to be an S corporation under section 1362(a) and that we have examined this consent statement, including accompanying schedules and statements, and to the best of our knowledge and belief, it is true, correct, and complete. We understand our consent is binding and may not be withdrawn after the corporation has made a valid election. (Sign and date below.)		**L** Stock owned or percentage of ownership (see instructions)		**M** Social security number or employer identification number (see instructions)	**N** Share-holder's tax year ends (month and day)
	Signature	Date	Number of shares or percentage of ownership	Date(s) acquired		

Under penalties of perjury, I declare that I have examined this election, including accompanying schedules and statements, and to the best of my knowledge and belief, it is true, correct, and complete.

Signature of officer ▶   Title ▶   Date ▶

For Paperwork Reduction Act Notice, see page 4 of the instructions.   Cat. No. 18629R   Form **2553** (Rev. 3-2005)

Part II   Selection of Fiscal Tax Year (All corporations using this part must complete item O and item P, Q, or R.)

O Check the applicable box to indicate whether the corporation is:

1. ☐ A new corporation **adopting** the tax year entered in item I, Part I.

2. ☐ An existing corporation **retaining** the tax year entered in item I, Part I.

3. ☐ An existing corporation **changing** to the tax year entered in item I, Part I.

P Complete item P if the corporation is using the automatic approval provisions of Rev. Proc. 2002-38, 2002-22 I.R.B. 1037, to request **(1)** a natural business year (as defined in section 5.05 of Rev. Proc. 2002-38) or **(2)** a year that satisfies the ownership tax year test (as defined in section 5.06 of Rev. Proc. 2002-38). Check the applicable box below to indicate the representation statement the corporation is making.

1. Natural Business Year ▶ ☐ I represent that the corporation is adopting, retaining, or changing to a tax year that qualifies as its natural business year as defined in section 5.05 of Rev. Proc. 2002-38 and has attached a statement verifying that it satisfies the 25% gross receipts test (see instructions for content of statement). I also represent that the corporation is not precluded by section 4.02 of Rev. Proc. 2002-38 from obtaining automatic approval of such adoption, retention, or change in tax year.

2. Ownership Tax Year ▶ ☐ I represent that shareholders (as described in section 5.06 of Rev. Proc. 2002-38) holding more than half of the shares of the stock (as of the first day of the tax year to which the request relates) of the corporation have the same tax year or are concurrently changing to the tax year that the corporation adopts, retains, or changes to per item I, Part I, and that such tax year satisfies the requirement of section 4.01(3) of Rev. Proc. 2002-38. I also represent that the corporation is not precluded by section 4.02 of Rev. Proc. 2002-38 from obtaining automatic approval of such adoption, retention, or change in tax year.

Note: *If you do not use item P and the corporation wants a fiscal tax year, complete either item Q or R below. Item Q is used to request a fiscal tax year based on a business purpose and to make a back-up section 444 election. Item R is used to make a regular section 444 election.*

Q Business Purpose—To request a fiscal tax year based on a business purpose, check box Q1. See instructions for details including payment of a user fee. You may also check box Q2 and/or box Q3.

1. Check here ▶ ☐ if the fiscal year entered in item I, Part I, is requested under the prior approval provisions of Rev. Proc. 2002-39, 2002-22 I.R.B. 1046. Attach to Form 2553 a statement describing the relevant facts and circumstances and, if applicable, the gross receipts from sales and services necessary to establish a business purpose. See the instructions for details regarding the gross receipts from sales and services. If the IRS proposes to disapprove the requested fiscal year, do you want a conference with the IRS National Office?
☐ Yes   ☐ No

2. Check here ▶ ☐ to show that the corporation intends to make a back-up section 444 election in the event the corporation's business purpose request is not approved by the IRS. (See instructions for more information.)

3. Check here ▶ ☐ to show that the corporation agrees to adopt or change to a tax year ending December 31 if necessary for the IRS to accept this election for S corporation status in the event (1) the corporation's business purpose request is not approved and the corporation makes a back-up section 444 election, but is ultimately not qualified to make a section 444 election, or (2) the corporation's business purpose request is not approved and the corporation did not make a back-up section 444 election.

R Section 444 Election—To make a section 444 election, check box R1. You may also check box R2.

1. Check here ▶ ☐ to show the corporation will make, if qualified, a section 444 election to have the fiscal tax year shown in item I, Part I. To make the election, you must complete **Form 8716,** Election To Have a Tax Year Other Than a Required Tax Year, and either attach it to Form 2553 or file it separately.

2. Check here ▶ ☐ to show that the corporation agrees to adopt or change to a tax year ending December 31 if necessary for the IRS to accept this election for S corporation status in the event the corporation is ultimately not qualified to make a section 444 election.

Part III   Qualified Subchapter S Trust (QSST) Election Under Section 1361(d)(2)*

Income beneficiary's name and address	Social security number
Trust's name and address	Employer identification number

Date on which stock of the corporation was transferred to the trust (month, day, year) . . . . ▶   /   /

In order for the trust named above to be a QSST and thus a qualifying shareholder of the S corporation for which this Form 2553 is filed, I hereby make the election under section 1361(d)(2). Under penalties of perjury, I certify that the trust meets the definitional requirements of section 1361(d)(3) and that all other information provided in Part III is true, correct, and complete.

_____   _____
Signature of income beneficiary or signature and title of legal representative or other qualified person making the election   Date

*Use Part III to make the QSST election only if stock of the corporation has been transferred to the trust on or before the date on which the corporation makes its election to be an S corporation. The QSST election must be made and filed separately if stock of the corporation is transferred to the trust **after** the date on which the corporation makes the S election.

Instructions for Form 2553

Department of the Treasury
Internal Revenue Service

(Rev. March 2005)

Election by a Small Business Corporation

Section references are to the Internal Revenue Code unless otherwise noted.

General Instructions

Purpose

A corporation or other entity eligible to elect to be treated as a corporation must use Form 2553 to make an election under section 1362(a) to be an S corporation. An entity eligible to elect to be treated as a corporation that meets certain tests discussed below will be treated as a corporation as of the effective date of the S corporation election and does not need to file Form 8832, Entity Classification Election.

The income of an S corporation generally is taxed to the shareholders of the corporation rather than to the corporation itself. However, an S corporation may still owe tax on certain income. For details, see *Tax and Payments* in the Instructions for Form 1120S, U.S. Income Tax Return for an S Corporation.

Who May Elect

A corporation or other entity eligible to elect to be treated as a corporation may elect to be an S corporation only if it meets all the following tests.

1. It is (a) a domestic corporation, or (b) a domestic entity eligible to elect to be treated as a corporation that timely files Form 2553 and meets all the other tests listed below. If Form 2553 is not timely filed, see Rev. Proc. 2004-48, 2004-32 I.R.B. 172.

2. It has no more than 100 shareholders. A husband and wife (and their estates) are treated as one shareholder for this test. A member of a family can elect under section 1361(c)(1) to treat all members of the family as one shareholder for this test. All other persons are treated as separate shareholders.

3. Its only shareholders are individuals, estates, exempt organizations described in section 401(a) or 501(c)(3), or certain trusts described in section 1361(c)(2)(A).

For information about the section 1361(d)(2) election to be a qualified subchapter S trust (QSST), see the instructions for Part III. For information about the section 1361(e)(3) election to be an electing small business trust (ESBT), see Regulations section 1.1361-1(m). For guidance on how to convert a QSST to an ESBT, see Regulations section 1.1361-1(j)(12). If these elections were not timely made, see Rev. Proc. 2003-43, 2003-23 I.R.B. 998.

4. It has no nonresident alien shareholders.

5. It has only one class of stock (disregarding differences in voting rights). Generally, a corporation is treated as having only one class of stock if all outstanding shares of the corporation's stock confer identical rights to distribution and liquidation proceeds. See Regulations section 1.1361-1(l) for details.

6. It is not one of the following ineligible corporations.

a. A bank or thrift institution that uses the reserve method of accounting for bad debts under section 585.

b. An insurance company subject to tax under subchapter L of the Code.

c. A corporation that has elected to be treated as a possessions corporation under section 936.

d. A domestic international sales corporation (DISC) or former DISC.

7. It has or will adopt or change to one of the following tax years.

a. A tax year ending December 31.

b. A natural business year.

c. An ownership tax year.

d. A tax year elected under section 444.

e. A 52-53-week tax year ending with reference to a year listed above.

f. Any other tax year (including a 52-53-week tax year) for which the corporation establishes a business purpose.

For details on making a section 444 election or requesting a natural business, ownership, or other business purpose tax year, see Part II of Form 2553.

8. Each shareholder consents as explained in the instructions for column K.

See sections 1361, 1362, and 1378, and their related regulations for additional information on the above tests.

A parent S corporation can elect to treat an eligible wholly-owned subsidiary as a qualified subchapter S subsidiary. If the election is made, the subsidiary's assets, liabilities, and items of income, deduction, and credit are treated as those of the parent. For details, see Form 8869, Qualified Subchapter S Subsidiary Election.

When To Make the Election

Complete and file Form 2553 (a) at any time before the 16th day of the 3rd month of the tax year the election is to take effect, or (b) at any time during the tax year preceding the tax year it is to take effect. An election made no later than 2 months and 15 days after the beginning of a tax year that is less than 2½ months long is treated as timely made for that tax year.

An election made after the 15th day of the 3rd month but before the end of the tax year generally is effective for the next tax year. However, an election made after the 15th day of the 3rd month will be accepted as timely filed if the corporation can show that the failure to file on time was due to reasonable cause.

To request relief for a late election, the corporation generally must request a private letter ruling and pay a user fee in accordance with Rev. Proc. 2005-1, 2005-1 I.R.B. 1 (or its successor). However, the ruling and user fee requirements may not apply if the following revenue procedures apply.

• If an entity eligible to elect to be treated as a corporation (a) failed to timely file Form 2553, and (b) has not elected to be treated as a corporation, see Rev. Proc. 2004-48, 2004-32 I.R.B. 172.

• If a corporation failed to timely file Form 2553, see Rev. Proc. 2003-43, 2003-23 I.R.B. 998.

• If Form 1120S was filed without an S corporation election and neither the corporation nor any shareholder was notified by the IRS of any problem with the S corporation status within 6 months after the return was timely filed, see Rev. Proc. 97-48, 1997-43 I.R.B. 19.

Where To File

Send the original election (no photocopies) or fax it to the Internal Revenue Service Center listed below. If the corporation files this election by fax, keep the original Form 2553 with the corporation's permanent records.

If the corporation's principal business, office, or agency is located in:	Use the following Internal Revenue Service Center address or fax number:
Connecticut, Delaware, District of Columbia, Illinois, Indiana, Kentucky, Maine, Maryland, Massachusetts, Michigan, New Hampshire, New Jersey, New York, North Carolina, Ohio, Pennsylvania, Rhode Island, South Carolina, Vermont, Virginia, West Virginia, Wisconsin	Cincinnati, OH 45999 Fax: (859) 669-5748
Alabama, Alaska, Arizona, Arkansas, California, Colorado, Florida, Georgia, Hawaii, Idaho, Iowa, Kansas, Louisiana, Minnesota, Mississippi, Missouri, Montana, Nebraska, Nevada, New Mexico, North Dakota, Oklahoma, Oregon, South Dakota, Tennessee, Texas, Utah, Washington, Wyoming	Ogden, UT 84201 Fax: (801) 620-7116

Acceptance or Nonacceptance of Election

The service center will notify the corporation if its election is accepted and when it will take effect. The corporation will also be notified if its election is not accepted. The corporation should generally receive a determination on its election within 60 days after it has filed Form 2553. If box Q1 in Part II is checked, the corporation will receive a ruling letter from the IRS in Washington, DC, that either approves or denies the selected tax year. When box Q1 is checked, it will generally take an additional 90 days for the Form 2553 to be accepted.

Care should be exercised to ensure that the IRS receives the election. If the corporation is not notified of acceptance or nonacceptance of its election within 2 months of the date of filing (date faxed or mailed), or within 5 months if box Q1 is checked, take follow-up action by calling 1-800-829-4933.

If the IRS questions whether Form 2553 was filed, an acceptable proof of filing is (a) a certified or registered mail receipt (timely postmarked) from the U.S. Postal Service, or its equivalent from a designated private delivery service (see Notice 2004-83, 2004-52 I.R.B.

1030 (or its successor)); (b) Form 2553 with an accepted stamp; (c) Form 2553 with a stamped IRS received date; or (d) an IRS letter stating that Form 2553 has been accepted.

 Do not file Form 1120S for any tax year before the year the election takes effect. If the corporation is now required to file Form 1120, U.S. Corporation Income Tax Return, or any other applicable tax return, continue filing it until the election takes effect.

End of Election

Once the election is made, it stays in effect until it is terminated. IRS consent generally is required for another election by the corporation (or a successor corporation) on Form 2553 for any tax year before the 5th tax year after the first tax year in which the termination took effect. See Regulations section 1.1362-5 for details.

Specific Instructions

Part I

Name and Address

Enter the corporation's true name as stated in the corporate charter or other legal document creating it. If the corporation's mailing address is the same as someone else's, such as a shareholder's, enter "c/o" and this person's name following the name of the corporation. Include the suite, room, or other unit number after the street address. If the Post Office does not deliver to the street address and the corporation has a P.O. box, show the box number instead of the street address. If the corporation changed its name or address after applying for its employer identification number, be sure to check the box in item D of Part I.

Item A. Employer Identification Number (EIN)

Enter the corporation's EIN. If the corporation does not have an EIN, it must apply for one. An EIN can be applied for:

• Online—Click on the EIN link at *www.irs.gov/businesses/small*. The EIN is issued immediately once the application information is validated.

• By telephone at 1-800-829-4933 from 7:00 a.m. to 10:00 p.m. in the corporation's local time zone.

• By mailing or faxing Form SS-4, Application for Employer Identification Number.

If the corporation has not received its EIN by the time the return is due, enter "Applied for" in the space for the EIN. For more details, see Pub. 583.

Item E. Effective Date of Election

 Form 2553 generally must be filed no later than 2 months and 15 days after the date entered for item E. For details and exceptions, see When To Make the Election *on page 1.*

A corporation (or entity eligible to elect to be treated as a corporation) making the election effective for its first tax year in existence should enter the earliest of the following dates: (a) the date the corporation (entity) first had shareholders (owners), (b) the date the corporation (entity) first had assets, or (c) the date the corporation (entity) began doing business. This same date will be entered for item H.

A corporation (entity) not making the election for its first tax year in existence that is keeping its current tax year should enter the beginning date of the first tax year for which it wants the election to be effective.

A corporation (entity) not making the election for its first tax year in existence that is changing its tax year and wants to be an S corporation for the short tax year needed to switch tax years should enter the beginning date of the short tax year. If the corporation (entity) does not want to be an S corporation for this short tax year, it should enter the beginning date of the tax year following this short tax year and file Form 1128, Application To Adopt, Change, or Retain a Tax Year. If this change qualifies as an automatic approval request (Form 1128, Part II), file Form 1128 as an attachment to Form 2553. If this change qualifies as a ruling request (Form 1128, Part III), file Form 1128 separately. If filing Form 1128, enter "Form 1128" on the dotted line to the left of the entry space for item E.

Column K. Shareholders' Consent Statement

For an election filed before the effective date entered for item E, only shareholders who own stock on the day the election is made need to consent to the election.

For an election filed on or after the effective date entered for item E, all shareholders or former shareholders who owned stock at any time during the period beginning on the effective date entered for item E and ending on the day the election is made must consent to the election.

If the corporation filed a timely election, but one or more shareholders did not file a timely consent, see Regulations section 1.1362-6(b)(3)(iii). If the shareholder was a community property spouse who was a shareholder solely because of a state community property law, see Rev. Proc. 2004-35, 2004-23 I.R.B. 1029.

Each shareholder consents by signing and dating either in column K or on a separate consent statement. The following special rules apply in determining who must sign.
• If a husband and wife have a community interest in the stock or in the income from it, both must consent.
• Each tenant in common, joint tenant, and tenant by the entirety must consent.
• A minor's consent is made by the minor, legal representative of the minor, or a natural or adoptive parent of the minor if no legal representative has been appointed.
• The consent of an estate is made by the executor or administrator.
• The consent of an electing small business trust (ESBT) is made by the trustee and, if a grantor trust, the deemed owner. See Regulations section 1.1362-6(b)(2)(iv) for details.
• If the stock is owned by a qualified subchapter S trust (QSST), the deemed owner of the trust must consent.
• If the stock is owned by a trust (other than an ESBT or QSST), the person treated as the shareholder by section 1361(c)(2)(B) must consent.

Continuation sheet or separate consent statement. If you need a continuation sheet or use a separate

consent statement, attach it to Form 2553. It must contain the name, address, and EIN of the corporation and the information requested in columns J through N of Part I.

Column L

Enter the number of shares of stock each shareholder owns on the date the election is filed and the date(s) the stock was acquired. Enter -0- for any former shareholders listed in column J. An entity without stock, such as a limited liability company (LLC), should enter the percentage of ownership and date(s) acquired.

Column M

Enter the social security number of each individual listed in column J. Enter the EIN of each estate, qualified trust, or exempt organization.

Column N

Enter the month and day that each shareholder's tax year ends. If a shareholder is changing his or her tax year, enter the tax year the shareholder is changing to, and attach an explanation indicating the present tax year and the basis for the change (for example, an automatic revenue procedure or a letter ruling request).

Signature

Form 2553 must be signed and dated by the president, vice president, treasurer, assistant treasurer, chief accounting officer, or any other corporate officer (such as tax officer) authorized to sign.

If Form 2553 is not signed, it will not be considered timely filed.

Part II

Complete Part II if you selected a tax year ending on any date other than December 31 (other than a 52-53-week tax year ending with reference to the month of December).

Note. Generally, the corporation cannot obtain automatic approval of a fiscal year under the natural business year (Box P1) or ownership tax year (Box P2) provisions if it is under examination, before an area office, or before a federal court with respect to any income tax issue and the annual accounting period is under consideration. For details, see section 4.02 of Rev. Proc. 2002-38, 2002-22 I.R.B. 1037.

Box P1

Attach a statement showing separately for each month the amount of gross receipts for the most recent 47 months. A corporation that does not have a 47-month period of gross receipts cannot automatically establish a natural business year.

Box Q1

For examples of an acceptable business purpose for requesting a fiscal tax year, see section 5.02 of Rev. Proc. 2002-39, 2002-22 I.R.B. 1046, and Rev. Rul. 87-57, 1987-2 C.B. 117.

Attach a statement showing the relevant facts and circumstances to establish a business purpose for the requested fiscal year. For details on what is sufficient to establish a business purpose, see section 5.02 of Rev. Proc. 2002-39.

If your business purpose is based on one of the natural business year tests provided in section 5.03 of

Rev. Proc. 2002-39, identify if you are using the 25% gross receipts, annual business cycle, or seasonal business test. For the 25% gross receipts test, provide a schedule showing the amount of gross receipts for each month for the most recent 47 months. For either the annual business cycle or seasonal business test, provide the gross receipts from sales and services (and inventory costs, if applicable) for each month of the short period, if any, and the three immediately preceding tax years. If the corporation has been in existence for less than three tax years, submit figures for the period of existence.

If you check box Q1, you will be charged a user fee of $1,500 ($625 if your gross income is less than $1 million) (subject to change — see Rev. Proc. 2005-1 or its successor). Do not pay the fee when filing Form 2553. The service center will send Form 2553 to the IRS in Washington, DC, who, in turn, will notify the corporation that the fee is due.

Box Q2

If the corporation makes a back-up section 444 election for which it is qualified, then the section 444 election will take effect in the event the business purpose request is not approved. In some cases, the tax year requested under the back-up section 444 election may be different than the tax year requested under business purpose. See Form 8716, Election To Have a Tax Year Other Than a Required Tax Year, for details on making a back-up section 444 election.

Boxes Q3 and R2

If the corporation is not qualified to make the section 444 election after making the item Q2 back-up section 444 election or indicating its intention to make the election in item R1, and therefore it later files a calendar year return, it should write "Section 444 Election Not Made" in the top left corner of the first calendar year Form 1120S it files.

Part III

In Part III, certain qualified subchapter S trusts (QSSTs) may make the QSST election required by section 1361(d)(2). Part III may be used to make the QSST election only if corporate stock has been transferred to the trust on or before the date on which the corporation makes its election to be an S corporation. However, a statement can be used instead of Part III to make the election. If there was an inadvertent failure to timely file a QSST election, see the relief provisions under Rev. Proc. 2003-43.

Note. Use Part III only if you make the election in Part I (that is, Form 2553 cannot be filed with only Part III completed).

The deemed owner of the QSST must also consent to the S corporation election in column K of Form 2553.

Paperwork Reduction Act Notice. We ask for the information on this form to carry out the Internal Revenue laws of the United States. You are required to give us the information. We need it to ensure that you are complying with these laws and to allow us to figure and collect the right amount of tax.

You are not required to provide the information requested on a form that is subject to the Paperwork Reduction Act unless the form displays a valid OMB control number. Books or records relating to a form or its instructions must be retained as long as their contents may become material in the administration of any Internal Revenue law. Generally, tax returns and return information are confidential, as required by section 6103.

The time needed to complete and file this form will depend on individual circumstances. The estimated average time is:

Recordkeeping	9 hr., 19 min.
Learning about the law or the form	3 hr., 9 min.
Preparing, copying, assembling, and sending the form to the IRS	4 hr., 38 min.

If you have comments concerning the accuracy of these time estimates or suggestions for making this form simpler, we would be happy to hear from you. You can write to Internal Revenue Service, Tax Products Coordinating Committee, SE:W:CAR:MP:T:T:SP, 1111 Constitution Ave. NW, IR-6406, Washington, DC 20224. Do not send the form to this address. Instead, see *Where To File* on page 2.

AS/RP1
Web-Fill
10-05

Registration Application for
Income Tax Withholding, Sales and Use Tax, and
Machinery, Equipment, and Manufacturing Fuel Tax
North Carolina Department of Revenue

I. Identifying Information

1. Federal Employer ID No. [   ] **or** Proprietor's Social Security No. [   ]

2. Type of Ownership: [   ] If other, please identify type of ownership here: [   ]

   If a corporation, state of incorporation: [   ] If N.C. Corporation or LLC, enter N.C. Secretary of State ID No. [   ]

3. Legal Business or Owner's Name: [   ]

4. Trade Name(DBA Name): [   ]

5. Daytime Business Phone: [   ] 6. Fax Phone: [   ]

7. Business Location in N.C. Street [   ]
   (Not P.O. Box Number) City [   ] State [   ] Zip Code [   ] County [   ]

8. Is the business located within city or town limits? [   ] 9. Number of locations in N.C. [   ] Enclose list if more than one.

10. Mailing Address: Street or P.O. Box [   ]
    City [   ] State [   ] Zip Code [   ]

11. List primary partners or corporate officers *(President, Vice President, Secretary, and Treasurer)*:

Name	Title	Social Security No.	Address

II. Withholding Tax Section - *Complete this section if you are applying for an Income Tax Withholding Number.*

Do you have employees who are subject to N.C. withholding? [   ] Date on which wages were or will first be paid in N.C. [   ]

Do you make pension payments to N.C. residents? [   ] If yes, do you choose to report the pension payment withholding separately? [   ]

Do you pay compensation *(other than wages to employees)* to a nonresident entity or a nonresident individual for personal services performed in N.C.? [   ] If yes, do you choose to report this withholding separately? *(See instructions.)* [   ]

Amount of tax you expect to withhold each month: ○ Less than $250 (Quarterly) ○ $250 - $2,000 (Monthly) ○ More than $2,000 (Semiweekly)

If your business is seasonal, fill in circles Jan Feb Mar Apr May Jun Jul Aug Sep Oct Nov Dec
for months employees are paid: ○   ○   ○   ○   ○   ○   ○   ○   ○   ○   ○   ○

III. Sales and Use Tax Section - *Complete this section if you are applying for a Sales and Use Tax Number.*

When will you start selling or purchasing items subject to N.C. sales or use tax? [   ]
(You are required to file returns beginning with the month or quarter you indicate.)

Will your sales be? ○ Retail (to users or consumers) ○ Wholesale (to registered merchants for resale) ○ Both Retail and Wholesale

What will you sell? (Be specific) [   ]

Are you registering only to remit use tax on your purchases? [   ]

Will you sell electricity or telecommunications, cable, or satellite services? [   ]

Will you lease motor vehicles to others? [   ] Will you sell new tires? [   ]

Will you sell new appliances? [   ] What accounting method will you use? [   ]

Amount of sales tax expected each month: ○ Less than $100 (Quarterly) ○ $100 - $10,000 (Monthly) ○ $10,000 or more (Semimonthly)

Jan Feb Mar Apr May Jun Jul Aug Sep Oct Nov Dec
If your business is seasonal, fill in circles for months of sales: ○   ○   ○   ○   ○   ○   ○   ○   ○   ○   ○   ○

IV. Machinery, Equipment, and Manufacturing Fuel Tax Section - *Complete this section if you are applying for a number to remit tax on your purchases of machinery, equipment, or manufacturing fuel.*

Are you registering to remit tax on purchases of machinery or recycling equipment? [   ]

Are you registering to remit tax on purchases of fuel to operate a manufacturing industry or plant? [   ]

IV. Signature: _____ Title: _____ Date: _____
I certify that, to the best of my knowledge, this application is accurate and complete.

Mail to: N.C. Department of Revenue, P. O. Box 25000, Raleigh, NC 27640-0100

Form AS/RP1 Instructions

Income Tax Withholding

Wages: North Carolina (N.C.) law requires withholding of income tax from salaries and wages of all residents regardless of where earned and from wages of nonresidents for personal services performed in this State. The tax must be withheld from each payment of wages, and is considered to be held in trust until it is paid to the Department of Revenue. Due date requirements for reporting and paying the tax depend on the amount of tax withheld each month. Employers withholding less than $250 per month report and pay quarterly. Employers who, on average, withhold at least $250 but less than $2,000 per month report and pay monthly. Employers who, on average, withhold $2,000 or more per month make payments on the dates federal deposits are required and file quarterly reports.

Pension Payments: If you are required to withhold federal tax under section 3405 of the Internal Revenue Code on a pension payment to a N.C. resident, you must also withhold State income tax unless the recipient elects no withholding. You must withhold on periodic payments as if the recipient is a married person with three allowances unless the recipient provides an exemption certificate (Form NC-4P) reflecting a different filing status or number of allowances. For nonperiodic distributions, 4% of the tax must be withheld. **Reporting and Paying Pension Withholding:** If you already have a wage withholding identification number, you can report and pay the pension withholding with your wage withholding **or** you may choose to report and pay the withholding tax separately. If you choose to pay pension withholding with wage withholding, you do not have to complete this form. However, if you choose separate reporting of wage and pension withholding, or if you report only pension withholding, you must complete and file this form to obtain a new identification number.

Other Compensation: If you pay non-wage compensation of more than $1,500 during the calendar year to a nonresident contractor for personal services performed in N.C. in connection with a performance, an entertainment or athletic event, a speech, or the creation of a film, radio, or television program, you must withhold N.C. income tax at the rate of 4% from this non-wage compensation. **Reporting and Paying Withholding from Non-wage Compensation:** If you already have a wage withholding identification number, you can report and pay the non-wage withholding with your wage withholding **or** you may choose to report and pay the withholding tax separately. If you choose to pay non-wage withholding with wage withholding, you do not have to complete this form. However, if you choose separate reporting of wage and non-wage compensation, or if you report only non-wage withholding, you must complete and file this form to obtain a new identification number. **For detailed instructions on reporting and paying tax withheld from wages, pensions, and other compensation, see Form NC-30, Income Tax Withholding Tables and Instructions for Employers. Form NC-30 is available on the Department's website at www.dornc.com.**

Sales and Use Tax

Every person who engages as a retailer or wholesale merchant in the business of selling, renting, or leasing taxable tangible personal property in this State or who operates a laundry, dry cleaning plant, or similar business in this State, or a hotel, motel, or similar business in this State must obtain a Certificate of Registration. A Certificate of Registration allows the merchant to issue a Certificate of Exemption to obtain property for resale without paying the sales tax. A purchaser is liable for a $250 penalty for misuse of a Certificate of Exemption. See the certificate for instructions on its proper use.

Every business that buys taxable tangible personal property from out-of-state vendors for storage, use, or consumption in North Carolina is required to obtain a Users or Consumers Use Tax Registration unless the business is registered for sales and use tax or has paid all taxes due on their purchases. Individuals making non-business purchases should remit the use tax due on their North Carolina Individual Income Tax Return and are not required to register.

Machinery, Equipment, and Manufacturing Fuel Tax

Every manufacturing industry or plant, major recycling facility, and every contractor or subcontractor that performs contracts with a manufacturing industry or plant is required to register and remit the 1% tax with an $80 maximum per article when purchasing mill machinery, mill machinery parts or accessories, or recycling equipment for storage, use, or consumption in this State. Every manufacturing industry or plant that purchases fuel to operate that industry or plant is also required to register and remit the 1% tax on the sales price of fuel.

Registration Application Instructions

Step 1 - Complete Section I, Identifying Information. Use blue or black ink.

Line 1 Enter your Federal Employer's Identification Number. If you have applied for the number, but have not yet received it, enter "applied for" and furnish the number as soon as it is available. **Important:** Federal employer identification numbers are required of all partnerships. If the business is a proprietorship, enter the Social Security Number of the owner.

Line 3 If the business is a sole proprietorship, enter the name of the owner. If the business is a corporation or a LLC, enter the legal name. The legal name of the N.C. corporation or LLC is the name shown on the Articles of Incorporation or Articles of Organization filed with the Secretary of State. The legal name of an out-of-state corporation or LLC is the name shown on the Certificate of Authority issued by the Secretary of State. If the business is a partnership, enter the legal name of the partnership and list the partners' names in Item 11.

Line 4 Enter the trade name by which your business is known to the public.

Line 7 Enter the address of the actual business location, not the home address of an individual owner or a representative in N.C.

Step 2 - Complete Section II if you are applying for an Income Tax Withholding Number.

Step 3 - Complete Section III if you are applying for a Certificate of Registration, also known as a Sales and Use Tax Number, or for a Users or Consumers Use Tax Registration.

Step 4 - Complete Section IV if you are applying for a number to remit the machinery, equipment, and manufacturing fuel tax.

Step 5 - Sign the application and mail it to P.O. Box 25000, Raleigh, NC 27640-0100. The application must be signed by the owner, a partner, a corporate officer, or another authorized individual.

NOTE - The Department will assign you a withholding and sales and use tax account number, as appropriate, after this application is processed. Use the assigned number to make your withholding and sales and use tax payments. The amount of tax withheld or any sales tax collected is deemed by law to be held in trust by you for the State of N.C. Failure to remit or any misapplication of these funds to the Department of Revenue could result in criminal action.

SCTC-111
(Rev. 2/22/06)

8011

SOUTH CAROLINA DEPARTMENT OF REVENUE
BUSINESS TAX APPLICATION

INTERNET REGISTRATION: **www.sctax.org**
TELEPHONE (803) 898-5872
Mail TO: SC DEPARTMENT OF REVENUE,
      REGISTRATION UNIT, COLUMBIA, SC 29214-0140

FOR OFFICE USE ONLY
SID# _____
W/H _____
SALES _____
USE _____
LICENSE TAX _____
14-2601

TAXES TO BE REGISTERED FOR THIS BUSINESS LOCATION

☐ WITHHOLDING (complete section A)
☐ Nonresident Withholding Exemption (complete section B)
☐ SALES (complete section C; $50.00 license tax is required)
☐ PURCHASER'S CERTIFICATE (complete section D)

COMPLETE BOTH SIDES OF THIS APPLICATION   **PLEASE PRINT OR TYPE ALL INFORMATION**

1. OWNER, PARTNERSHIP, OR CORPORATE CHARTER NAME

2. TRADE NAME (DOING BUSINESS AS)

3. PHYSICAL LOCATION OF BUSINESS REQUIRED (NO P.O. BOX)

_____
STREET

_____
CITY   **COUNTY** (REQUIRED)   STATE   ZIP

6. MAILING ADDRESS (FOR ALL CORRESPONDENCE)

_____
IN CARE OF

_____
STREET

_____
CITY   COUNTY   STATE   ZIP

9. LOCATION OF RECORDS (NO P.O. BOX)

4. BUSINESS PHONE NUMBER | DAYTIME PHONE NUMBER

5. FEDERAL IDENTIFICATION NUMBER

7. TYPE OF BUSINESS

☐ AGRICULTURE, FORESTRY, FISHING & HUNTING (11)
☐ MINING (21)
☐ UTILITIES (22)
☐ CONSTRUCTION (23)
☐ MANUFACTURING (31 -33)
☐ WHOLESALE TRADE (42)
☐ RETAIL TRADE (44 - 45)
☐ TRANSPORTATION & WAREHOUSE (48-49)
☐ INFORMATION (51)
☐ FINANCE & INSURANCE (52)
☐ REAL ESTATE, RENTAL & LEASING (53)

☐ PROFESSIONAL, SCIENTIFIC, & TECHNICAL SERVICES (54)
☐ MANAGEMENT OF COMPANIES & ENTERPRISES (55)
☐ ADMINISTRATIVE AND SUPPORT, WASTE MANAGEMENT & REMEDIATION SERVICES (56)
☐ EDUCATION SERVICES (61)
☐ HEALTH CARE & SOCIAL ASSISTANCE (62)
☐ ARTS, ENTERTAINMENT, & RECREATION (71)
☐ ACCOMMODATION & FOOD SERVICES (72)
☐ OTHER SERVICES (81)
☐ PUBLIC ADMINISTRATION (92)

10. TYPE OF OWNERSHIP

☐ SOLE PROPRIETOR (one owner)   ☐ PARTNERSHIP (two or more owners, other than LLP)
☐ UNINCORPORATED ASSOCIATION, ENTER LEGAL NAME. _____
☐ FOREIGN CORPORATION (ATTACH COPY OF ARTICLES OF CERTIFICATE OF AUTHORITY).
☐ SOUTH CAROLINA CORPORATION DATE INCORPORATED _____
☐ OTHER (EXPLAIN) _____
☐ LLC/LLP FILING AS: ☐ CORPORATION ☐ PARTNERSHIP ☐ SINGLE MEMBER

8. MAIN BUSINESS (I.E., RETAIL FURNITURE SALES)

8A. CHECK IF YOU SELL THESE PRODUCTS (for Solid Waste Purposes):
☐ MOTOR OIL ☐ LEAD ACID BATTERIES ☐ TIRES ☐ LARGE APPLIANCES

8B. DO YOU SELL AVIATION GASOLINE? ☐ YES ☐ NO

8C. DO YOU PROVIDE SERVICE TO CELLULAR AND PERSONAL COMMUNICATIONS USERS? ☐ YES ☐ NO

11. NAME(S) OF BUSINESS OWNER, GENERAL PARTNERS, OFFICERS OR MEMBERS:

SOCIAL SECURITY NUMBER	NAME/TITLE/GENERAL PARTNERS	HOME ADDRESS	IF PARTNER PERCENT OWNED

ARE YOU A SC RESIDENT? (Y/N) _____ HOW LONG HAVE YOU LIVED IN SC? _____ (YEARS, MONTHS)

12. HAVE YOU:

A. ACQUIRED ANOTHER BUSINESS? ☐ YES ☐ NO
MERGED WITH ANOTHER BUSINESS? ☐ YES ☐ NO
FORMED A CORPORATION OR PARTNERSHIP ☐ YES ☐ NO
MADE ANY OTHER CHANGE IN THE OWNERSHIP? ☐ YES ☐ NO

B. DID YOU ACQUIRE: ALL OF THE SOUTH CAROLINA OPERATIONS?
PART OF THE SOUTH CAROLINA OPERATIONS?
PERCENTAGE ACQUIRED:

C. DATE ACQUIRED OR CHANGED: _____
WAS THE BUSINESS OPERATING AT THE TIME OF ACQUISITION OR CHANGE? ☐ YES ☐ NO
DATE CLOSED: _____
DOES THE FORMER OWNER OR LEGAL ENTITY CONTINUE TO HAVE EMPLOYEE? ☐ YES ☐ NO

D. FORMER OWNER'S S.C.E.S.C. ACCOUNT NUMBER:

FORMER OWNER'S S.C. TAX ACCOUNT NUMBER:

_____

E. NAME OF BUSINESS ACQUIRED:

_____
(Full organization name including trade name)
ADDRESS OF FORMER OWNER:

_____

13. FIRST DATE OF EMPLOYMENT IN S.C.
mo/day/year

14. ANTICIPATED DATE OF FIRST S.C.PAYROLL
mo/day/year

15. ESTIMATE NUMBER OF EMPLOYEES IN S.C.

16. IS BUSINESS WITHIN SC MUNICIPAL LIMITS?
☐ YES ☐ NO   WHICH CITY? _____

17. IS YOUR BUSINESS SEASONAL?
☐ YES ☐ NO   IF YES, LIST MONTHS ACTIVE. _____

COMPLETE REVERSE SIDE OF THIS FORM

I CERTIFY THAT ALL INFORMATION ON THIS APPLICATION, INCLUDING ANY ATTACHMENTS, IS TRUE AND CORRECT TO THE BEST OF MY KNOWLEDGE

_____   _____   _____
SIGNATURE OF OWNER, ALL PARTNERS, OR CORPORATE OFFICER   TITLE   DATE

80111610

SECTION A: TO APPLY FOR WITHHOLDING NUMBER   Every employer having employees earning wages in SC must register for withholding. Other types of payments also require state tax withholding.

STATUS OF EMPLOYER (CHECK ONE):

☐ RESIDENT - Principal place of activity inside SC

☐ NONRESIDENT - Principal place of activity outside SC

CLASSIFICATION OF **RESIDENT** EMPLOYER (CHECK ONE):

☐ 01 Tax withheld from sources that do not require withholding (Ex.: Domestic Help, Farmers, Fishermen)

☐ 02 FEDERAL withholding (941 total) does not exceed $2,500.00 per quarter

☐ 03 FEDERAL withholding (941 total) is less than $50,000 during 12-month lookback period

☐ 04 FEDERAL withholding (941 total) is greater than $50,000 during 12-month lookback period

CLASSIFICATION OF **NONRESIDENT** EMPLOYER (CHECK ONE):

☐ 01 Tax withheld from sources that do not require withholding (Ex.: Domestic Help, Farmers, Fishermen)

☐ 05 SC State withholding is less than $500 per quarter

☐ 06 SC State withholding Totals $500 or more per quarter

SECTION B: EXEMPTION FROM WITHHOLDING ON NONRESIDENTS

☐ Check the appropriate block to administratively register with the Department and claim exemption from nonresident withholding required by SC Code Sections 12-8-540 (rents and royalties), 12-8-550 (temporarily doing business or performing services in SC), or 12-8-570 (trust or estate beneficiaries). The exempt person agrees to be subject to the jurisdiction of the Department and the S.C. courts to determine S.C. tax liability, including withholding, estimated taxes, and interest and penalties, if any. Registering is not an admission of tax liability, and, does not, by itself, require the filing of a tax return. See instructions for further information.

☐   I agree to file SC tax return   ☐   I am not subject to SC Tax Jurisdiction (no NEXUS)

SECTION C: TO APPLY FOR RETAIL SALES LICENSE   ($50.00 LICENSE TAX IS REQUIRED.)

In and out-of state sellers. A retail license will not be issued to a person with any outstanding state tax liability. Any license tax paid with this application will be applied to the tax liability.

☐   IN-STATE SELLER   ☐ OUT-OF-STATE SELLER

If applying for Retail License, a $50.00 Sales License Tax is required with this application.

ANTICIPATED DATE OF FIRST SALES mo/da/yr	HOW MANY RETAIL SALES LOCATIONS DO YOU OPERATE IN S.C. UNDER YOUR OWNERSHIP?

SECTION D: TO APPLY FOR PURCHASER'S CERTIFICATE OF REGISTRATION FOR USE TAX S. C. Use Tax is imposed on the storage, use, or consumption of tangible personal property on which S.C. sales tax has not been previously paid.

EFFECTIVE DATE OF REGISTRATION
mo/da/yr

SECTION E: If mailing address for returns is different from front of application indicate type of tax this applies to.

☐ SALES   ☐ WITHHOLDING   ☐ PURCHASERS CERTIFICATE

_____   _____
STREET OR BOX   IN CARE OF

_____   _____
CITY   STATE   ZIP   PHONE

IF CURRENTLY OR PREVIOUSLY REGISTERED WITH SC DEPARTMENT OF REVENUE UNDER THIS OWNERSHIP, INDICATE ACCOUNT NUMBER(S) IN THIS SPACE _____

NAME OF BANKING INSTITUTION USED

Enter Internet/E-mail address _____

UPON COMPLETION OF **BOTH SIDES, SIGN AND DATE ON FRONT OF APPLICATION.**

MAIL TO: SC DEPARTMENT OF REVENUE, REGISTRATION UNIT, COLUMBIA, SOUTH CAROLINA 29214-0140

80112618

INSTRUCTION FOR FORM SCTC-111 (Rev. 6/17/03)
APPLICATION MUST BE COMPLETED IN ITS ENTIRETY (FRONT AND BACK).
CHECK APPROPRIATE BLOCK TO INDICATE TYPES OF TAXES TO BE REGISTERED FOR BUSINESS.
COMPLETE APPROPRIATE SECTIONS AS INDICATED.

REGISTER OVER THE INTERNET AT www.sctax.org

ITEM 1 - Enter owner, partnership, or corporate charter name.

ITEM 2 - Enter trade name or business name.

ITEM 3 - Enter the physical location of business (STREET ADDRESS REQUIRED, NOT POST OFFICE BOX).

ITEM 4 - Enter business and daytime telephone number, including area code.

ITEM 5 - Enter Federal Employer Identification Number. To apply for a FEI number, contact the IRS and request Form SS-4. If you have not received your FEI number from the IRS, please notify this office as soon as it is received. Contact IRS at 1-800-829-3676.

ITEM 6 - Enter mailing address for all correspondence if different from business address.

ITEM 7 - Check appropriate block to indicate type of business.

ITEM 8 - Describe main business activity:
(a) If retail, describe the products you sell (apparel, furniture, cars, groceries, sell at flea markets, etc.).
(b) If manufacturer, describe the product you manufacture.
(c) If service, describe the type of service you offer.

ITEM 8A- The specific items listed are subject to a solid waste excise tax. Check appropriate block to indicate if you sell any of these items.

ITEM 8C- Check the appropriate block to indicate if you are providing service to wireless telephone users in South Carolina (include cellular and personal communication service).

ITEM 9 - Enter the location where your records are going to be kept, if different from Item 3. (NO POST OFFICE BOX)

ITEM 10 - Check the appropriate block to indicate type of ownership. Corporations that transact business in SC as well as LLCs/LLPs must qualify with the office of the SC Secretary of State. If ownership type is LLC, indicate the filing method of the LLC (i.e. - partnership, corporation or single-member disregarded entity). If LLC is a disregarded entity, indicate "single member" in item 10 and provide single member information in Item 11.

ITEM 11 - Enter social security number. Enter owner, general partners, officers and/or members by name and title. This item should include general partners only; do not include limited partners. Enter home address. Indicate percentage owned for general partners. Attach additional sheet if necessary. Indicate if you are a SC resident and years lived in SC.

Social Security Privacy Act
It is mandatory that you provide your social security number on this tax form. 42 U.S.C 405(c)(2)(C)(i) permits a state to use an individual's social security number as means of identification in administration of any tax. SC Regulation 117-1 mandates that any person required to make a return to the SC Department of Revenue shall provide identifying numbers, as prescribed, for securing proper identification. Your social security number is used for identification purposes.

ITEM 12 - Indicate if you acquired the business in SC and date of acquisition. Show the previous owner's name, address, South Carolina Employment Security Commission account number, and SC retail, corporate and/or withholding tax account number(s). Check appropriate blocks to indicate if the predecessor is completely out of business and if you continued at least 95% of the previous owner's business.

ITEM 13 - Enter date employees first worked for you in SC.

ITEM 14 - Enter anticipated date of the first SC payroll for the business.

ITEM 15 -   Enter estimated number of employees working in SC.

ITEM 16 -   Check appropriate block to indicate if business is located within SC municipal limits. Enter name of city.

ITEM 17 -   Indicate if your business is seasonal and enter which months the business is active.

SIGNATURE -   Application must be signed by owner, all partners, or corporate officer. **IF THE SIGNATURE(S) IS OMITTED, THE APPLICATION WILL BE REJECTED.** Attach additional sheets for signatures, if necessary.

SECTION A: **WITHHOLDING**
Check appropriate block to indicate separate returns for each location or consolidated returns for all locations.
Check appropriate block for status and classification of employer.

SECTION B: **NONRESIDENT/CONTRACT WITHHOLDING EXEMPTION**
SC statutes require state income tax to be withheld from payments on contracts in excess of $10,000 made to nonresidents. Nonresidents who have no activity and no employees in South Carolina are granted exemption from statute requirements by completing Section B of the application (SCTC-111). Provide a completed form I-312 (Affidavit of Registration) to the withholding agent with whom you are contracting. Form I-312 is not furnished to the South Carolina Department of Revenue.

SECTION C: **RETAIL SALES LICENSE**
Retailers selling in/into this state are required to have a South Carolina Retail Sales Tax License.

License tax in the amount of $50.00 is required. **APPLICATION WILL BE REJECTED IF THE LICENSE TAX IS NOT ENCLOSED.**

Check appropriate block for in-state or out-of-state seller.

Enter the anticipated date retail sales will begin (open date). **APPLICATION WILL BE REJECTED IF THE DATE IS OMITTED.**

Enter the number of retail sales locations in SC under your ownership.

SECTION D: **PURCHASER'S CERTIFICATE OF REGISTRATION FOR USE TAX**
Enter effective date of registration (open date).

SECTION E: Enter mailing address if different from front of application.

Enter account number(s) in the space provided if currently or previously registered with SC Department of Revenue under this ownership.

Enter the name of the Financial institution (Bank, Credit Union ...) used by the Business.

Enter your Internet/E-mail address.

Index